THE SCRUMBAN [R]EVOLUTION

The Agile Software Development Series

Alistair Cockburn and Jim Highsmith, Series Editors

Visit **informit.com/agileseries** for a complete list of available publications.

Agile software development centers on four values, which are identified in the Agile Alliance's Manifesto*:

1. Individuals and interactions over processes and tools
2. Working software over comprehensive documentation
3. Customer collaboration over contract negotiation
4. Responding to change over following a plan

The development of Agile software requires innovation and responsiveness, based on generating and sharing knowledge within a development team and with the customer. Agile software developers draw on the strengths of customers, users, and developers to find just enough process to balance quality and agility.

The books in The Agile Software Development Series focus on sharing the experiences of such Agile developers. Individual books address individual techniques (such as Use Cases), group techniques (such as collaborative decision making), and proven solutions to different problems from a variety of organizational cultures. The result is a core of Agile best practices that will enrich your experiences and improve your work.

* © 2001, Authors of the Agile Manifesto

Addison-Wesley   **informIT.com** | **Safari** Books Online

ALWAYS LEARNING

PEARSON

THE SCRUMBAN [R]EVOLUTION

GETTING THE MOST OUT OF AGILE, SCRUM, AND LEAN KANBAN

AJAY REDDY

✦ Addison-Wesley

New York • Boston • Indianapolis • San Francisco
Toronto • Montreal • London • Munich • Paris • Madrid
Capetown • Sydney • Tokyo • Singapore • Mexico City

Library of Congress Cataloging-in-Publication Data
Reddy, Ajay.
 The Scrumban [r]evolution : getting the most out of Agile, Scrum, and lean Kanban / Ajay Reddy.
   pages   cm
 Includes index.
 ISBN 978-0-13-408621-7 (pbk. : alk. paper)—ISBN 0-13-408621-X (pbk. : alk. paper)
 1. Project management—Data processing. 2. Lean manufacturing. 3. Agile software development.
 4. Scrum (Computer software development) I. Title. II. Title: Scrumban evolution. III. Title:
scrumban revolution.
 T56.8.R43 2016
 005.1068'4—dc23
                                                                                2015016226

ISBN-13: 978-0-13-408621-7
ISBN-10: 0-13-408621-X

Text printed in the United States on recycled paper at RR Donnelley in Crawfordsville, Indiana.
First printing, July 2015

I dedicate this work to my first born, Nehemiah Subhinay, named after Nehemiah 400–450 B.C., who ran the first successful Agile project in history, completing the wall around Jerusalem in 52 days.

CONTENTS

FOREWORD
BY DAVID J. ANDERSON

"Scrum is hard," says Ken Schwaber, one of the creators of the method. It's a defined process with a prescriptive set of rules that are known to work in combination. Scrum is known to work in the context for which it was designed. The real challenge for those adopting Scrum is in changing their context to enable Scrum to be effective for them. Changing the context of your business and the demands of your customers isn't easy—and hence, "Scrum is hard."

Back in 2002, when I was first contemplating what we now know as the Kanban Method, Scrum was not the dominant Agile method that it is today. Agile was new and the term "Agile software development" had been around for only one year. The best known of the Agile methods was Extreme Programming. Many software development organizations were still practicing methods developed in the 1980s and 1990s and using techniques such as use cases to capture requirements. Project planning was done with Gantt charts, and phase-gate governance processes that forced entire large-scale projects known as "phases" were commonplace. There would be a requirements gathering phase, a systems analysis phase, a design phase, and so on. Agile methods, with their small deliverable increments and iterative approaches to coding and testing, were scary and adoption was slow. Where I saw the greatest resistance was in adoption of looser approaches to requirements definition, such as the use of user stories, and in the dismantling of phase-gate governance processes often controlled by program/portfolio management offices or an audit or quality function often reporting into the PMO.

I came to the conclusion that if we were to deliver true business agility for the masses of technology development companies around the world, we had to adopt a new approach to improvement. Rather than trying to replace existing methods with new (but scary) Agile methods, we should instead pursue an evolutionary approach where we "start with what you do now" and look for specific problems that exist, and then seek specific ways to fix those.

By 2004, I saw a pattern where IT departments and product development groups would commit to too much work, too early; make plans often based on idealistic assumptions; and then fail to deliver on their promises, leading to unhappy customers. The causes of the failures formed a common pattern. Committed work would change in scope and definition, while new work would arrive, and the ongoing work would be interrupted often for information gathering reasons, or for rework, or for servicing production problems. Committed work in progress would get put aside and blocked for many reasons, and insufficient risk management planning had taken place to allow for these problems. The solution for many of these problems was to adopt a kanban system as a first step in a process of evolutionary improvement. Kanban systems encourage us to defer commitment, limiting work in progress and limiting our exposure to many of the common problems that cause promises to be broken and projects to fail to deliver on expectations.

These two things were separate: We needed an evolutionary approach to improving service delivery in IT work and product development, and kanban systems were a good solution to unrealistic early commitment and the problems of interruptions, changing and growing scope, and work blocking for a multitude of reasons. It turned out that the pattern that required use of a kanban system was so common that by 2007 the concepts had effectively merged into one single management approach we now know as the "Kanban Method."

So Kanban was "agility for the rest of us." Kanban was designed to bring agility to those who couldn't or wouldn't adopt defined Agile methods in the 2000s. What does this have to do with Scrum? Well, Scrum is hard. It has probably been oversold to an eager audience keen to find a simple solution to their delivery challenges. Many firms have adopted Scrum without fulfilling its full requirements—they haven't changed their context to one that's truly suitable for Scrum. Indeed, in many cases, it simply isn't possible to control the context of your business; instead, your customers and your market do that for you. They don't change to fit the way you want to work; rather, you must change to fit the way in which they expect you to do business with them. This has left a world full of troubled, incomplete, or lackluster Scrum implementations.

It turns out that despite the smaller increments of sprints, many Scrum implementations suffer from all the same ailments that I observed with traditional project management and software development life-cycle methods more than a decade ago. Hence, adopting Kanban is an appropriate way to help a challenged Scrum deployment evolve and adjust to the context in which it is being used. This doesn't make the purists happy. It's not "Scrum by the defined set of rules," so, according to Ken Schwaber, it isn't Scrum. The question you have to ask yourself is, "Is our goal to do Scrum perfectly and be first-class citizens in the worldwide Scrum community? Or is our goal to improve the service delivery of IT work, software development, and new products to our customers?" If you recognize the latter as your true goal, then you have to accept that some degree of tailoring is required to develop a process that is unique to your own situation and "fit for purpose." The fact that you've picked up this book and taken the trouble to read the foreword would suggest that you already recognize that strictly following the rules of Scrum isn't working for you, and you need help to evolve to something that better matches the context of your business.

Ajay Reddy is an experienced Scrum practitioner who has been through the same journey you find yourself on. He, too, discovered that he needed help, and he found that the message of the Kanban Method resonated with him and enabled him to deliver solutions to what had appeared to be intractable problems. If Scrum hasn't been working for you, maybe the issue doesn't lie with you and your ability to follow its strict rules properly. Maybe the truth is that you need a different process solution, uniquely tailored to your situation. Let Kanban help you achieve that, and allow Ajay to guide you in how to do it.

If there is a single message I want you to take away from this foreword, it is contained in this quote from my own book, *Kanban: Successful Evolutionary Change for Your Technology Business*: "You have permission to try Kanban. You have permission to modify your process. You have permission to be different. Your situation is unique and you deserve to develop a unique process definition tailored and optimized to your domain, your value stream, the risks that you manage, the skills of your team, and the demands of your customers." Be proud of what you've achieved so far with Scrum, and embrace the idea that there is so much more you can do in future. Let Kanban help you get there.

—David J. Anderson
  Sequim, Washington

FOREWORD
BY JIM BENSON

If there was one central tenet of Lean, one that no one ever talks about, it would simply be this:

You have to pay attention to your project.

That is simply it. To continuously improve or to deliver a quality product, we need to actually know, as a team, what we are doing and why.

When we abandon our projects or our understanding of our customers to prescriptive management techniques, we are saying that we (our team and our product) are just another run-of-the-mill software factory. Predictable, mechanical, uncreative. Certifiable.

But very few projects can claim to have reached this level of the mundane. Software creation gains profitability only because of differentiators. Differentiators require vision. Vision requires creativity. And creativity requires experimentation and imagination.

We are not robots. Software is not an assembly line—far from it. Therefore, software developers and those drawn to the industry have some key shared characteristics:

1. They are problem solvers.
2. They are inventors.
3. They are craftspeople.
4. They get really angry when they are denied to be 1–3.

In 2008, when my colleague Corey Ladas wrote *Scrumban: Essays on Kanban Systems for Lean Software Development*, he was extending the definition of increasingly prescriptive Agile techniques by providing two important things:

- A toolkit to pay attention
- Permission to pay attention

Software development is a system that is creating other systems. It is intricate. It is social. It is complex. We don't have shelves and shelves of books on how to develop software because it is easy. Each project has many potential implementation paths, many potential life cycles, and many decisions.

In turn, each website, app, or embedded program we create is itself a system. It interacts with the user, it interacts with other software, it breaks, it needs to be maintained. Our software products live within social, financial, and digital worlds that we must at least appreciate, if not understand, to craft appropriate code.

So I must honestly ask of you and your current Agile practice:

- Are you setting your development teams up with a system that allows them to really see the real-time context of their work?
- Does your system allow your team to notice early when there are problems?
- Does it allow them to change not just the features, but also your processes?
- Does it really allow them a sustainable pace (develop a quality product) or are you always trying to improve your velocity (increase utilization)?

To do any of these things, we cannot afford to separate the developers from the design. Current versions of popular Agile techniques incorporate mechanisms to divide developers from the vision of their product. Our original goals with Agile were to liberate the programmers. Instead, we have come full circle. Scrum masters have become project managers; product owners have become product managers. We have recreated waterfall in Scrum clothing.

The Kanban Method, Personal Kanban, Scrum (Types A, B, C), Scrumban, SAFe, RUP, XP . . . none of these things is THE answer. There is no one, single answer. If there was, it would be obvious and we'd all just do it. Taken alone, these approaches are as healthy as a prepackaged microwave dinner. When these and other techniques are used as ingredients, then you can make a real meal.

There would be no Kanban today without Kent Beck, Eliyahu Goldratt, Taiichi Ohno, and W. Edwards Deming. David's, Corey's, and my experiences in launching Kanban were themselves the products of learning and paying attention—of combining many ideas into one.

Just as a driver's manual from Tokyo won't tell you precisely how to drive in Akron, so the methods and ideas mentioned earlier won't tell you precisely how to steer your projects if they are used in isolation. To steer, you have to pay attention. To pay attention, you need to see your work and reduce distractions.

Lean and Kanban will *help* you do these things, but they are frustrating.

Why?

Because you and your team are likely overworked and don't have the time or perhaps even the permission to pay attention to or change your working environment. Open-ended Lean systems are therefore hard to start. You need to have clear direction and descriptions of work for your team members, your bosses, and other stakeholders. *Who has time for that?*

That's where this book comes in.

Ajay is taking Corey's ideas a step further, providing some more potential implementations for teams who would rather be successful than blind followers of canned processes. This book will help you to pay attention, to see the work you are taking on, to demonstrate to others the load you are dealing with, and to begin to take control of your work in process. *But don't stop here: Ajay calls it (r)evolution on purpose. Evolving is a continuous process.*

Think of this book as that first glimmer of light at the end of the tunnel. But remember, simply seeing that light is not enough: You need to keep moving forward, keep improving your processes, and keep creating and maintaining the best product possible.

Software never sleeps.

—Jim Benson
   Author of the Shingo Award-winning *Personal Kanban:*
   Mapping Work | Navigating Life
   Ocean Shores, Washington

PREFACE

Although Scrumban has evolved as a framework over the years, it has no definitive guide or definition. In fact, as highlighted early in this book, several "authoritative" sources disagree about what Scrumban actually represents. Scrumban deserves better.

The objective of this book is to transform a confusing set of conflicting representations into a comprehensive, coherent, and practical resource that brings value to the individuals and organizations wishing to harness the power of Scrumban in their own environments. This book is not about new advances in thinking, but rather about demonstrating how a broad set of proven Lean and Agile principles can be effectively interwoven and managed within the context of a single framework. In the same vein, it's not a recipe book. Although it incorporates recommendations and practice tips, this book is primarily intended as a guide to allow individuals and organizations to expand their thinking in ways that effectively support their ultimate aims.

How to Use This Book

There are a couple of different strategies for approaching this book. Before addressing them, let's consider the different levels of learners.

New practitioners want to seek out concrete steps to implement and follow. Scrumban presents a couple of unique challenges for these "Shu-level" learners. First, it calls for practitioners to engage in systems thinking and to acknowledge the notion that we can't improve the systems of which we're a part without first gaining a holistic understanding of those systems. Second, though some of Scrumban's practices and principles lend themselves to defining concrete steps, most do not. Consequently, the concrete steps early learners will be asked to embrace represent incremental building blocks to larger understandings.

Now for the two strategies. Which one you select depends on what you want to get out of this book:

- If you're interested in understanding the big picture and want to master Scrumban in its full context (something I strongly encourage), then moving through this book from beginning to end is the way to go. Should you find yourself reading something that you think is irrelevant or puts you to sleep, then by all means skip ahead. But I don't suggest doing this too often— gaining a comprehensive understanding of the full context is especially important to helping new practitioners avoid common pitfalls.

- If you're interested in learning more about a specific topic, you can jump straight to the chapter that covers it. Each chapter is a self-contained vehicle of knowledge on a broad topic, but the chapters are also ordered to lend a sense of continuity to the journey that is Scrumban.

Throughout the book I've sprinkled stories about how teams and organizations have used Scrumban. In some cases, teams or organizations accelerated their mastery of Scrum's roles and practices. In other cases, Scrumban served as an alternative path to Agility (which meant the teams following this path were no longer practicing Scrum). Both kinds of outcomes delivered pragmatic, bottom-line results—the thing teams and organizations care most about. If you don't care about these things, then this book is not for you.

Although this book predominately focuses on software development, the Scrumban framework can be adopted across a variety of business functions, it facilitates shared languages and shared understandings, and it integrates and aligns efforts effectively. This aspect of the framework is particularly relevant to challenges associated with scaling Lean and Agile practices across the enterprise, and is what ultimately makes Scrumban so powerful.

How This Book Is Organized

This book is organized into four main sections, each consisting of several chapters.

- Part I, Introduction
    - Chapter 1, Manifestations: Scrumban Demystified
      An overview of Scrumban's origins and current states of understanding in Lean and Agile circles.
- Part II, Foundations—Starting with the End in Mind
  Chapters 2, 3, and 4 are intended to provide readers with a holistic overview of Scrumban's roots and the reasons to employ it. The holistic nature of these chapters makes the material relevant for all levels of learners (Shu, Ha, and Ri—I'll talk more about these levels in Chapter 1), but especially for managers and executives. Because deep foundational understandings at every level drive better outcomes, I encourage individuals at the team level to avoid giving these chapters short shrift—especially Chapter 2.
    - Chapter 2, The Matrix and the Mess: Where It All Begins
      This chapter introduces key considerations that often go unrecognized in quests for improvement. I visit historical factors that often influence the performance of IT organizations, explore why efforts to become Agile (which often involves introducing Scrum into an environment)

can stall or fail, and how Scrumban is generally structured to help overcome these impediments.

■ **Chapter 3, The Mission: Clarifying the Relationship between Purpose, Values, and Performance**

Organizations are most successful when they maximize the alignment of efforts across four key areas. In this chapter, I highlight how Scrumban can be used to improve organizational alignment across all business functions.

■ **Chapter 4, Motivations: Why Scrumban Works**

Why Scrumban? I take a closer look at the core principles and practices that make Scrumban such a robust framework for improving worker satisfaction and creating high performance.

■ **Part III, Execution—Putting Scrumban into Practice**

Chapters 5, 6, and 7 are where the rubber meets the road, emphasizing the "how to" versus the "why." Because I strongly discourage new practitioners from diving into the "how to" with little understanding of the "why," readers will still find a significant amount of explanatory material embedded within content that's intended to serve as a practical guide.

■ **Chapter 5, Mobilize: Rolling Out Scrumban**

A close look at one approach for kickstarting Scrumban within a team or organization.

■ **Chapter 6, Method: Working under the Hood**

A concrete exploration of how Scrumban's specific values, principles, and methods can be applied and used at different stages of adoption.

■ **Chapter 7, Measurements: Gaining Insights and Tracking Progress**

The metrics I rely on to provide new perspective and enable more reliable forecasting.

■ **Part IV, Improving—Advanced Topics and Practices**

Chapters 8, 9, and 10 represent advanced thinking—a "graduate"-level course. Unseasoned practitioners are less likely to fully understand the relevance and power of the topics discussed, as that understanding comes only with experiencing Scrumban in action. Nonetheless, the content provides perspective on the many options and capabilities the framework exposes over time.

■ **Chapter 8, Management: Management Is Doing Things Right—Leadership Is Doing the Right Things**

Though Scrumban doesn't have to be driven from a top-down direction to achieve initial success, this chapter reviews why good leadership is essential to sustaining high performance over the long term.

- Chapter 9, Maturing: Like a Fine Wine, Scrumban Can Get Better with Age
  Approaches that help teams continue to mature, and common evolutions that might be encountered.
- Chapter 10, Modeling: To Boldly Go Where Few Men and Women Have Gone Before
  Even more advanced techniques for more precise forecasting and adaptive management.
- Appendix, More: For the Stout of Heart
  An appendix containing definitions and additional reference material.

Conventions

I've employed a couple of simple conventions to help readers navigate through certain categories of information. For example, some topics are especially suited to executives and those in portfolio or program management roles. You'll encounter illustrations of executive and manager types introducing these topics (I've borrowed these illustrations from GetScrumban, an online game I co-created as a training tool).

Similarly, "Sanjay" the coach will direct your attention to concepts of particular importance, call out traps and pitfalls for the unwary, and otherwise offer tips based on experiences helping many teams leverage Scrumban in their environments.

I also try to let you know when more advanced topics are addressed so you can elect to revisit them as your understanding grows over time.

ACKNOWLEDGMENTS

This work would not have been possible without the contributions and support of many people. In particular, I would like to thank. . . .

. . . my dear wife Diana, our four children, and my mother Susheela for their exuberant and selfless support to making this work possible.

. . . my friend and colleague at CodeGenesys, Jack Speranza, for his help in making this book possible. As CodeGenesys Chief Operating Officer, he provided a pedagogical perspective in presenting this book's material to a variety of audiences.

. . . Marc Hughes, my friend and partner, and my team at ScrumDo for supporting this work with invaluable data and analysis.

. . . clients of CodeGenesys and ScrumDo.com who gave us permission to share their stories.

. . . other colleagues at CodeGenesys—especially Haritha and Bernard—for their support and help.

. . . Dimitar Bakardzhiev and Frank Vega for their invaluable feedback.

. . . David Anderson, Jim Benson, and Russell Healy for their kind support.

. . . Corey Ladas, creator of Scrumban, without which this book obviously could not exist.

. . . and the too-many-to-name members of the Lean and Agile communities who agreed to let us incorporate portions of their work and are always making many contributions for the greater good.

—Ajay Reddy
Boston, Massachusetts

ABOUT THE AUTHOR

Ajay Reddy has been helping technology teams and organizations improve how they work for more than a decade. Emphasis on a hands-on approach and collaborative experimentation, verified business outcomes, and improved team satisfaction are a hallmark of his engagements.

Ajay began his professional journey as a software engineer, a role in which he was first exposed to Agile approaches like Extreme Programming. He soon transitioned to coaching others in adopting Agile mindsets and practices, constantly seeking out ways to improve this process based on the variety of challenges associated with different settings.

Ajay founded CodeGenesys, a Lean–Agile consulting boutique, in 2009. In 2010, he co-developed ScrumDo, a Scrum and Kanban management tool, with the express purpose of facilitating Agile implementations across the industry. Over the past five years, he has helped organizations both large and small employ Scrumban with great success. Ajay believes Scrumban is a particularly simple, yet powerful framework with a great amount of untapped potential. In addition to writing this book, he recently co-created the GetScrumban game as a practical and effective aid for helping individuals and organizations orient themselves to the true capabilities of this framework.

As the chief product strategist and lead coach for ScrumDo, Ajay is helping teams and organizations in 145 countries realize the benefits of Scrumban. He teaches Scrumban across the United States, India, and Europe, and is a regular speaker at Scrum and Kanban meetups and conferences across the globe.

In 2012, Ajay became disillusioned with the debate over frameworks, seeing it as putting too much emphasis on the frameworks rather than on the human systems and business concerns those frameworks were created to facilitate. He believes using frameworks as tools to effectively support desired outcomes is more important than the mechanics of any framework. It was this realization that led directly to his spending the last two years writing this book.

Ajay Reddy lives in Massachusetts with his wife, Diana, and their four children. You can find him on Linkedin, at www.ajayreddy.net, at codegenesys.com, at www.scrumdo.com, and as @ajrdy on Twitter.

PART I
INTRODUCTION

Chapter 1

MANIFESTATIONS: SCRUMBAN DEMYSTIFIED

I estimate that 75% of those organizations using Scrum will not succeed in getting the benefits that they hope for from it . . . Scrum is a very simple framework within which the "game" of complex product development is played. Scrum exposes every inadequacy or dysfunction within an organization's product and system development practices. The intention of Scrum is to make them transparent so the organization can fix them. Unfortunately, many organizations change Scrum to accommodate the inadequacies or dysfunctions instead of solving them.

—*Ken Schwaber, co-creator of Scrum*

Scrum is an incredibly simple, effective, and popular software development framework; its value increases as teams and organizations develop their understanding and application of its core principles and practices.

Despite its simplicity, Scrum can be difficult to master. While it empowers both individuals and teams to discover factors that impede Agility and address how they should be tackled, it relies on their collective motivation, effort, and capabilities to make this happen. An entire industry now exists around delivering services to help individuals, teams, and organizations rise to higher levels of capability.

Scrumban is also a simple framework. It's a relative newcomer to the world of software development and has yet to fully evolve; it's also often misunderstood by people in Lean and Agile circles. Many people have never even heard of it. Some believe it to be nothing more than using virtual kanban systems within the Scrum framework, while others believe it to be a new software development framework that combines "the best" elements of Scrum and the Kanban Method. Neither of these viewpoints captures the true essence of Scrumban.

A Helpful Perspective

In the early 2000s, Alistair Cockburn introduced "Shu-Ha-Ri" to the software development world. It provided a way of thinking about the three distinct phases people pass through as they master a new skill or concept. Cockburn borrowed this concept from Japanese martial arts and believed it could be effectively applied within the context of improving software development processes and practices.

I invite you to embrace a learning style that is loosely based on Shu-Ha-Ri in learning to understand Scrumban. Let's quickly review the three stages:

- *Shu (Beginner)*: The first stage of learning. New learners seek to reproduce a given result by following a set of instructions that are practice focused. They focus on how to perform a task with a basic understanding of the underlying principles. Success in this stage is measured by whether a procedure works and how well the student understands why it works.
- *Ha (Intermediate)*: Once a student has mastered basic practices, values, and principles, he or she begins to identify the limits of these practices and techniques. The student seeks to expand his or her awareness of alternative approaches, learning when an alternative applies and when it breaks down. Success in this stage is measured by how well the student learns to apply adaptive capabilities to varying circumstances.
- *Ri (Advanced)*: The student has become a master. It no longer matters whether he or she is following a given procedure or practice. His or her knowledge and understanding are the product of repeated thoughts and actions. The master has developed a fully adaptive capability within the context of his or her experience in the environment. Success is measured by consistently successful outcomes.

Informed readers should not confuse the concept of Shu-Ha-Ri with something like Carnegie Mellon University's Capability Maturity Model Integration (CMMI) process improvement training and appraisal program. Those who adopt and practice Scrumban principles would not be as inclined to direct harsh criticisms at the model as have some individuals in Lean and Agile circles.

Although I disagree that CMMI's prescribed "destinations" or "characteristics" correlate with capability in all contexts, this model does present a menu of potential catalysts to employ in a Scrumban framework when pursuing desired business outcomes. Viewed from the opposite direction, the flow management capabilities that Scrumban enables may provide a useful catalyst for organizations pursuing prescribed levels of CMMI capability to achieve their desired outcomes.

A Framework for [R]Evolution

When Corey Ladas introduced the world to Scrumban in his seminal book, *Essays on Kanban Systems for Lean Software Development* (Modus Cooperandi Press, 2009), he defined Scrumban as a transition method for moving software development teams from Scrum to a more evolved development framework. Over the past five years, my own research and work experience have unearthed the many ways in which Scrumban itself has evolved.

Since Corey wrote his book, organizations have layered the Kanban Method alongside Scrum to help them achieve several different kinds of outcomes. For example, I've successfully helped organizations apply Scrumban principles and practices in a variety of contexts—from startups to Fortune 50 companies, in industries ranging from professional services to software product development. Across these contexts, I've used Scrumban for the following purposes:

- Help teams and organizations accelerate their transitions to Scrum from other development methodologies
- Enable new capabilities within teams and organizations to help them overcome challenges that Scrum (purposefully) causes them to confront
- Help organizations evolve new Scrum-like processes and practices that work for them—not to accommodate the inadequacies and dysfunctions that Scrum exposed, but rather to resolve them in a manner that is most effective for their unique environment

These experiences demonstrate that Scrumban has evolved to become a family of principles and practices that create complementary tools and capabilities. And like any living organism, these principles and practices will continue to evolve as practitioners share their experiences and learnings.

Now, let's consider the three different outcomes summarized previously within the context of Shu-Ha-Ri:

- Scrumban provides the discipline and structure needed by practitioners in the Shu phase of learning. The Scrumban framework enables teams and organizations to manage the introduction of the artifacts and ceremonies of Scrum or the enhanced metrics and flow management practices of Kanban—disciplines and structures that new learners require in limited scope.

  For example, Scrum's ceremonies are essential to creating desired levels of performance and agility. Although it is a relatively simple framework, Scrum can seem overwhelming when it is first introduced. In a misguided effort to ease adoption, many organizations modify or omit ceremonies or, even worse, ignore the importance of understanding the basic principles and values. This rarely, if ever, produces the desired outcomes.

  Additional capabilities provided by the Scrumban framework can substitute for the functions served by the modified or omitted Scrum ceremonies. Scrumban's visualizations and other mechanics improve the effectiveness while reducing the time and effort associated with conducting ceremonies. Scrumban more effectively connects the practice of ceremonies with the principles and values that the ceremonies serve.

- Scrumban exposes new tools and capabilities that aid the experiments and discoveries pursued in the Ha phase. Meeting the challenges that teams and organizations commonly face as they implement Scrum or other Agile practices represents one aspect of this dimension.

  Consider creating and managing a product backlog. This Scrum artifact, and the events surrounding it (grooming and planning sessions), is intended to manage risk and optimize value by enabling better decision making due to maximized transparency and understanding of work. This can be especially frustrating when organizations effectively assign multiple product owners to a backlog because individual limitations interfere with realizing a full set of capabilities, or because of wide variations in subjective assessments.

  The Scrumban framework visualizes information and integrates capabilities other frameworks don't inherently provide. It helps provide improved contextual understandings and more accurately measures the outcome of different approaches (directly appealing to the Ha phase practice and understanding). For instance, Scrumban visualizes all sources of work demands and a more objective economic impact over time (cost of delay) to help prioritize work, lending greater transparency to the overall picture and expanding ways to adapt.

- Scrumban is flexible enough to provide Ri-level masters with a robust process within which to operate at hyper-performing levels. By emphasizing systems thinking, experimentation, and discovery, Ri-level masters are free to mold their ways of working in whatever fashion will produce the best results—from both performance and worker satisfaction standpoints. It makes no difference whether the resulting process is true to any particular set of practices.

- Scrumban supports both "revolution" and "evolution." More importantly, it's structured in a way that strongly supports all levels of learning and understanding—at a level of quality that is greater than that provided by either Scrum or Kanban alone.

All of Scrumban's added capabilities can be *optionally* applied to a Scrum context in a variety of ways. They can also be extended across multiple areas of an organization to drive better business outcomes. Scrum's software development framework lies at its foundation, as does the Kanban Method. However, neither of these frameworks represents a prescribed destination for organizations practicing Scrumban.

Beyond representing a significantly evolved mindset from the framework expressed by Ladas, today's Scrumban is quite different from the definitions used by other respected leaders in the Lean/Agile community.[1] In many respects, these perspectives view Scrumban as a vehicle for moving teams from Scrum to another software development process. While this remains *one* potential outcome, real-world

---

1. See, for example, http://tiny.cc/badcomparisonsSK (July 2013).

applications demonstrate Scrumban has come to entail more than this across a broad range of contexts.

Over the years, Scrumban has been used to help teams and organizations accelerate their transitions to Scrum from other development methodologies. It's been used to help teams and organizations overcome a variety of common challenges that Scrum is designed to force them to confront. When the context requires, it's been used to help organizations evolve new Scrum-like processes and practices that work best for them—not simply as a means to accommodate inadequacies and dysfunctions Scrum exposed, but rather as a strategy to resolve those problems in a manner that is most effective for that environment. This latter outcome is obviously not something for which Scrum itself provides. These different paths reflect Scrumban's bottom line—the service-oriented pragmatism that most businesses value.

Ultimately, Scrumban has become a framework of empowerment. David J. Anderson, pioneer of the Kanban Method, recently stated:

> *Empowerment isn't about letting people do whatever they want, or assuming they'll somehow self-organize to produce the right outcome. Empowerment is about defining boundaries, and we do the same with children when bringing them up; we tell them things like when their bedtime is, where they're allowed to play, whether they're allowed to go outside the yard of the house, they're allowed to swim at the shallow end of the pool, they aren't allowed to jump from the diving board . . . all these things. So empowerment is about giving people clear boundaries, and then letting them use their initiatives inside the boundaries.*[2]

Scrumban is distinct from Scrum because it emphasizes certain principles and practices that are quite different from Scrum's traditional foundation. These include the following:

- Recognizing the role of management (self-organization remains an objective, but within the context of specific boundaries)
- Enabling specialized teams and functions
- Applying explicit policies around ways of working
- Applying laws of flow and queuing theory

Scrumban is distinct from the Kanban Method in the following ways:

- It prescribes an underlying software development process framework (Scrum) as its core.
- It is organized around teams.
- It recognizes the value of time-boxed iterations when appropriate.
- It formalizes continuous improvement techniques within specific ceremonies.

---

2. http://tiny.cc/DavidAKanban (March 2013).

Stop Drinking the Kool-Aid

Mike Cohn, a leader in the Agile/Scrum community, recently "criticized"[3] Scrum teams for not being "focused on finding innovative solutions to the problems they [teams] are handed." He wasn't actually criticizing Scrum; rather, he was criticizing a mindset that has evolved among Scrum practitioners—a mindset that favors a safe approach to completing work over innovation.

I see a related phenomenon in my coaching engagements. The biggest impediment to improvement often lies with team members who are either unable or unwilling to think about improving the way work is done (or how their work is relevant to creating business value).

I believe the problem runs even deeper than this. A cult of Scrum has arisen that permeates the industry that has developed around Scrum. Not only are Scrum practitioners failing to pursue innovation in their work, but they are also failing to pursue innovation in the process. Scrum has evolved over the years as new information was discovered, yet there seems to be a growing resistance among its most ardent practitioners to reflecting on how to support its fundamental purpose.

I saw this reluctance most recently during a presentation to an Agile community in Boston. At the beginning of the presentation, I asked the audience how many of them were using Scrum in their environments. About half the audience members raised their hands. Then I asked how many had experienced challenges in adopting Scrum in their organizations. Not a single hand went down.

As I began describing some of the alternative ways Scrumban enables teams and organizations to achieve their desired purposes, debates erupted over whether prescribed or popular approaches associated with Scrum were ineffective. Despite my repeated emphasis that Scrumban simply represents *alternative* or *additional* paths when some aspect of the Scrum framework isn't fulfilling its intended purpose in a particular context, the majority of people in the room—even those who acknowledged challenges with their Scrum adoptions—were more interested in defending their existing process than in considering whether an alternative approach could help them overcome a challenge.

This cult-like mentality is not limited to the Scrum community. Pick your method or framework, and you'll find a lot of similar behavior—even in Kanban.

Fortunately, most day-to-day practitioners are pragmatists and realists. Simple pragmatism and a willingness to experiment are why Scrumban has evolved to become the framework described in this book. Unfortunately, there will always be a fringe set of "thought leaders" who perpetuate framework debates because they are unwilling to promote the benefits of an approach that "competes" with models in which they've invested significant amounts of both time and money. Scrumban may

---

3. http://tiny.cc/cohnscrumcricism.

be somewhat less threatening because of its familiar elements, but they will criticize it anyway.

Scrumban is a framework that almost forces its practitioners to accept the reality that good ideas can come from anywhere. It encourages people to actively pursue this reality at every turn. The question readers must answer for themselves is whether they're ready to accept this reality and embrace exploration, or whether they will remain trapped within a narrower perspective, justifying this mindset by the existence of a "debate" that is perpetuated more out of fear than out of fact.

Let's Get Started

One of the most powerful characteristics of Scrumban is the fact it can be implemented at any level of the organization—you don't need the authority of someone in command and control to begin making a difference in how you work (though it's certainly easier if you do have some degree of buy-in).[4] It also tends to be contagious.

So whether your goal is to have your company become a market leader or simply to gain better control over your own environment, I invite you to join the Scrumban community's Scrumban.io[5] LinkedIn group or www.facebook.com/Scrumban and to follow the Scrumban blog at www.scrumban.io.

---

4. This can be true even in environments where development processes are subject to audit, though the nature and extent of evolutionary change may be more limited than in less restrictive contexts.
5. The Linkedin group is available at www.theagilecollaborative.net, which redirects to https://www.linkedin.com/groups/Scrumbanio-7459316.

PART II

FOUNDATIONS—STARTING WITH THE END IN MIND

Chapter 2

THE MATRIX AND THE MESS: WHERE IT ALL BEGINS

IN THIS CHAPTER

- Scrumban's Roots and the Importance of Systems Thinking
- The Relevance of Alignment
- A High-Level Overview of How Scrumban Complements Scrum's Capabilities

Learning Levels:

The foundational concepts covered in this chapter are relevant to all learners.

You're reading this book for a reason. Perhaps you want to evaluate Scrumban as a potential solution for a current problem. Or maybe you have some professional curiosity about the framework. Regardless of your motivation, there's probably a "mess" lurking behind it, along with preconceived notions of what's causing it.

As a management framework, Scrumban emphasizes the discovery of knowledge by layering new principles and practices alongside existing ways of working. As you begin this journey, I challenge you to test whether preconceived notions about your reality may be interfering with your discovery of new ways of understanding it.

It's also important to begin the journey by clarifying the destination. Defining an explicit destination can help you avoid aimless wandering. The next few chapters are focused on concepts that help you identify and understand your intended destination.

During the first leg of this journey, I'll show you the foundations upon which Scrumban is built and outline how they're relevant to solving common challenges. Some of this may seem esoteric or irrelevant to your particular needs. I encourage you to dive in, though, as experience shows they are relevant to your ultimate success.

Bon voyage!

Scrumban Stories

Throughout this book I call out experiences from a variety of case studies that reflect how various teams and business units employed Scrumban to build a better way of working for themselves and drive better results for their companies. Some organizations are explicitly identified, while others are incorporated into a fictional entity I've called Mammoth Bank. However, the data and experiences are very real and can be read in their entirety in the Appendix.

Part 1: The Matrix (Scrumban's Origins)

Unfortunately, the Internet is replete with blog articles and other resources that incorrectly define Scrumban. In large measure, these erroneous descriptions arise from the framework's evolution over time. For this reason, I believe the best way to understand Scrumban is to invest some time in understanding its origins.

What Scrumban Is and What It Is Not

Understanding Scrumban starts with understanding its roots—Scrum and Kanban. In my experience, both can be horribly misunderstood.

Jeff Sutherland and Ken Schwaber state, "Scrum is a framework for developing and sustaining complex products."[1] In this vein, Scrum is both a project management methodology and a framework for catalyzing change and emergent behavior.

As a project management framework, Scrum prescribes formalized processes (e.g., sprint planning sessions, iterations, retrospectives) and roles (product owners, Scrum masters, team members). As a change catalyst, it has historically relied upon the concept of commitment as its preferred control mechanism for bringing about desired modifications. Although some Certified Scrum Trainers (CSTs) continue to instruct on commitment, this factor has been downplayed in more recent years. The "modern" viewpoint places greater emphasis on the mechanics of inspection and adaption. Unfortunately, the concepts of both commitment and inspection/adaptation have pragmatic limitations.

A common example of this can be found in some of my most recent work with a large financial institution. Despite extensive coaching efforts by multiple consultants, most managers and senior executives at this bank simply could not adjust their mindset to avoid treating work assigned to a sprint as anything other than a commitment. The Scrum framework allows for the possibility that "commitments" may need

---

1. Jeff Sutherland and Ken Schwaber. (July 2013). *The Scrum Guide: The Definitive Guide to Scrum*, p. 3.

to be renegotiated as the team discovers more information about work in the sprint backlog. Nevertheless, the framework offers little guidance and few mechanics for helping the organization overcome pragmatic realities such as the staunch resistance displayed by management in this example.

As a process framework, Scrum tends to be extremely effective at the team level.[2] However, it's not *naturally* well suited to whole-system management.[3] Scrum prescribes four formal events for inspection and adaptation—Sprint Planning, Daily Scrum, Sprint Review, and Sprint Retrospective—all of which are focused on optimizing work that's undertaken by small teams of 7–12 people.

Scrum isolates the team's work inside time-boxed batches of development (sprints). It encourages techniques to make these batches of work as predictably as possible (to help the team meet its sprint commitments). Scrum seeks to isolate the team from outside influences as much as possible. Its primary mechanics for exposing process inadequacies and organizational dysfunction are purposely team-centric.

Similarly, Scrum doesn't prescribe specific ways to help measure or manage problems and dysfunctions before they actually manifest themselves. In those situations, it encourages organizations to use other tools best suited to address the issues. In my estimation, Scrumban is such a tool.

From an implementation standpoint, Scrum often represents a very different approach to software development than those methods previously used by the adopting organization. Introducing Scrum into such environments often leads to radical and disruptive change. As a consequence, Scrum has come to be unfairly characterized as being naturally disruptive. In fact, not all radical change is necessarily disruptive. Similarly, change that is disruptive in one environment will not necessarily be disruptive in another. The when, how, where, and who factors of Scrum implementation often play far more significant roles in determining its disruptive nature than the framework itself.

Now let's consider the Kanban Method. It is primarily a framework for catalyzing evolutionary change and enabling continuous improvement. It achieves this, in part, by using kanban systems that visually emphasize improved understanding of existing conditions. The Kanban Method can help inform us about which kinds of changes will and won't be disruptive for an organization.

The Kanban Method is purposely structured to promote evolutionary change. Such evolutionary changes tend to initially manifest as process optimizations. As organizational capability matures, the Kanban Method can support substantially larger and more dramatic managed changes.

---

2. User data from two Scrum management platforms (ScrumDo.com and Rally Software) supports this finding.
3. There are examples, however, of efforts that scale Scrum across the enterprise. See, for example, http://tiny.cc/JeffSutherland.

It's critical to recognize that the Kanban Method is neither a project management framework nor a software development framework.[4] In fact, it doesn't tell us *how* to do these things at all. More significantly, it must be layered with an existing process.

Coaching Tip!

Important Concept Ahead

Ultimately, the Kanban Method is a framework that enables individuals, teams, and organizations to *better understand* how they work. It employs a handful of mechanisms to *simplify coordination across whole systems* and to maximize resource flexibility across multiple subsystems. Ambiguity is purposely built in so the framework can be successfully applied in any context—Scrum or otherwise.

Key Take-Away

Scrumban is *not* about using just a few elements of both Scrum and Kanban to create a software development process. Rather, it emphasizes applying kanban systems within a Scrum context, and layering the Kanban Method alongside Scrum as a vehicle for evolutionary change. Ultimately, it's about aiding and amplifying the capabilities already inherent in Scrum, as well as providing new perspectives and capabilities.

Managing Knowledge Work

It's important to address the concept of "knowledge work"—a term coined by Peter Drucker in the mid-20th century. It's the kind of work that dominates modern business arenas. Architecture, engineering, law, medicine, and much of finance are all examples of knowledge work. Software development and most IT functions also constitute knowledge work.

Knowledge work is differentiated from most other types of work by its primary characteristic of "non-routine problem solving that requires a combination of convergent, divergent, and creative thinking"[5] (a tip of the hat to Reinhardt, Schmidt, et al. for this). Though the process of producing completed knowledge work is similar to the process of manufacturing hard goods in many ways, it is uniquely different in several key aspects.

---

4. This definition of the Kanban Method has been rigorously applied by its pioneer, David J. Anderson, for many years. That said, Anderson and other leaders in the Kanban community created a "Project Management with Kanban" curriculum in the fall of 2014 designed to show how the framework can be used to serve essential project management functions.

5. Reinhardt, W.; Schmidt, B.; Sloep, P.; Drachsler, H. (2011). "Knowledge Worker Roles and Actions: Results of Two Empirical Studies." *Knowledge and Process Management.*

More than 25 years ago, Eliyahu Goldratt penned a business novel titled *The Goal*. Rejected by most publishers and panned by many critics (both literary and business-centric), Goldratt's book went on to sell millions of copies. Why? Because people discovered the principles and theories he illustrated in his story brought a new perspective to manufacturing processes that led to substantial results. The style of his book also provided a great way to evangelize for needed changes in the organizations that adopted them.

The principles espoused in Goldratt's book work well when applied to a manufacturing process. When attempts were made to apply them to knowledge work, however, matters proved more challenging. The Kanban Method was born out of the recognition of knowledge work's unique characteristics. Let's look at some examples.

Knowledge work is a dynamic process that incorporates both learning and creativity throughout "production." In contrast, manufacturing is largely separated from the brainpower necessary to conceive both the product and the production process. As complex as they may be, most manufacturing processes "simply" repeat a series of steps to consistently produce a product of known value. Considerations that need to be taken with regard to optimizing knowledge work have no bearing in a manufacturing process, and vice versa.

For example, one way Goldratt's theory of constraints (TOC) can be applied to improve a manufacturing process is to identify system bottlenecks (places in the workflow where capacity is most limited). Maximizing the productivity of bottlenecks improves overall system throughput because the output is constrained by its lowest-producing component. Unfortunately, it is not always practical in a knowledge work setting.

Perhaps the "bottleneck" lies with a junior developer who hasn't acquired the skills to be as productive as more senior members of the team. Though it may be possible to improve throughput by "swapping" that junior developer for a more productive senior resource, doing so may actually increase overall business risk—that is, the failure to develop junior team members may leave the production process vulnerable in other ways. This dynamic doesn't exist when you're talking about swapping out one production machine for another.

Or perhaps the "bottleneck" lies in a senior team member whose "full" productivity is impeded because 25% of his or her time is devoted to helping other team members. It may be more important to maintain slack for such a senior resource because doing otherwise would actually decrease the productivity of the team as a whole. This dynamic is also not present in a manufacturing setting.[6]

---

6. Dimitar Bakardzhiev has suggested a seemingly valid application of TOC within a similar context. Though the scenario we describe reflects different conditions, his article shows how TOC can be successfully applied to many knowledge work problems. http://tiny.cc/DimiterBakLiquidity (June 2013).

In addition, there's a distinct difference in the manner in which critical information arrives in the work process. In a manufacturing process, the requirements are usually set before work begins; the design is fixed before production starts. However, in knowledge work, both design and enhancements are a part of the production process.

Finally, one of the most fundamental differences between manufacturing and knowledge work is variability. There is a very high degree of variability across all aspects of knowledge work—from the nature of the work performed to the amount of time and resources necessary to complete it. Accounting for this variability introduces complexities for which theories and practices in other settings don't have to account.

Scrumban is my chosen framework for arming individuals, teams, and organizations with capabilities to maximize their ability to manage knowledge work effectively.

Start the Journey with Systems Thinking

Analytical thinking is so entrenched in work and educational systems that many people are effectively conditioned to always analyze information rather than synthesize it. This practice represents a significant hindrance to improving work habits because analytical thinking involves viewing systems as a collection of independent things, causing people to ignore the interactions and dependencies that influence the results of each individual's actions. As the saying goes, "No man is an island"; it takes the collective interaction of many things to sustain the production of goods and services. Even lone rangers and experts rely on other people and systems to conduct their businesses.

> **Coaching Tip!**
>
> Important Concept Ahead

If we want to improve the conditions of our work and maximize the value of our actions, then we must recognize the best way to achieve this is to *avoid* focusing our attention on any specific component of a system in isolation. Doing so requires a substantial and conscious effort, and it explains why we start our journey with an emphasis on systems thinking.

Unfortunately, the systems we interact with are camouflaged. Although frameworks like Scrum are built on systems thinking, they do not extend to helping discover and manage system influences. Scrumban enables capabilities that make this extension easier.

Key Take-Away

Dr. W. Edwards Deming was a pioneer of systems thinking. He produced demonstrations, created statistical models, and curated real-world business studies that showed how thinking in terms of a system is critically important to solving a wide range of problems.

Deming estimated that 94% of business problems are derived from the processes we put in place rather than the people who work within those processes. Improving the system usually eliminates most problems.

So what are systems and what makes them unique? Here are some basic characteristics:

- A system is a set of components with a unifying purpose.
- Each component has an effect on the whole.
- Each component depends on at least one other component.
- There are often delayed responses, making cause and effect relationships difficult to perceive.
- System inputs, processes, and outputs have natural variation.
- The sum of the output of the components is not equal to the output of the system.
- Systems have a tendency to move toward disorganization (entropy).

A car is a great example of a system. It's made up of many components that work together to transport the driver and passengers from one place to another. These components include the motor, the transmission, the passenger compartment, the trunk, and so on.

When we take a car apart, it loses all of its essential characteristics; it ceases to be a car and becomes merely a collection of parts. As this example demonstrates, a system is never the sum of its parts—it's the product of the interaction of those parts.

Now suppose you want to improve your car's performance so it's more fun to drive and more economical. If you devoted all your attention to the motor, you probably wouldn't achieve your goal. That's because the system output you want to achieve relies on the interaction of many components, not just the performance of the motor. If you understand how this systems perspective applies to your car, then you're ready to extend this way of thinking to your work.

Practice Tip

How can you tell when efforts that are ostensibly designed to improve the performance of the "car" (a systemic improvement) are really only tuning the "motor" (a localized optimization)? By adopting the principles and practices outlined in this book! Specific examples presented here focus on evaluating metrics that directly measure your desired system outputs, applying disciplined approaches to problem solving, and much more. Once put into practice, these tools enable us to detect telltale signs by recognizing when addressing system bottlenecks or constraints is simply "moving the problem around" rather than truly changing the capabilities of the system.

Scrumban Can Incorporate Other Models and Frameworks

Next-Level Learning:

Evolving to More
Advanced Practices

Both Scrum and the Kanban Method are frameworks that are meant to be employed in conjunction with other processes and techniques. Kanban's capability to seamlessly integrate a broad variety of models and methods into the visualization and measurement aspects of its framework is what makes it such a powerful vehicle for success. These functions play a particularly important role as organizations extend Scrumban's capabilities across the enterprise. Teams and organizations just beginning to adopt Scrumban principles are best served by seeking to master one thing at a time. Introducing more than one framework or model is not conducive to maximizing efforts or accelerating through the Shu level of learning.

Later in this book, we'll consider the impact of integrating multiple models and frameworks within Scrumban, such as A3 Thinking, the Cynefin framework, and advanced statistical modeling.

Why Systems Thinking Is Relevant

Learning Levels:

The foundational concepts covered in this section are relevant to all learners.

IT organizations are systems, as are the organizations to which they belong. They are made up of distinct parts (individuals, other teams, and even other systems) that interact as a functional unit to produce software. They have processes that transform inputs into outputs (where information is what flows in and out).

Scrumban Stories: Mammoth Bank

The year is 2013. The IT organization at a large bank is eight years into an "Agile transformation." An outside firm was retained to lead the initial transition. A different company was hired several years ago to assist with ongoing efforts. And now a third firm has just been engaged to help the institution finally realize the full extent of benefits it had originally targeted from this major undertaking.

The IT organization is under fire for slow and unreliable delivery of work. The bank is losing customers and opportunities because of lagging capabilities in its technology applications. Senior executives are frustrated because the

good outcomes they've seen from the transformation are scattered and dispro-
portionate to the herculean investment of time, money, and effort.
    The bank finds itself in this position primarily because the organization has
focused on improving individual components, rather than the entire system.
The system has dampened their efforts. Had they recognized this dynamic early
on, they could have avoided a lot of pain and expense—not to mention accelerated the process of getting the results they were seeking.
    Read the full story of Mammoth Bank in the Appendix.

Deming demonstrated that an organization can achieve great results when all of
its connections and interactions are working together toward a shared objective. You
won't make the process of developing software more pleasurable for your developers
(or provide better results for your customers) if you simply improve the performance
of one team, or even a group of teams. For this reason, we're committed to highlighting how Scrumban can be leveraged at all layers of an organization to align understanding and effort across four key arenas:

- Leadership's ability to understand the needs of the marketplace and articulate
  a vision designed to address those needs (Figure 2.1). The better a company's
  leadership understands the needs of the marketplace, the better it can define
  products and services to satisfy those needs.

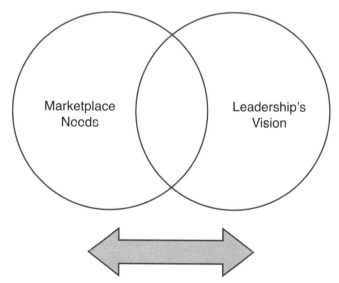

FIGURE 2.1   Aligning organizational vision with actual needs in the marketplace is
the first step toward creating sustained success.

How Scrumban Boosts Scrum's Capabilities

As an Agile framework, Scrum seeks to help product owners and the IT organization better understand the marketplace by creating short feedback loops using formal mechanisms (such as the Sprint Review and Release Planning events). These mechanisms are designed to foster greater collaboration between the end users of an IT application and its developers.

Outside of prescribing these basic roles and processes, however, Scrum is silent as to how organizations can achieve what should be one of their most important goals—an improved understanding of the marketplace.

With Scrumban, however, organizational leaders can leverage the framework's service-oriented and sustainability agendas to improve their understanding of the marketplace. For example, business leaders can learn to apply the principles and practices of "Discovery Kanban" to aid in a continuous sensing and visualization of options and risks. Discovery Kanban helps firms recognize and address the challenge of simultaneously executing and refining their proven business models while also exploring options for new business opportunities.[7]

■ Leadership's ability to effectively communicate its vision and the employees' ability to develop a shared understanding of how their work relates to achieving that vision (Figure 2.2). An organization's goods and services are ultimately produced by a system of systems. No matter how well leadership may understand the needs of the marketplace, the organization will suffer unless its employees also understand it and appreciate how their work relates to achieving the company's vision for the marketplace.

How Scrumban Boosts Scrum's Capabilities

Scrum relies on defined roles and the collaborative process to help achieve this kind of alignment. Because its prescribed mechanics are team-centric, the basic framework doesn't address achieving strategic alignment across multiple teams throughout a larger system.

In Scrum's defense, Scrumban does not prescribe specific approaches for achieving strategic alignment, either. Instead, it provides a framework that integrates tools and techniques such as the following, which foster wider alignment:

- ■ Visualization techniques that broaden shared understandings
- ■ An emphasis on using empirical data and the scientific method to make better decisions

---

7. http://tiny.cc/DeliveryDiscovery.

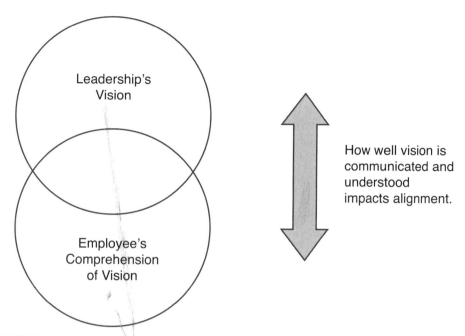

FIGURE 2.2   Ensuring your employees' understanding of organizational vision is consistent with what is intended to be communicated is a critical area of alignment.

- Techniques that minimize or eliminate barriers created by natural, human psychological responses

    More significantly, these and other additional capabilities can be extended beyond the software development process. Having a framework that can be used to improve shared understandings and collaboration across multiple business functions is critical to improving overall alignment.

- Employees' ability to effectively translate their understanding of leadership's vision into actions (i.e., products, services), as represented in Figure 2.3. Just as leadership must be able to effectively communicate its vision across the system, so employees must be able to translate their understanding of that vision and the marketplace into actions that enable the system to produce goods and services in alignment with their understandings.

How Scrumban Boosts Scrum's Capabilities

Both Scrum and Scrumban seek to maximize alignment in this arena through improved quality and throughput. Scrumban complements

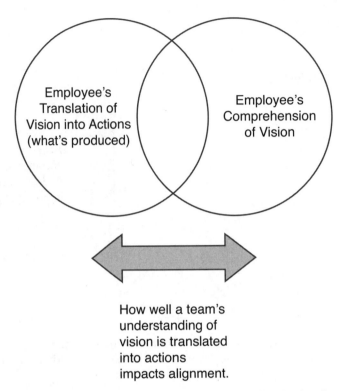

Employee's
Translation of
Vision into Actions
(what's produced)

Employee's
Comprehension
of Vision

How well a team's
understanding of
vision is translated
into actions
impacts alignment.

FIGURE 2.3   Enabling employees to work in a way that effectively allows them to take action in alignment with their understandings is important to successfully achieving organizational objectives.

Scrum's inherent capabilities by providing alternative views into product/ service delivery (for example, by making it easy for teams to analyze a quantifiable metric like lead time versus relying on a subjective measurement like velocity). The framework also exposes additional ways to maximize return on investment (ROI), such as by integrating advanced prioritization and adaptive risk management capabilities into daily workflow decisions.

- Employees' effectiveness at aligning the results of their actions with marketplace needs (Figure 2.4). The organization's products and services must satisfy the needs of the marketplace. Total alignment across these arenas is not required to achieve success, but greater alignment means a greater ability to sustain operations and fuel continued growth.

Every individual and team within an organization contribute toward maximizing organizational alignment. This is why systems thinking is relevant, and why it is

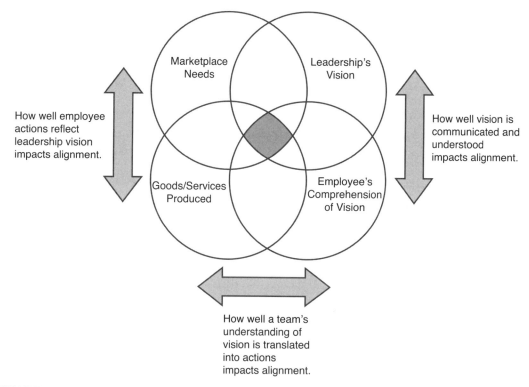

FIGURE 2.4   The more we are successful in aligning these arenas, the more we enable ourselves to achieve mutual success.

found at the starting line in the process of discovery. Scrumban helps us discover the right questions to ponder, the right information to analyze, and the right solutions to implement.

Systems in Our Work Environments

Conceptualizing systems is one thing; identifying them is another. It can be especially challenging to identify key systems when we're immersed within them. The first hurdle emerges from the tendency to focus attention on systems defined by visible roles and functions. These systems are only the tip of the iceberg, however. There are many different kinds of systems to consider.

Practice Tip

Identifying and visualizing core systems is one of the first and most important steps in using Scrumban effectively. Though Scrum's foundation rests, in part, in systems thinking principles, this framework does not focus on helping us understand the systemic interaction of their components—a necessary step to improving systemic versus purely local outcomes.

- Formal Systems
  - Usually the most visible systems. Examples include the documentation of processes, organizational charts (often hierarchical), and suppliers and customers (often viewed as terminal nodes).
  - Formal systems tend to reflect the structure of management versus the structure of work.
- Informal Systems
  - Examples include "shadow" organizations that perform actual work, networks that cross organizational boundaries, cooperative efforts outside formally defined roles, and cross-functional/self-directed teams.
  - These systems are not usually formally documented but are typically recognized within the workplace.
- Intangible Systems
  - Examples include the knowledge and lore of an organization that sets limitations and reflects where people really stand.
  - These systems are typically ignored by traditional management frameworks, yet they reassure employees that their efforts are valued and tied to the organization's ultimate success.
  - For better or for worse, management influences these systems most directly.

Scrumban Stories: Mammoth Bank and Siemens Health

Like any large company, Mammoth Bank was replete with visible systems. It also had its share of hidden systems. For example, Agile coaches reported to an invisible layer of management at the third-party vendor. How do you think this reality influenced outcomes?

Similarly, the influences of preexisting cultural systems didn't disappear when their physical manifestations were stripped away. For example, high-performing employees who had worked in quiet workspaces for years (in some cases, decades) didn't automatically become valued collaborators when thrust into shared workspaces.

The bank's failure to recognize and manage all of these systemic influences is what ultimately dampened the impact of its investment in a very large Agile transformation process. Investing time to discover and map these influences was a key factor in the significant gains I was able to make with their teams.

This approach can be contrasted with that taken by leadership at Siemens Health Services. In 2005, this organization elected to adopt Agile practices—specifically, Scrum/XP. By 2011, their teams had achieved high levels of maturity, but they continued to struggle with a number of challenges at the program and portfolio levels.

Leadership decided to insert the Kanban Method into this environment. Rather than discover the organization's existing systems, they elected to employ an "idealized design" approach (essentially assuming the organization was completely destroyed, and implementing a new design based on their ideal). I'll explore this strategy in more detail as we take a deeper dive into systems thinking.

Read the full stories of Mammoth Bank and Siemens Health Services in the Appendix.

Scrumban's Approach to Understanding Systems

We know from Deming's work that people who don't view their organization as a system tend to create complexity and problems. On the flip side, we also know that reducing complexity ultimately increases leverage (doing more with less), produces more breakthroughs, and leads to easier problem solving. Scrumban incorporates several core principles loosely correlated with Deming's System of Profound Knowledge that support us in truly understanding the systems within which we work:

- *Every system has variation.* All of the information we need to create optimal systems is both unknown and unknowable. Expecting identical performance from a system in different circumstances is foolish.
- *Favor the scientific method.* We can discover many helpful things about systems that are not immediately known. Using the scientific method allows us to discover these things more rapidly.
- *Only stable systems can be improved.* Observing systems at work enables us to detect and isolate their built-in flaws. We must stabilize a system before improving it, however, and we must rely on dynamic interactions rather than static observations. We can use Scrumban practices to first stabilize our system and then to improve it.
- *Tampering is counterproductive.* Both complexity and entropy (the tendency to move toward disorder) can be reduced by removing inherent flaws. Management is often the main source of increased complexity because of misguided efforts to work around missing resources, over-adjustment, and imposition of nonlinear workflows.

Practice Tip

Although Scrumban's core principles and practices can facilitate our discovery of systems and their properties, these capabilities don't relieve practitioners of their responsibility to make systems thinking a conscious effort!

Part 2: The Mess (Reasons Scrumban Is Needed)

Although the forces driving them are typically unique, teams and organizations share common motivations in seeking out new ways of working. How many of these are familiar to you?

Why We Want to Be "Agile"

> **Learning Levels:**
>
> The foundational concepts covered in this chapter are relevant to all learners.

Let's face it—nobody seeks to be Agile simply for the sake of being Agile. Rather, the drive to become Agile is intended to address an underlying need or issue that has captured someone's attention.

A common concern among the companies with which I've worked is a lack of a shared understanding among employees as to why their organization seeks to be "Agile." That knowledge gap explains why it's useful to review some of the more common *business* reasons companies and IT organizations choose to invest their efforts in adopting Agile frameworks like Scrum. Those reasons are explored in the following sections.

Faster Time to Market

The business side of the house can get tired of long delivery cycles that delay the realization of value and produce inadequate products. The promise of short delivery cycles and periodic releases emphasized by Agile practices is very appealing.

How Scrumban Boosts Scrum's Capabilities

As an Agile software development methodology, Scrum excels at helping teams bring applications to markets rapidly. Throughout this book, I'll highlight how Scrumban's Lean and systems thinking foundations add new capabilities that can improve the speed at which we deliver the right products and services to our customers. One simple example is how the framework helps identify and measure waste, such as excessive waiting (nonworking) time in workflows.

Earlier ROI

Early and incremental delivery of working software can make a huge difference to a business. Among other things, being able to show customers and end users working versions of applications can positively influence sales.

How Scrumban Boosts Scrum's Capabilities

Scrum excels with helping organizations achieve a positive ROI earlier in the development process. Scrumban's ability to tightly integrate practices that help organizations identify the right ROI to pursue, and to better manage the risks associated with work, serves to strengthen an already significant benefit. A specific example would be the mechanisms Scrumban uses to identify and measure work based on a defined risk profile.

Building the Right Products

Even if you're building applications that your customers say they want, Agile practices help ensure you build products in such a way that your customers will actually use them. Short delivery cycles let customers experience an emerging product, respond to it, and communicate needed adjustments throughout the development process.

How Scrumban Boosts Scrum's Capabilities

This is another arena in which Scrum shines, but the rewards here often rely on achieving a level of maturity in practices—something that many organizations struggle with. Organizations employing Scrumban will find it easier to integrate customer feedback throughout the entire product and service life cycles.

For example, Scrumban frameworks can help organizations actually influence customer demand before development begins, rather than resigning them to simply responding to feedback after the product is in use. I recently leveraged this ability at ScrumDo.

Like most Software as a Service (SaaS) providers, ScrumDo is constantly using customer feedback to inform and prioritize future product development decisions. Unlike many companies, it actively shapes customer demand through bidirectional communication. In my experience, the product development team was able to quickly assess the urgency of product enhancement requests against the development team's capacity to deliver them. This triggered direct communications with customers, which in turn improved their own understanding of their actual needs. As a result, ScrumDo was able to make early revisions in the enhancement requests, leading to a better balance between real customer demands and ScrumDo's capacity to respond to those demands—a better outcome for all involved.

Better Quality

There are four primary dimensions to software development projects: time, cost, scope, and quality. Traditionally, businesses have set strict limits on time, cost, and scope. As a consequence, unless a business is willing to compromise its established limits, the only dimension you can adjust is quality.

How Scrumban Boosts Scrum's Capabilities

Agile methods like Scrum set limits on time, cost, and quality, leaving scope as the variable dimension. This works because the Pareto principle tells us 80% of a product's value is derived from 20% of its functionality, rendering scope almost irrelevant once the critical 20% is achieved.

Scrum provides a solid framework for managing to this objective, but its overall effectiveness is often reliant upon the individual capabilities of a limited number of people within the organization. Moreover, the framework requires that firm commitments to produce certain features be made at the beginning of each sprint. In highly dynamic markets, committing to complete work even two weeks before delivery may be too early. Scrumban emphasizes the use of scientific methods to continually prioritize work at every decision point in the value stream, allowing organizations to integrate information and measures relevant to making those decisions right within the visual management framework.

Greater Predictability

Unfortunately, many IT organizations struggle with the challenge of providing the business unit with any idea of what it's going to get for its money or when it will see that benefit. This has led to business customers caring more about how predictably teams can deliver work rather than how quickly they can produce work. While important, predictability shouldn't have to be the paramount concern.

How Scrumban Boosts Scrum's Capabilities

Agile frameworks are designed to help teams make and meet commitments with stability and confidence. While methodologies like Scrum allow teams to better predict their own efforts, a team's output is rarely a self-contained function. Moreover, traditional Scrum techniques like team estimating do not scale effectively across an organization.

Scrumban adds capabilities that can not only help teams improve their estimates' precision, but also make it easier for organizations to reliably forecast and coordinate efforts across multiple teams and programs. For example, layering virtual kanban systems within the Scrum framework allows for objective performance indicators like lead time measurements. Unlike story points, which while not technically part of the Scrum framework are widely utilized in practice, the meaning of the numbers doesn't vary between teams. Basic queuing system mathematics enables probabilistic forecasting—which is typically more reliable than pure estimates-based forecasting.

Why Agile Adoptions Stall or Fail

| Especially For: |
| Managers & Executives |

Regardless of the specific reasons an organization seeks to adopt Agile practices, why are some successful in becoming lean, high-performing units whereas others meet with mixed results?

Both the Scrum and Kanban frameworks represent paths to Agility. Both are susceptible to being poorly implemented. In particular, both frameworks are vulnerable to practitioners who focus too intently on efficiency gains and ignore critical components like systems thinking and organizational culture.[8] This stifles creativity, innovation, and sustainability—all of which are important outcomes for the organization.

Scrum is actually very good at exposing systemic problems and dysfunctions. However, it wasn't designed to help individuals and organizations understand or manage the *systemic interactions* that lurk behind them. This isn't a shortcoming any more than the inability of a screwdriver to nail two boards together means the screwdriver is an ineffective tool.

Scrumban is simply another tool in the Agile toolbox. It's probably more apt, however, to describe it as a Swiss Army knife. It's something you can use to accelerate the maturing of Scrum practices. You can also use it as a "crutch" to satisfy an essential Scrum purpose that would otherwise go unmet because of some deficiency in the organization, team, or individuals involved. It can even influence work processes totally outside an organization's IT/software development domain. Let's consider some of these in context.

Viewing Agile as a Process, Rather Than as a Mindset

Transitioning to Agile methodologies is not a linear process. Roles are different, values are different, and successful transitions require changes in culture and mindset as much as in process.

There is no single recipe for Agility, yet many organizations attempt to implement Scrum as just that. Deming and the systems thinkers who've followed in his wake understood a fundamental truth: Identical processes introduced into different systems produce different outcomes, as do identical processes applied to the same system at different times. This variation occurs because no two systems are the same, and individual systems are always changing over time.

---

8. See, for example, http://tiny.cc/ScrumCriticism (July 2014).

While some benefit may be derived from following the directions in a "recipe," the extent of those benefits will be dictated by local factors. Scrum is flexible, but it doesn't explain how to implement changes in a way that individuals and business cultures will necessarily be ready to accept. This is where Scrumban can play a major role.

If the underlying intent is to improve an organization's ability to respond to marketplace needs, then we need to equip that organization's employees with an ability to understand the systems in which they work and enable them to discover and determine an optimal approach for a given context. Consider the current spectrum of approaches used to manage employees to meet this goal.

At one end of the spectrum is perhaps the most common approach, the top-down mandate. When an organization embraces a top-down management approach, its leaders decide their company needs to "become Agile," they prescribe an approach to achieve it (e.g., adopting Scrum), and then they expect everyone to fall in line behind the initiative.

At the other end of the spectrum are approaches like Dan Mezick's "open Agile adoption." This framework incorporates concepts like invitation (participation is optional), experimentation, game mechanics, rites of passage, and others. Many of these concepts are reminiscent of Toyota's quality circles. Peter Drucker might assess this approach as one that encourages "human energy" because it provides a way to manage the period of time when individuals no longer hold on to pretransition methods and status but haven't fully transitioned to their new way of working.

Mezick's approach embraces many of the concepts associated with holacracy— a management structure based on the tasks a company needs to accomplish rather than a standard reporting structure. In this social system of organizational governance, authority and decision-making processes are distributed across self-organizing teams rather than vested at the top of a hierarchy. Open Agile adoption is intended to provide a defined process in which individual team members take the initiative and express their concerns or ideas openly.[9]

How Scrumban Boosts Scrum's Capabilities

Scrum doesn't help us determine which approach to favor. In fact, critical aspects of the "open Agile adoption" (or holacratic) approach could lead to just as much culture shock in some organizations as mandates from on high would produce in others.

Scrumban allows us to discover the best approach for a given context. Implementing its core practices and principles does not require significant change, and the framework serves as a vehicle through which change can be adopted at a pace that's comfortable and sustainable.

---

9. As of this writing, the most notable organization to adopt a holacratic structure is Zappos.com (announced in December 2013).

Scrumban Stories: Mammoth Bank

Mammoth Bank had an ongoing relationship with a major business consultancy. The "gurus" worked with executive management to define a custom framework for Agile practices. They essentially prescribed implementing a "Scrum-like" framework, albeit one lacking many essential characteristics, at the team level.

As coaches began confronting the realities of implementation, it became clear transitioning to this "custom framework" would present many issues. However, neither the company nor its high-priced consultants would entertain additional frameworks (such as Kanban) to aid their implementation.

I began using Scrumban as a tool for guiding new practitioners on Scrum practices, though I didn't give it a label. As far as everyone else was concerned, they were doing Scrum. The performance of teams employing Scrumban significantly outpaced the performance of all the other teams.

Even something as simple as a "label" can be both empowering and limiting.

Read the full story of Mammoth Bank in the Appendix.

Lack of Commitment or Effort

Far too often, Agile is sold as a panacea for many problems. Agile processes can improve many things, but they are not magic, nor do they obliterate organizational dysfunctions.

Ultimately, work is a human endeavor, and improving any human endeavor requires more than desire. That is, it takes a conscious commitment to making that desire a reality. It calls for enduring the struggle associated with breaking habits and adopting entirely new ones. It also requires a willingness to seek and accept outside perspectives as a guide.

Toyota was at the brink of bankruptcy in the middle of the 20th century; by the end of the century, it was the most successful auto manufacturer in the world. This incredible turnaround wasn't simply the outcome of improved processes; rather, it was the direct result of changes in thinking and in behavior across *every layer* of the organization.

Toyota embraced new values—including a serious commitment to continuous improvement. It took conscious steps to nurture these values in every employee, and purposely worked to better align company and employee goals. It emphasized long-term relationships, two-way communications, servant leadership, and disciplined approaches to problem solving. These factors were the underlying forces behind its turnaround, and they were the direct result of the incredible commitment and effort made at every level of the organization. If your aim is to create sustainable high performance in your organization, then take lessons from Toyota's journey.

How Scrumban Boosts Scrum's Capabilities

Both Scrum and Scrumban help build commitment and effort. The major distinction between the two lies in Scrumban's bias toward incremental, evolutionary change in harmony with the human elements necessary to make it happen. Organizations can use this approach to become better Scrum practitioners, or to discover and implement their own unique practices.

Put another way, Scrum prescribes a final form for many aspects of an organization's work processes. Scrumban focuses on the purpose underlying those forms, and helps an organization discover how they can be fulfilled in other ways when the context requires it.

Succumbing to Disillusionment

After making an investment of time, money, and effort in Agile processes, it's only human for disillusionment to set in when companies see their productivity decrease or when they fail to improve as expected. While many people possess amazing resilience, this factor is a wildcard—and a reservoir that decreases with successive unsatisfactory experiences.

How Scrumban Boosts Scrum's Capabilities

Scrum is a powerful framework, but some of its ceremonies can create disillusionment when they're not properly adopted. For example, it's not uncommon for project managers to assume the role of Scrum master, yet continue to function in substantially the same manner. Scrum doesn't work well when this happens.

Similarly, time-boxed sprints can be too rigid for many environments and may create a perception of too much overhead. Sprint planning typically consumes a half-day or more for an entire engineering team. If ensuring involvement and coordination across multiple functions is an issue, then Scrum's formalities can definitely improve matters. But what if they're not?

Team estimation, a core component of most Scrum environments, can also lead to problematic issues. Time spent trying to evaluate and debate a feature's or story's size can be counterproductive, especially if you're already breaking down items to their smallest viable scope. Poor estimation—an extremely common issue—can actually cause problems. When work turns out to be bigger than expected, the sprint becomes overloaded. Responding to this unexpected expansion requires both time and effort.

More significantly, flawed estimations lead to unrealistic expectations. In such a case, retrospectives often turn into critiques of estimation techniques, priority changes, and other practice elements—demoralizing outcomes that are counterproductive to trust building.

Productivity can also became "spiky" in a time-boxed sprint paradigm, with few inherent tools available to address and resolve this inconsistency. Crazy hours at the end of the sprint as team members struggle to get everything done to fulfill the commitment are often followed by crashes as team members "recover."

These examples show why disillusionment represents a significant reason for failed transformations. It is nearly impossible to recover from the resulting psychological burnout—especially in startup environments, with their already limited resources. Scrumban incorporates mechanisms that help minimize these kinds of experiences.

Failing to Account for Human Factors

Change is threatening to most people; disruptive change is especially so. Imposing rapid and/or drastic changes upon people is fraught with peril, if only because of the psychological barriers it creates.

That said, not all disruptive change is necessarily bad. In some cases, it's actually needed. Jack Welch alludes to this concept when discussing his philosophy on the four types of managers.

Welch contends that organizations face the challenge of developing and sustaining a culture that is both values centered and performance driven. When leaders tolerate employees who deliver results but exhibit behaviors inconsistent with the company's values, they are ultimately working to defeat their own agenda.

For example, a core value of Agility is continuous improvement. If a high-performing individual in your organization doesn't share that commitment, he or she will eventually sabotage any efforts you make to instill that value in others.

How Scrumban Boosts Scrum's Capabilities

Scrum is silent on how to best address these types of psychological barriers. More significantly, the way it tends to be implemented rarely addresses the implications of introducing that change. In contrast, these human factors are directly managed within Scrumban's framework.

For example, there is little to no immediate change in ways of working when Scrumban is introduced. Rather, the framework emphasizes the adoption of simple mechanisms such as visualization, which allow teams to gain more insight into their systems, improve their shared understandings, and set the scope and pace of change as they discover ways to improve.

Delegation to Outside Consultants

The long-term success of any effort to make an organization more Lean and Agile is dependent upon leadership's continued ownership of the effort and its ongoing emphasis on driving desired business outcomes through new processes. Too often, organizational leadership ends up inadvertently delegating this responsibility to outsiders.

I've been involved in a number of engagements where companies have hired outside firms to help them execute the tactical steps necessary to successfully adopt Agile methodologies. Often, management abdicated "ownership" of certain efforts to these firms—efforts it should have retained with its scope of control. Specific examples include ensuring employees understand how their efforts are tied to desired business outcomes, and ensuring the organization ultimately achieves those outcomes. No outside firm can direct these kinds of things.

Though not directly related to this concept, it's noteworthy how process improvement consulting has become an obscene business in the Western world. Executive management has come to view outside consultants as being better positioned to sustainably improve their organizations than their own leadership. This is seldom true—especially in large organizations. Nonetheless, this mindset explains why many consultants receive upward of $2000/day in Agile coaching fees (as of 2014). Experts are important tools. Organizations just need to ensure they're not being called upon to perform functions that properly lie within the purview of the organization.

Scrumban Stories: Siemens Health Services

When Siemens sought to introduce Scrumban into its organization, it took a perfect approach to engaging outside consultants. It knew from prior experience that to make a new process sustainable, it had to develop internal expertise and competency. It also recognized, however, that it couldn't be successful without outside help. Siemens retained a firm that could help the company establish the proper foundation through a combination of initial training and continued expert insight. These experts mentored internal coaches, deepening their understandings and making the organization aware of rubrics like Little's law and expanded metrics. Siemens executives readily admit they would not have been nearly as successful without the help of this outside expertise.

Read the full story of Siemens Health Services in the Appendix.

Failure to Stabilize Before You Improve

Deming demonstrated why it's necessary to stabilize existing systems before attempting to improve them. Scrum is a great framework, but it wasn't designed with facilitating systems stabilization in mind. It relies on its prescriptive team structure to create stabilization (e.g., it assumes the construction of Scrum teams of 7–12 members from existing stable teams' instability will eventually result in stabilization). Also, the framework doesn't really incorporate any mechanics that reveal when stability may be lacking. For this reason, many Scrum project teams believe stability isn't affected when people are moved in and out of teams, leading to performance issues for which the framework may unfairly be blamed.

Many consulting firms offer, and many companies buy, for example, "Agile health assessments," "Agile spaces," and similar services. Such schemes typically provide the organization with little more than a checklist of actions generated without any contextual understanding of the system into which they would be introduced. Using an imperceptive checklist to improve is counterproductive.

Scrumban's own capabilities, plus those of additional models and techniques that can be "plugged in" to Scrumban systems, help identify system states and the best approaches for managing in them. Some of the external models I've used include A3 Thinking, a disciplined approach to problem solving, and the Cynefin framework, which represents a pragmatic application of complexity theory.

Failure to Identify the Right Problems and Tampering with Things That Work

Another principle derived from Deming's work is the importance of failing to identify the right problems or tampering with things that are already working well. A common misstep of management is to work on the wrong problems or needlessly manipulate perceived problems that aren't problems at all, both of which can lead to managers forcing things into a predetermined mold.

How Scrumban Boosts Scrum's Capabilities

Scrum exposes problems and dysfunctions, but it wasn't designed to manage the process of correcting them. In contrast, Scrumban's evolutionary change framework directly provides for this kind of course correction.

For example, I once worked with a Scrum team that was very inconsistent in its ability to finish all work accepted into a sprint. A previous coach had elected to train team members on improved work breakdown techniques as a means of improving their ability to meet their sprint commitment. Though his intentions were admirable, he'd elected this course of action without truly understanding what was actually driving the outcome. The introduction of Scrumban's systems understandings and workflow visualizations helped the team and their new coach discover the root causes of their Sprint commitment issues.

Similarly, I worked with a large financial institution that was intent on constructing new Agile workspaces to support its new processes. In undertaking this major change in physical space, however, management failed to account for the psychological implications for workers who had worked in physical cubes for decades and the barriers to change this new approach created in other contexts. Teams were enabled to overcome many obstacles once Scrumban frameworks were implemented in affected environments.

Unhealthy Introspection during Retrospectives

We alluded to the problem of negatively focused retrospectives earlier when addressing disillusionment. Retrospectives can often devolve into inappropriate focus on individuals rather than on the system. They can also lead to improvements being treated separately from the system itself (e.g., the use of Kaizen boards, where efforts the team undertakes to improve are visualized separately from "ordinary work"). Scrumban helps counteract these tendencies by continually stressing a holistic systems viewpoint and encouraging the visualization and management of all efforts within a unified framework.

Unhealthy Focus on Speed and Results over Quality

Introducing a poor product to the market because of an over-emphasis on speed has produced negative long-term consequences for many organizations. The right results incorporate both appropriate quality and timing considerations. Scrumban enables practices and techniques that help organizations identify and manage to the appropriate balance.

Making Continuous Improvement the Responsibility of or Dependent on a Limited Number of Individuals

Peter Drucker has said the gravest indictment of any leader is for his or her organization to collapse as soon as the leader leaves or dies. There is an equivalent net effect for organizations that delegate the ownership of core Agile values to only a select few.

Roles: The Good, the Bad, and the Ugly

Roles carry a lot of baggage. We identify with our roles. The work we perform is embodied within our roles. When new processes define different roles or different functions for existing roles, we need to recognize that psychological elements must be overcome in that process.

How Scrumban Boosts Scrum's Capabilities

Because Scrum prescribes roles without speaking to this psychological agenda, those implementing it often fail to take the implications of role changes into consideration.

Artificial adherence to either existing roles or a prescribed definition of new roles often impedes an organization's ability to effectively evolve. Scrumban is inherently structured to deal with these challenges. Among its core principles is respect for existing roles, but with an eye toward encouraging teams and individuals to discover any needed changes on their own in a nonthreatening fashion.

Intentional versus Emergent Architecture

Finally, it's worthwhile to introduce another area of tension that Scrumban helps to illuminate—the degree to which we adopt intentional versus emergent approaches to software development. Traditional methods, like waterfall, dictate a lot of upfront work on architectural planning and design. The result is a very deliberate and intentional process.

Because Agile practices favor the creation of working software over extensive planning and documentation, most practitioners believe organizations wishing to become more Agile are better off allowing architecture to emerge from the work performed to complete small, customer-focused requirements. Rework will be necessary as a deeper understanding of the system is developed, but this approach helps avoid the tendency to over-engineer architecture past the point of usefulness. Scrum is biased toward this mindset. A symptom of an unwieldy technical debt typically suggests the presence of an insufficient architectural focus.

But consider the purpose of architecture: it exists to shape our solution, address foreseeable technical risks, and minimize the effect of changes. Solving larger problems and creating common ways of doing things (lightweight architectural mechanisms) are good architectural goals, but only if the solution is certain.

Environments consisting of large teams, reuse requirements, multiple integration and alignment requirements, and external governance requirements (among others) are probably better suited to an intentional architecture approach. Contrasting environments and markets, such as startups and smaller organizations, are usually better suited to an emergent architecture approach.

How Scrumban Boosts Scrum's Capabilities

At the end of the day, unless an organization has a framework that can withstand incremental development, it will end up with so much technical debt that it slows down the software delivery pipeline, as developers end up doing maintenance instead of new development. This is exactly what had started to happen at Mammoth Bank in our case study.

Scrum itself is silent about how best to deal with this issue. Scrumban helps organizations proactively address these kinds of developments—first by making the work and its consequences more visible, then by enabling teams and organizations to integrate a variety of mechanics to proactively address them as part of ongoing work.

Tying It All Together

And so ends our first step of discovery and understanding. The single most important learning you can take away from this chapter is that of systems thinking. Although systems thinking was first articulated in a meaningful way more than 70 years ago, it's still a novel mindset for most people in the business world. The sooner you can acclimate yourself to this new way of thinking, the sooner you'll be able to leverage the principles and practices detailed in this book.

Systems thinking enables improved understandings. Improved understandings, in turn, give us a better sense of what to look for as we seek out ways to improve. Having a better sense of what to look for enables us to recognize meaningful patterns that would otherwise go unobserved. Use this knowledge to your advantage as we continue our journey.

Chapter 3

THE MISSION: CLARIFYING THE RELATIONSHIP BETWEEN PURPOSE, VALUES, AND PERFORMANCE

IN THIS CHAPTER

- How Vision and Shared Purpose Impact Team Performance
- Why It's Important to Create Adaptive Capabilities
- Connecting the Work We Do to the Customers Whom We Serve

Learning Levels:

The foundational concepts covered in this chapter are relevant to all learners.

If systems thinking is central to effectively aligning systems across the organization, then shared purpose is central to effectively executing actions that move us closer to our desired outcomes. But what if neither purpose nor desired outcomes are clear?

In this chapter, we consider why organizational purpose and values are relevant to work. We then examine some of the ways teams and organizations can apply Scrumban to overcome challenges created by deficiencies in these arenas.

Why We're Paid to Work

Fundamentally, we're paid to work because we produce something of value. Put another way, we're paid for contributing something of value that's critical to delivering products customers are willing to exchange money for. In our quest for professional success, it's only natural to focus on improving our own capabilities, or those of our direct reports. Systems thinking demonstrates the potential foolhardiness of this approach.

Consider a team sport like baseball, where individual players are part of a team. A player can double his on-base percentage every year, yet never score a run if his teammates don't bring him home. Similarly, a team can improve its collective performance in every area, but they won't win more games if the other teams improve more.

> **Coaching Tip!**
>
> Important Concept Ahead

The organizations we work for are similar to the teams in a baseball league. They operate as systems of systems. Their overall performance is dictated first by how well they succeed in maximizing the collective performance of the systems within the team, and then by whether those efforts produce equal or better value than their competitors in the marketplace.

In a perfect meritocracy, individual compensation would be established by measuring the relative risk and contribution associated with our roles. Unfortunately, we live in a world where most of us overvalue the relative risk and value associated with our individual contributions, while management often undervalues them. One way to begin changing this dynamic is by improving the shared understanding of purpose and mission. Scrumban is naturally suited to help achieve this goal.

Key Take-Away

Deming often explained the concept of a system by comparing it to an orchestra, explaining that when listeners judge its performance, the illustrious play of the few is far less important than the way everyone performs together

According to Deming, "The conductor, as manager, begets cooperation between the players, as a system, every player to support the others. There are other aims for an orchestra, such as joy in work for the players and the conductor."[1]

Scrum provides tools and capabilities that enable teams to work together more effectively. In a system of systems, however, improving the performance of a single development team is like improving the performance of an individual player on a baseball team—it may or may not improve overall performance at the end of the day. Scrumban adds capabilities that help prioritize the right things to improve, and to identify and objectively measure which outcomes we want to influence.

The Importance of Shared Purpose

High performance and high satisfaction go hand in hand. Indeed, one of the most effective ways we can increase the value of our work as well as our own satisfaction with it is by ensuring our decisions are governed by the forces that define the purpose

---

1. The System of Profound Knowledge by Dr. W. Edwards Deming.

of our work. This is why I emphasize articulating the team's purpose when introducing Scrumban into my clients' way of working.

How Scrumban Boosts Scrum's Capabilities

As a framework, Scrum relies on individual practitioners to clarify shared purpose. For example, the product owner is charged with discovering and communicating an understanding of market effectiveness. Scrum doesn't offer any specific mechanisms to help product owners discover leadership's vision. Similarly, opportunities to create shared understanding of that vision are effectively limited to planning meetings and retrospectives, which do not contribute to improved alignment across multiple teams.

Scrumban's core practices and principles represent additional and alternative tools for the pursuit of information and improved alignment across the organization. This approach encourages visualizing and sharing work demands, work in progress, team capacities, explicit policies around that work, risks associated with the work, and the work's quantified value to the organization. It emphasizes behavior focused on service orientation and delivery.

The Importance of Adaptive Capabilities

> **Especially For:**
>
> Managers & Executives

When groups and organizations attain a shared motivation and approach to continuous improvement, they are exhibiting key characteristics of "thinking systems" (systems that have *adaptive capabilities*). When organizations foster consistent values and common disciplines to guide choices and decision making, they are providing the raw materials needed to sustain a culture of adaptive capability in their organizations.

Organizational learning closely correlates with adaptive capability, which is why minimizing or eliminating barriers to effective organizational learning is important if we want to create and sustain effective ways of working. Regardless of our role within a company, we can all work at recognizing and minimizing common impediments to organizational learning:

- Silo thinking
- Failure to make time for reflection
- Lack of a cogent long-term vision around which to unite
- Apathy
- Denial of the existence of problems
- Lack of a systemic framework for learning

How Scrumban Boosts Scrum's Capabilities

Philosophically, Scrum encourages breaking down impediments to learning. Its bias toward cross-functional teams helps avoid silo thinking. Its retrospective ceremonies encourage time for reflection and improvement. Its empowering capabilities help to minimize apathy. Other impediments, however, are influenced only indirectly, if at all.

Lurking behind Scrumban's core principles and practices is a strong bias toward the creation of thinking systems. This starts with the framework's focus on identifying the relative priority of organizational philosophies, values, vision, mission, and goals (Figure 3.1). The resulting hierarchy leads to local decision making that's in greater alignment with those aims.

Let's get acquainted with some of the ways Scrumban influences the adoption of conceptual frameworks, common disciplines, and habitual ways of thinking that foster adaptive capabilities.

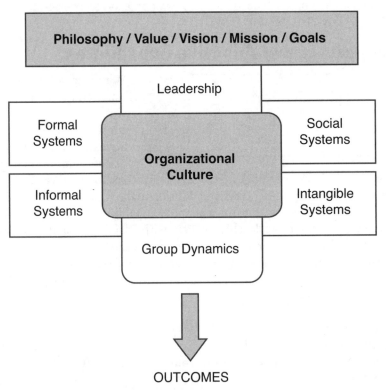

FIGURE 3.1   How the people in an organization approach their work and make decisions is driven by a confluence of many factors. Organizational values and the resulting culture they create serve as an "invisible hand" guiding these outcomes.

Communication and Application of Core Values to Decision Making

The difference between brilliant teams and mediocre ones doesn't lie so much in their collective mental capabilities, but in how well they're able to utilize those capabilities as a group. Core values enable these capabilities by changing environments so as to create like-minded "thinking systems" within organizations.

Core values are an organization's essential and enduring beliefs—a small set of guiding principles with intrinsic value. They guide employees in determining what should and shouldn't be done in a given situation, and also communicate their relative importance. Employees who understand and practice organizational values have a strong sense of what to trade off when choices must be made. In short, values are an essential way to integrate a common mindset in every employee, creating a system that moves in unison toward a common outcome. Ideally, this common mindset is clearly established by leadership.

To this end, high-performing companies understand it's more important to know "who you are" than "where you are going." Change is inevitable: Leaders will die, markets will change, products and services will become obsolete, and new technologies will emerge. Core values, however, endure as a source of guidance and inspiration through all of these changes. They are essential in holding an organization together and helping it maintain order as it changes.

As good systems thinkers and Scrumban practitioners, we recognize there are many sources of guidance and lessons from an endless variety of teachers. The principles of Judaism represent a particularly profound example of the power of values. Judaism's values held the Jewish people together for centuries despite the Diaspora; all Jews played an integral role in maintaining and practicing these values. Both leaders and employees can learn from history in this regard.

So what are the core values that enable organizations in this manner? They include many of the same values associated with the Agile Manifesto, Scrum, and Kanban:

- Respect
- Courage
- Commitment to continuous improvement
- Transparency
- Alignment
- Customer focus
- Commitment to empiricism
- Entrepreneurial culture

A review of companies that have experienced decades of continuous success reveals that most, if not all, maintained a fixed set of core values and purposes, even as they were simultaneously adopting different business strategies and practices to adapt to their changing world. For example, Hewlett-Packard has undergone several radical changes in operating practices, cultural norms, and business strategies without losing the spirit of the company's core principles. Johnson & Johnson continually questions its structure and revamps its processes while preserving its core ideals. In the 1990s, 3M sold off several of its large, mature businesses to refocus on its core purpose of innovating to solve problems.

So how can an organization know what should and should not change? The ability to manage both continuity and change is often associated with consciously practiced disciplines closely linked to a clear vision. Let's take a closer look at what vision means in this context.

Vision

High-performing organizations have a clarity and rigor associated with otherwise vague concepts of "vision." They create frameworks that offer practical guidance for articulating a coherent vision. Because "vision" can mean different things for different people, Scrumban can serve as a conceptual framework to help define it, to develop shared understandings of it, and to help employees discover it when clear articulation is lacking.

A well-conceived vision has two major components—a core ideology and an envisioned future. Core ideology defines what an organization stands for and why it exists. It is unchanging and complements the envisioned future (what an organization aspires to become, to achieve, and to create). The envisioned future will usually require significant change and progress to achieve.

A good vision is *neither* wishful thinking *nor* an ambitious plan that doesn't take into account the organization's current capabilities and past achievements. Instead, an effective vision recognizes and accounts for the fact change occurs both incrementally and through market-changing innovations (like Apple's knack for developing products that consumers doesn't even know they need).

While vision is critical, to be useful it must be translated into tangible objectives that employees can rally around. Steve Jobs put it this way: "If you are working on something exciting that you really care about, you don't have to be pushed. The vision pulls you." This is where values and vision intersect with mission and goals. If management doesn't communicate the organizational vision to its employees, then its employees need a framework through which these things can be discovered.

Team Members:

When either organizational vision or the way your work contributes to its realization is unclear, Scrumban's focus on service will enable you to gain clarity over time and encourage adoption of measures that more closely align your efforts to organizational objectives.

Scrumban starts by providing new measures of validation. Just as profitability, market position, and sales growth validate a company's value proposition, so Scrumban enables us to validate our organization's vision and mission through empirical measures.

Similarly, a vision cannot be so distant that it essentially negates the possibility of ever realizing it. Just as Scrum's time-boxes create realistic horizons to establish achievable commitments, so Scrumban provides mechanisms that allow us to ensure the visions used to guide our decisions are realistic enough to be useful. If an articulated vision appears too distant, Scrumban enables employees to articulate more relevant nearer-term objectives.

Lastly, poorly communicated visions sometimes suggest competing goals. Though core values can help resolve these dilemmas, an organization risks degraded performance unless other means are available to provide employees with needed guidance. Managers can lean on Scrumban's core principles to provide these alternative capabilities.

Mission and Goals

The mission identifies the business of an organization. It articulates (in a customer-focused way) why the organization exists, and it serves as a general guide for decision making. In more basic terms, a mission defines the purpose for undertaking work and explains how the organization pursues its vision.

Goals, by comparison, are concrete achievements that an organization wants to attain within a set period of time. They are the tactical stepping-stones to fulfilling the organization's mission. Scrumban can be used to clarify and articulate organizational mission and goals in the same way that it addresses and breaks down the broader vision.

As IT organizations gain greater understanding and control over their work processes, it's increasingly important to recognize and respond to how the risk paradigms associated with various business strategies can change. Scrumban allows us to integrate the adaptive management of strategic options into the context of our daily work. More importantly, it allows us to do so using models familiar to other units in the organization. This is essential to fostering greater alignment across multiple business functions.

Consider Ansoff's matrix. The Ansoff matrix was first published in *Harvard Business Review* in 1957 and is a tool that business leaders may use as a quick and simple method for thinking about the risks and rewards associated with alternative paths for growth. Risk increases as you move away from the lower-left corner of the matrix. Ansoff recognized four potential product growth strategies in this context of risk, as shown in Figure 3.2.

As the matrix reflects, new product development for an existing market is a medium-risk strategy. We don't know all the measures that go into assessing risk in this domain, but our ability to execute technology product development would likely be a significant component.

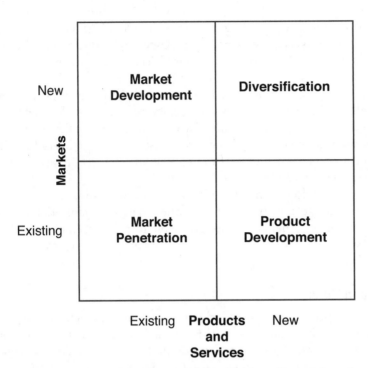

FIGURE 3.2   Ansoff's matrix is a simple tool for thinking about risk and reward in a product/services strategy context.

Development teams can easily integrate technical risk management into a Scrumban framework. The improved management and predictability can then be applied to positively influence and manage the risk matrix of new growth strategies. This is a prime example of how the Scrumban framework can be used to inform and positively influence non-IT processes in an organization.

Scrumban Stories: CodeGenesys

Scrumban was instrumental in helping CodeGenesys quickly ramp up a new business unit. More than half the employees in this unit were new to the company, many were new to the domain, and all were distributed across several locations.

An electronic kanban board was used to visualize the team's work. Despite cultural differences in style and communication, team members quickly gained a clear understanding of their common purpose. Within a matter of weeks, several members were leading efforts to improve the way work was being done in pursuit of the unit's objectives. Within a matter of months, the team was operating at very high efficiency; reliably delivering completed work at a comfortable cadence.

Read the full story of CodeGenesys at http://codegenesys.com/scrumban/case-study-CG.

All of the concepts discussed in this section—values, vision, mission, and goals—represent forces and attributes that influence the alignment between the leadership's vision and an organization's understanding of that vision. If these things are vague or poorly communicated, the systems involved are likely to be poorly aligned. Scrumban helps teams overcome such challenges by emphasizing the discovery and shared understanding of information needed to fill these gaps.

Being Disciplined about the Right Metrics

Organizations want to measure progress toward desired outcomes. Unfortunately, it's easy to fall into the trap of measuring the wrong things, especially when you view metrics as a static choice. While it's important to have a constant set of metrics to evaluate over time, it's equally important to recognize that different metrics help us understand different things. Scrumban recognizes that it may be important to track different sets of measurements at different points in time to help us better understand and overcome the challenges we are facing.

When organizations create a culture that elevates business value as the only benchmark, they produce forces that result in a superior alignment of their key systems. Most of the additional metrics that Scrumban introduces are directly tied to the creation or delivery of business value in one form or another.

In contrast, consider Scrum's primary metric of velocity. This team-based measurement is intended to provide a close approximation of throughput. While the process of estimating story points can be a very effective tool for teams to acquire a better shared understanding of work, these estimates don't necessarily correlate with either business value or the time it actually takes to complete work. Scrumban's visualization of work and policies, its inherent bias toward value delivery/service orientation, and its additional metrics represent alternative techniques teams and organizations can consider when points estimation isn't fully meeting the organization's overall needs.

It's especially important for larger organizations to maintain consistency across their measurements. This is one place where Scrum's reliance on velocity may actually be a shortcoming. Teams are different, and so are their estimations. Individual teams may be able to use velocity effectively for sprint planning and related needs, but that metric doesn't really help teams assess how their performance is delivering value to their customers, or help an organization manage the efforts of multiple teams contributing to a portfolio of efforts.

Ultimately, the value of a business or a system is determined by the consumer of its product or service. Cost is just one of many factors that determine value. As this book was being written, Apple commanded a significant market share for portable devices (smartphones and tablets), even though its products were more expensive than most competing products. Examples such as this illustrate why additional capabilities that help a team or organization understand and validate actual business value are invaluable.

Scrumban Stories: Siemens Health Services

Though Siemens had given some thought to the enhanced metrics it would be able to use under a Scrumban framework, the company discovered an unexpected benefit from its endeavor. Many of the "new" metrics it began utilizing were familiar to business stakeholders and related non-IT personnel. The importance and benefits of having a shared language cannot be underestimated.

Read the full story of Siemens Health Services in the Appendix.

Using Disciplined Approaches to Identify and Address the Most Important Problems

Toyota is famous for its relentless ability to improve performance. Central to this ability is a culture that instills structured problem solving in its employees. Toyota employs A3 Thinking, a disciplined approach to problem solving. Other frameworks also exist.

Although A3 Thinking or structured problem solving is not a formalized part of either Scrumban or the Kanban Method, it naturally "plugs in" to these frameworks and is particularly well suited to helping employees at all levels of an organization influence the alignment of its key systems.

For example, leadership can employ A3 techniques to identify problems and improve their ability to effectively communicate the organization's vision to employees. Similarly, employees can use the same structured processes to clarify which short-term objectives to pursue when leadership has provided only a vague framework of organizational values, vision, and goals.

More specifically, teams can effectively "substitute" target conditions from an A3 process for a vague vision or longer-term objectives. Structured processes help clarify whether a particular course of action will help achieve a target condition, the steps that should be taken to get there, any potential impediments, and more.

Improving systems alignment helps counteract entropy in our work systems—that is, their tendency to move from order to chaos. It also helps ensure we don't fall into the trap of expecting the results achieved in other contexts when we simply apply a prescribed way of doing things ("best practices") without consideration of the unique characteristics of our systems.

I've focused a great deal of attention on core values and principles because they are central to understanding how Scrumban adds new dimensions to how we view and manage work. As with most things, you will develop a more complete understanding of these considerations through implementation and practice. Don't lose sight of these core principles, as the context they provide can help you avoid many common pitfalls.

Tying It All Together

The topics discussed in this chapter might seem abstract and esoteric, especially to readers who are not in an executive or senior management role. Nevertheless, it would be a serious mistake to dismiss this content as irrelevant. Why? Because the responsibility is a two-way street. The first line of responsibility for aligning purpose, values, and performance lies with an organization's leaders and managers. Employees seeking greater opportunity, control, and satisfaction with their work, however, have an equal responsibility to discover ways to gain clarity when alignment is cloudy.

Arming ourselves with the knowledge of what we should expect from our managers and leaders is an avenue toward self-empowerment. Familiarizing ourselves with the tools we can use to get what we need enables us to become effective agents of change. Don't underestimate the power of this combination.

Chapter 4

MOTIVATIONS: WHY SCRUMBAN WORKS

IN THIS CHAPTER

- Scrumban's Origins
- How Scrumban Effectively Layers the Kanban Method Alongside Scrum
- How Scrumban Integrates Additional Frameworks and Models

Learning Levels:

The foundational concepts covered in this chapter are relevant to all learners.

This chapter is devoted to taking a closer look at some of the mechanics that make Scrumban tick. Because the Kanban Method represents a big part of the system, we're going to spend a significant amount of our time in Kanbanland. Let's start with a quick review of Scrumban's first incarnation.

Where It All Began

In his seminal book on Scrumban,[1] Corey Ladas makes the case that time-boxed iterations add no value to well-regulated pull systems (kanban systems). Because his book advocated evolving Scrum systems away from time-boxed sprints, many people have come to equate Scrumban with this approach. As previously noted, however, Scrumban has evolved to make this just *one* possible incarnation. Nonetheless, because Ladas was among the first to layer a kanban system within a Scrum context, it's instructive to review his thinking and the experience that brought him to this point.

Ladas posited that true Agile development is premised on achieving one-piece flow—in other words, developing the capability to produce one feature at a time. As it takes a considerable breadth of talent to design and develop a product of any consequence, one-piece flow necessitates assembling and coordinating a team of experts.

---

1. *Scrumban: Essays on Kanban Systems for Lean Software Development* (Modus Cooperandi Press, 2008).

Ladas began his overview by illustrating some of the pros and cons associated with "craft production," using a small team of generalists whose idle members would pull (take ownership and work upon) a single work item as it appeared in the work queue as an example. Working on one item at a time, each team member would continuously apply the workflow until that item was integrated and deployed. Upon completing his or her work, the member would return to an idle pool for reassignment. Ladas suggested the resulting flow would look something like that shown in Figure 4.1.

While this craft style of producing work controls the flow and establishes some degree of predictability, it essentially entails a series of one-off pieces produced by generalists. Drawbacks to this approach include losing key elements of specialized workflows (including reviews at hand-offs), a lack of knowledge transfer from one team member to another, and a general decrease in quality as workers focus on task completion versus task quality.

Ladas then considered a "feature crew" approach. The primary distinction between this approach and the "craft" approach lies in how work is processed. Here, work is handed off among specialists with complementary skill sets rather than being completed end to end by a single generalist. Although resource utilization with the feature crew approach is lower than with the craft method, Ladas claimed it would be offset by the efficiency benefits gained from specialization. Still, outcomes were not ideal.

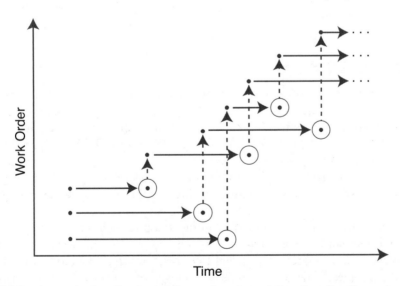

FIGURE 4.1   A rough visualization of "one-piece" workflow in a "craft production" model.

Source: Corey Ladas. *Scrumban: Essays on Kanban Systems for Lean Software Development* (Modus Cooperandi Press, 2008).

Ladas next explored the notion of synchronized workflow. The software development world has traditionally recognized two approaches to partitioning work: by schedule or by workflow. Traditional project management frameworks schedule large work orders and align resources by workflow. Agile frameworks schedule small work orders and align resources by schedule (in Scrum, this is the time-boxed sprint). Synchronized workflow represents an approach that schedules small work orders just as Agile frameworks would do but also includes an alignment of resources by workflow as traditional frameworks would do.

Assuming the same kind of craft development team as with the feature crew approach (one specialist for each step in the workflow), Ladas's first thought experiment was to synchronize work according to a clock, creating a discrete pipeline.

At the first tick of the clock, a work item is pulled and placed in the first processing state. At the second tick, the first work item enters the second processing state and a new item is set in motion. Once the pipeline is full, each tick represents completion of one work item and the beginning of another. The resulting flow can be visualized as shown in Figure 4.2.

Unfortunately, this model can't really work in a software development environment. The size of work items is rarely identical, and the same is true of the amount of time each spends in a given phase of production. You might be able to achieve synchronization if you set the clock tick equal to the worst-case duration of any given work item state (assuming you could establish that measurement), but this would result in a substantial waste of human talent.

Breaking work items up into grouped tasks and leveling them so they can be completed within the same amount of time is one way to manage variability, and it would definitely make the synchronized approach described previously more attractive. Moving work through multiple "pipelines" would further reduce the negative impact associated with stalled work. The overall synchronization issue, however, would still be a problem.

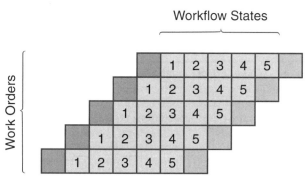

FIGURE 4.2   Visualization of workflow in a "feature crew" model.

Source: Corey Ladas. *Scrumban: Essays on Kanban Systems for Lean Software Development* (Modus Cooperandi Press, 2008).

This point is where Ladas ultimately began to take on the view that time-oriented synchronization represents waste. By relaxing synchronization requirements and using buffers to smooth out variation (i.e., using a kanban pull system managed with work in progress [WIP] limits and minimal queue buffers for synchronization), Ladas demonstrated that flow-based development in a craft environment represents a powerful path to true Agility.

It's hard to argue with Ladas's conclusions about the continuous flow mode, especially when they are combined with the dissatisfaction that teams experience with time-boxed sprints. Ladas ultimately took the position that "first generation" Agile frameworks like Scrum are a historical necessity to achieve improved approaches and a great "starting point" on the path to Agility. I'm inclined to adopt a slightly more pragmatic viewpoint.

The continuous flow model is powerful, but rhythms of synchronized commitment points (i.e., time-boxed iterations) can be extremely useful and even the best choice in some contexts. Factors favoring time-boxed practices include the depth of skills and "maturity" of your teams, the stability of the members in those teams, and the extent to which key resources must be shared.

Ultimately, Scrumban emphasizes pragmatism. It rests on the principle that management and workers are in the best position to decide which commitments make sense for their circumstances. Rather than forcing a constraint upon a system because it makes sense in most circumstances, Scrumban should, like the Kanban Method, favor facilitating discovery and understanding of systems to make intelligent choices. Continuous flow was the right choice for Ladas and his organization—but it may not be the best option for yours.

To be fair, when Ladas coined the term "Scrumban" in 2008, the Kanban Method had not matured to the level of definition it currently enjoys, and the variety of contexts in which it applied were more limited. These continuing evolutions are why we maintain that today's Scrumban framework is far broader than the single context that Ladas described.

Scrumban Stories: Contrasting Approaches

Siemens Health Services and Objective Solutions (a Brazilian company) both chose to adopt Ladas's continuous flow model in their Scrumban implementations. Some of their reasons were the same, while others differed. Both organizations had fairly mature and stable teams, both had implemented extreme programming (XP) practices, and both were experiencing difficulties coordinating, planning, and estimating large sprint backlogs across multiple teams (15–50 teams). These challenges related more to business factors than to team needs.

The Objective Solutions teams saw continuous flow as a solution for managing sprint starvation. Their flagship product is a large, complex software product for which a new version is released every month. They initially synchronized their sprint duration to this delivery cadence, but found teams were often starved for work by the end of their sprints. They saw continuous flow as a solution to this dilemma.

The teams at Mammoth Bank took a mixed approach. Most teams continued to employ time-boxed iterations in their Scrumban frameworks. Mammoth's teams were generally less mature in their understanding and execution of Scrum practices, so regular interactions around the work were beneficial in helping members improve their shared understanding of both the work and the sprint goals.

Read the full stories of these organizations in the Appendix.

The importance and benefits of having a shared language cannot be underestimated.

Layering the Kanban Method

The evolution of the Kanban Method since Ladas's initial efforts has also caused Scrumban to evolve over time. To understand Scrumban's capabilities, it's necessary to understand the influences that layering of the Kanban Method alongside Scrum brings to the table.

Attending to the Psychological Agenda

| **Especially For:** |
| Managers & Executives |

Companies that evolve from good to great usually have no name for their transformation, nor are they likely to have followed a specific program. Instead, what they share in common are pragmatic, committed-to-excellence processes and frameworks that keep the company, its leaders, and its people on track for the long haul—that is, frameworks that prioritize discipline over a quick fix.

So how do you get a company with 10,000, 25,000, or 50,000 or more people to immediately embrace and adopt a new strategy that will eventually change substantial aspects of your operations? You don't—and certainly not with a single program.

What organizations must do is gradually build momentum, by constructing tangible evidence that their plans make sense and deliver results. Scrum supports this need in some ways, but in most adoptions its implementation entails a radical and abrupt transformation over a more deliberate creation of evidence and trust building.

In a fundamental way, the Scrumban framework parallels the concepts set forth by Stephen Covey in his book *The Seven Habits of Highly Effective People*. Covey posits that everyone begins life in a state of dependence. In other words, we feel and take no responsibility for the events of our lives because we are totally dependent on others (usually our parents). Most of us eventually transition to a state of independence, where we gain stability through self-reliance. If we are to become truly effective, however, Covey claims that we must learn to build interdependent relationships. In many ways, the process of gaining independence allows us to better understand the benefits of dependency.

It's easy to extend Covey's work into an organizational or systems context. Nurturing people and systems that learn to build healthy, interdependent relationships is the key to evolving teams and organizations toward sustainable performance. The Scrumban framework moves organizations in this direction by emphasizing systemic understandings, building trust across the organization (recognizing one key way to build trust lies in consistently fulfilling promises), and leveraging the natural desires of individuals:[2]

1. *Curiosity*: Having things to think about and investigate.
2. *Honor*: Pride that our personal values are reflected in how we work.
3. *Acceptance*: The people around us approve of who we are and what we do.
4. *Mastery*: Work that challenges our competence but remains within our abilities.
5. *Power*: The ability to influence what happens around us.
6. *Freedom*: Some independence from others in our work and responsibilities.
7. *Relatedness*: Good social contacts with the people with whom we work.
8. *Order*: Enough rules and policies to create a stable environment.
9. *Goal*: Our purpose in life is reflected in what we do.
10. *Status*: Our position is good, and recognized by those who work with us.

Similarly, Scrumban buttresses key principles of persuasion and influence—abilities that are both necessary and valuable when looking to set expectations with others or when seeking service level agreements. Consider, for example, how Robert Cialdini's core principles of persuasion can be leveraged within a Scrumban framework:[3]

1. *Reciprocity*: People tend to return favors. As Scrumban imparts greater predictability around work delivery, teams can confidently approach the creation of explicit service level expectations as "favors" that position the team for reciprocity.

---

2. Jurgen Appelo (http://www.noop.nl/2013/02/champfrogs.html).
3. These principles are identified in Cialdini's book on persuasion and marketing, *Influence: The Psychology of Persuasion* (William Morrow & Company, 1984).

2. *Commitment and consistency*: If people expressly commit to something, they are more likely to honor that commitment. Scrum already emphasizes commitment and consistency; Scrumban raises that up a notch through its visualization of work and service-oriented agenda.

3. *Social proof*: People will do things they see other people doing. Scrumban is infectious, and the people using it usually turn out to be its strongest advocates.

4. *Authority*: People tend to obey authority figures, even if they are asked to perform objectionable acts. Scrumban can support (and sometimes even create) authority through its scientific foundation—especially when it exposes a course of action that is counterintuitive (or objectionable on the surface).

5. *Liking*: People are more easily persuaded by people they like. Scrumban doesn't make people more likable, but it does create a framework for less contentious discussions on core issues by expanding shared understandings and helping avoid different interpretations of the same data.

6. *Scarcity*: Perceived scarcity will generate demand. Scrumban visualizes where scarcity actually exists and encourages striking a better balance between demand and capacity.

The Kanban Method's Agendas

The Kanban Method brings three main agendas to Scrumban that emphasize creating sustainable results from better service delivery while maintaining resilience in changing external conditions: sustainability, service orientation, and survivability.

Sustainability

"Sustainable pace" is one of several objectives we associate with true Agility, and Kanban's sustainability agenda is driven by the concept of limiting work-in-progress, in tandem with its larger theme of achieving balance.

More than any other framework (including Scrum), the Kanban Method directly addresses the challenge of balancing demand against capability and introduces the need for "demand shaping" through capacity allocation. It also helps to improve awareness of non-value-adding demands and encourages their reduction (eliminating waste—a Lean principle). An oft-encountered example in software development would be responding to requests for information about future work that may or may not occur, or reserving capacity so as to be able to respond to unpredictable and disruptive demands and expedite work.

Scrumban Stories: Sustainability in Common

The Scrumban stories in the Appendix highlight various ways the framework makes our jobs easier—whether at the team level or when seeking to manage at a project, program, or portfolio level. One characteristic all of these stories share is sustainability—sustainability produced by respecting psychological barriers, by driving decisions from discoveries, and by allowing teams to achieve appropriate balance.

Read the full stories of the organizations we highlight in the Appendix.

Service Orientation

Kanban's service orientation agenda is distinctive and often represents a radical change of thinking. In many cases, it also produces immediate benefits.

Using a service orientation as a lens through which to view both process and organization drives clarity around what we deliver, to whom we deliver it, and why we deliver it. It deepens our knowledge discovery and improves service delivery by minimizing variability, improving lead times, and enhancing predictability. You can scale Kanban across an organization in a service-oriented fashion by designing each service with a systems thinking approach.

Survivability

Kanban's bias toward evolutionary improvement directly translates into reduced resistance to change and more sustainable institutional improvements. This is why the simple notion of "starting with what you do" can have such a large and immediate impact.

Kanban's use of "fitness criteria metrics" that evaluate the organization's goals also supports sustained improvement. These metrics emphasize identifying the service capabilities that external stakeholders really value. Delivery time, quality, predictability, and safety are the values external stakeholders usually want. Measuring its achievements against such criteria allows the business to evolve in a fashion that makes it more fit for its intended purpose.

The Kanban Method's Core Principles and Practices

The Kanban Method is deceptively simple, and Scrumban incorporates its four principles (guidance for a mindset) and six practices (high-level guidance for creating fine-grained practices) to achieve its purposes:

- *Four Principles*
  - Start with what you do now.
  - Respect the current process, roles, responsibilities, and titles.

- Agree to pursue incremental, evolutionary change as opportunities are discovered.
- Encourage acts of leadership at all levels of the organization.
- *Six Practices*
    - Visualize.
    - Limit WIP.
    - Manage flow.
    - Make policies explicit.
    - Develop feedback mechanisms at the workflow, inter-workflow, and organizational levels.
    - Improve collaboratively using model-driven experiments.

Kanban's first three principles (starting with what you currently do, respecting current responsibilities and roles, and agreeing to pursue evolutionary adaptations) are directed at breaking down psychological barriers to learning and change. These barriers are often the main reasons why efforts to adopt new ways of working fail.

Scrum is largely silent about the psychological elements of learning and change. Although this is by design, it does render implementation more challenging.

Scrum emphasizes local decision making and empowers practitioners to choose how to do things within the context of its framework using whatever models and tools make sense for them. The Kanban Method comprises mechanisms that ease the introduction of new learnings and processes. Integrating its capabilities with Scrum is wholly consistent with how each framework was designed to operate.

At the end of the day, all of the Kanban Method's principles and practices emphasize pragmatism. This pragmatism, however, will sometimes conflict with the philosophy of process "purists"—that is, people who believe that frameworks work well only when everything they prescribe is "properly" adopted. I suspect purists see *all* perceived shortcomings in the adoption of their particular framework as a signal that organizational problems need to be addressed. Scrumban practitioners contend otherwise.

For example, Scrum is designed to work best when development team members possess cross-functional skill sets. Teams and organizations transitioning to Scrum may require a significant amount of time to realign and nurture teams to an appropriate level of cross-functional capability.

In contrast, the Kanban Method—and by extension Scrumban—emphasizes clarity about current context and capabilities. It is only in this context that an organization can determine how to move forward in a way that enables improvement before all of Scrum's prescribed capabilities are in place.

If the goal is to increase adoption of Agile methods and sustain that adoption over time, then what really matters is finding ways to help people work as productively as possible at any given moment, while remaining committed to continuous improvement. In some environments, this may ultimately lead to mature Scrum practices; in others, it may lead to Scrum-like practices. Scrumban takes the position that either path represents an acceptable outcome.

The Kanban Lens

If the Kanban Method's agendas represent core outcomes that the framework is designed to help achieve, then the "Kanban lens" is the apparatus that helps forge a path to achieving them. In fact, it's the "Kanban lens" that enables us to see how an organization is currently structured and functioning.

Acquiring this view is the only way that teams can "kanbanize" existing structure without having to reorganize it (because sometimes all it takes to reveal conflicting policies and catalyze improvements is a different perspective). The specific enabling concepts are as follows:

- *Service orientation*: Looking at an organization through a service-oriented lens enables teams, and organizations, to begin to apply a systems thinking perspective to their context. Seeing services delivered to customers where you once envisioned only a collection of functions and specializations creates a whole new level of understanding.
- *Understanding service delivery involves workflow*: Appreciating the concept of flow—the notion that service delivery consists of work flowing through a series of stages—is similarly important to gaining a new perspective.
- *Understanding work flows through a series of knowledge discovery activities*: This is the concept most early practitioners tend to have trouble with— especially those familiar with value stream concepts from Lean manufacturing. When mapping value streams, Lean practitioners recommend that you "follow the work." In knowledge work, however, this can lead to visualizing stages of work through a series of specialists. This completely misses the point, and can result in overly complicated visualizations or, even worse, institutionalize hand-offs. Instead, the focus should lie with identifying and understanding the dominant activity associated with discovering the knowledge necessary for work to pass through its current stage. This leads to simpler visualizations and more meaningful discoveries.

Perhaps most significantly, viewing organizations through a Kanban lens enables organizations to create networks of interdependent kanban systems. A "system of systems feedback loop" lets us scale an enterprise in a service-oriented fashion, and self-levels enable us to optimize service delivery across a complex set of services, customers, and their demands.

Kanban Kata and Related Practices

> **Coaching Tip!**
>
> Important Concept Ahead

As mentioned earlier, much of Toyota's success as an automaker has been attributed to its establishment of common disciplines around continuous improvement. In his book *Toyota Kata* (McGraw-Hill, 2009), Mike Rother notes, "Toyota's tools and techniques, the things you see, are built upon invisible routines of thinking and acting, particularly in management, that differ significantly from those found in most companies." This is a good reference point from which to begin discussing the concept of a kata and considering how it is exercised in Scrumban.

Kata is a Japanese word describing detailed patterns of movement. It's essentially a teaching protocol—a way for individuals to create habits through repeated practice. Katas are not thoughtless, mundane habits, but rather value-adding habits that reinforce important values. Toyota has applied the concept of katas to continuous improvement. A3 Thinking, for example, is both a disciplined approach to problem solving and a kata for members of the organization to practice (instilling a common approach and vocabulary throughout the organization).

When an organization's employees and managers seek out improvements day after day, without having to think about it, then high performance becomes sustainable. Toyota achieved this by creating a culture around A3 Thinking—that is, by experimenting on a small scale with a very specific direction in mind. Each experiment represents a step toward a desired outcome. Teams leap toward a target condition that's set just outside their comfort zone. Over time, this experimentation and leaping have become as natural to the company's employees as breathing.

A3 Thinking represents an outstanding choice of kata for many reasons. Other options, such as the Cynefin framework, are also possible. Scrumban naturally supports many different katas. If you want to create and sustain high performance in your environment, use the framework to seek out what works best for you.

Key Take-Away

Though adopting a common kata across an organization represents the ideal, adopting some habitual discipline is a key ingredient to accelerating individual and organizational learning. Remember, early Shu learners yearn for concrete steps to repeat and follow. Katas represent an ideal structure for achieving this around many principles and practices that would otherwise remain abstract.

The Significance of Complementary Values

Good frameworks rely on core sets of values for their successful practice. Scrum, Kanban, and Scrumban are no different. Let's quickly review what they are and contemplate how they interact.

Scrum

Because of its emphasis on fostering agility, teamwork, and continuous improvement, Scrum's core set of values are team-centric [Scrum Alliance]:

- *Focus*: By focusing on only a few things at a time (the sprint backlog), teams will work well together, produce higher-quality work, and deliver valuable items sooner.
- *Courage*: A sense of team ownership (rather than individual ownership) means individuals are not alone. They feel supported and have more resources at their disposal, giving them the courage to undertake greater challenges.
- *Openness*: As teams work together, they practice expressing how they're doing and what's in their way. They learn that expressing concerns allows problems to be addressed.
- *Commitment*: Because teams have greater control over their own destiny, they become more committed to success.
- *Respect*: As teams work together (sharing both failure and success), they come to respect each other and to help each other become worthy of respect.

Kanban

Because of its emphasis on service delivery and catalyzing evolutionary change, Kanban's values extend across other arenas:

- *Understanding*: A process that can't defend itself is a sure sign the people using it have forgotten what they want and believe. Regaining that perspective is essential to moving forward.
- *Agreement*: Meaningful and sustainable performance cannot be achieved without agreement.
- *Respect*: Kanban applies the value of respect in slightly different ways, starting with the principle of respecting current roles and ways of working. In this vein, Kanban recognizes and manages psychological barriers to improvement.

- *Leadership*: Good leadership and good management create the conditions in which self-organization thrives.
- *Flow*: People are happiest and most productive when they are in a state of flow—a state of complete absorption with the activity at hand. Kanban encourages the improved management of flow at organizational, team, and individual levels.
- *Transparency*: Workflow, work states, parameters, policies, and constraints should all be visible. Visualization enhances understanding, enables us to see patterns, and improves our decision making.
- *Balance*: Systems that behave well in the face of variety possess a resilience that is good for the customer, the organization, and the worker. Kanban helps us evolve resilient systems that deliver predictability for a variety of work item types within a range of performance expectations. This is a killer feature of the framework.
- *Collaboration*: Collaboration creates the expectation that we'll look beyond our own team's boundaries in addressing impediments to flow. It also speaks to working systematically to improve understanding through observation, model building, experimentation, and measurement (empiricism).
- *Customer focus*: A customer-focused concern means going beyond an activity-centric ("task completed") or a product-centric ("potentially shippable product") perspective. This is a surprisingly challenging concept that can have a dramatic impact.

Scrumban

As an independent framework focused on bottom-line results, Scrumban brings three additional values to the table:

- *Empiricism*: Empirical approaches are always favored over theories, as are verifiable results over dogma.
- *Humility*: Systems are constantly changing, and we are constantly learning. We must always be ready to challenge our understanding. Improved understandings and approaches can come from any source.
- *Constructive interaction*: There will always be competing management frameworks and methods. Scrumban emphasizes constructive debate that improves understanding of the strengths and limitations of each over blind acceptance that any one framework represents the "only" or "best" way of achieving a particular outcome.

Scrumban's Relationship to Agile Thinking

The Agile Manifesto outlines four core principles:

1. Individuals and interactions over processes and tools
2. Working software over comprehensive documentation
3. Customer collaboration over contract negotiation
4. Responding to change over following a plan

Clearly, Scrum embeds these principles quite effectively. It prescribes short periods of incremental software delivery. Its built-in feedback loops are designed to facilitate an "inspect-and-adapt" approach rather than gathering requirements. It prescribes customer involvement at the team level.

How Scrumban Boosts Scrum's Capabilities

In many software development contexts, the Scrum framework doesn't provide specific guidance on things like interoperability between development teams, and it purposely excludes any formal framework for managing dependencies on outside resources. Scrumban helps with such challenges because of its emphasis on optimizing the flow of work through an existing Scrum process. It catalyzes the maturation of key Scrum/Agile characteristics rather than introducing something new or different.

Other Frameworks and Models

Next-Level Learning:

Evolving to More
Advanced Practices

For teams and organizations in the initial stages of adopting Scrumban, it's sufficient to be aware that many frameworks can be layered with one another to manage software development more effectively. As individuals and organizations master core practices, Scrumban enables practitioners to integrate other frameworks within its capabilities to visualize, measure, and direct work. It's this ease of integration that makes it such a powerful management framework.

A3 Thinking

A3 Thinking is a disciplined approach to problem solving that gives those employing it a deeper understanding of a problem or opportunity. It facilitates cohesion and alignment around a best course of action—core principles that should sound familiar.

When teams and organizations employ A3 Thinking, they undertake specific actions that precipitate the "right way" of thinking about something. This leads to the articulation of the next action and deeper thinking, producing a never-ending cycle of thought and action to produce continuous improvement. People often associate A3 Thinking with root cause analysis, but that's just one aspect of this framework.

The mindset behind A3 Thinking can be distilled into seven basic elements:

- Employing a logical thought process
- Presenting information in a nonjudgmental fashion
- Summarizing results achieved and processes used
- Visualizing only critical information
- Demonstrating alignment with the organization's strategy and objectives
- Maintaining consistency throughout the organization
- Employing a systemic approach to problem solving

Root cause analysis helps ensure our understanding of a current condition is both accurate and complete. Many Lean practitioners find the "Five Whys" method emphasized by Toyota to be particularly effective.

While "Five Whys" is a powerful tool to help unearth the causes of problems, it can sometimes be too basic. If people aren't rigorous in holding themselves to deep thinking, they may stop their inquiry at a level of symptoms before identifying the actual root cause. Similarly, the methodology doesn't provide a means for inquiring beyond your own level of knowledge. Moreover, different people employing the approach can come up with different causes for the same problem because it creates a tendency to isolate a single cause when, in fact, many factors might be combining to produce the issue under investigation.

Teams and organizations that employ a disciplined process like A3 Thinking across all of their problem-solving inquiries fare much better than those that don't, so we make it a point to introduce this or some other technique whenever feasible.

The Cynefin Framework

The Cynefin framework—a practical application of complexity theory to the science of management—is an example of another model that Scrumban teams can employ to improve their understanding of their work and ultimately enhance their decision-making capabilities. Cynefin can be applied in many different ways, but perhaps the most relevant relates to improving our assessment of inherent risks—from market and regulatory risks (which inform how work should be prioritized) to skill and technology risks (which inform the expected variability of time and effort needed to complete a particular feature or story). Scrumban lets us visualize and manage this intelligence in a variety of ways (from board and work card design to establishing classes of service).

Real Options

Real Options is a powerful approach for making better-informed decisions. It responds to the psychological effects that uncertainty has on our behavior (both as individuals and within groups).

The framework possesses two core origins—one mathematical, the other psychological. The math side was developed in the context of financial markets (appropriately enough, to better inform the trading of "options"). It defines the optimal decision for what and when to trade.

The psychological side is based on theories in neuro-linguistic programming and cognitive behavior. These theories help us understand why humans are naturally disinclined to follow optimal decision-making processes and instead end up making irrational decisions.

In many ways, some of Scrum's core practices limit our ability to employ Real Options theory. Consider the sprint backlog. The Scrum methodology forces us to commit to completing items selected for the backlog. While sprints are usually short enough to minimize the risk of committing to user stories "too early," any sprint backlog stands in sharp contrast to the "just-in-time" decision making associated with continuous flow.

Another example of early commitment (and potential waste) in a traditional Scrum context derives from the breakdown of work itself. Most of the epics that get planned in Scrum are never executed, yet teams often expend effort breaking these epics before they're ultimately discarded. The Real Options framework allows us to adopt disciplined approaches to better understand how late in the process we can defer work breakdown. Recently, I took one step in this direction with a client by starting with a specific subset of product backlogs and breaking down work further only if and when it proved necessary—and sometimes that meant in the middle of a sprint.

That said, sometimes the structure of a sprint outweighs any benefits associated with extending the commitment point to the last possible moment (which requires continuous flow). The context should dictate what makes the most sense for a given team or organization.

Some Final Thoughts on Systems Thinking

This chapter has discussed at length how systems thinking is a discipline for understanding things holistically—that is, a framework for seeing interrelationships rather than simply a static collection of discrete entities. The importance of each component of a system is tied to its relationship to the whole, and examining a single component in isolation does not allow us to truly attain a realistic picture of its importance.

Understanding systems can be challenging. Cause and effect are not always closely related in time and space, and a system's components are continually influencing and being influenced by their environments. Feedback loops can amplify or dampen the effect of actions, meaning the smallest of actions can have great effect and the largest of actions can have little effect.

We encourage you to apply this mindset to understanding Scrumban. Like a system, it consists of many component principles. If you want to be fully capable of understanding the true nature and capabilities that Scrumban offers and to influence the systems in which you work, then you must adhere to the following practices:

- *Commit to real learning.* If we fail to keep learning, then we're doomed to mediocrity.
- *Be prepared to be wrong.* If there were an obvious way of doing something well within a system, chances are we'd already be doing it. Ongoing problems and mediocre performance are as much a function of our own mental models as anything else. If we're not prepared to challenge how we view things, we won't be able to leverage nonobvious areas for improvement.

    To this end, information theory tells us the "maximum potential" for learning is reached when our experiments are wrong approximately 50% of the time. If we're trying to improve our process, we need to experiment. If we want to maximize our learning, we need to make mistakes!
- *Rely on collective intelligence over individual intelligence.* We need to gather different people with different points of view to see things collectively that none of us would see as individuals. This can be a difficult concept to accept, especially in a culture that idolizes individual performance.

There's a great deal of symmetry between these three needs and Scrumban's three core values.

Tying It All Together

Congratulations! With this review of Scrumban's foundations under your belt, you've just attained a deeper knowledge of the framework than most of the people who profess to understand what it is, including many consultants and coaches! Let's quickly review some key highlights that will be useful to keep in mind as you continue your journey.

First, Scrumban was conceived as a continuous flow delivery model representing a "next generation" evolution of Scrum. Although it has since evolved to represent something different, this origin explains why many continue to perceive it in its original form.

Second, the Kanban Method itself has substantially evolved during the same time period. Because the Kanban Method leverages kanban systems as part of its framework, many people perceive it as an "alternative" process methodology rather than as a lens through which we can better understand and improve our existing ways of working.

Third, as a layering of the Kanban Method alongside Scrum, Scrumban has evolved to become much more than just the "best elements of both." It encourages us to seek out improved understandings from all sources, and enables us to easily integrate other models and frameworks in this quest.

PART III

EXECUTION—PUTTING SCRUMBAN INTO PRACTICE

Chapter 5

MOBILIZE: ROLLING OUT SCRUMBAN

IN THIS CHAPTER

- How Framework Choices Influence Outcomes
- A Step-by-Step Guide to Getting Started
- Using Scrumban to Stabilize a Team before You Improve

Having outlined the foundational principles and mechanics that make Scrumban successful, it's time to discuss how teams and organizations can start employing Scrumban. Rolling out Scrumban doesn't have to require a lot of effort. In fact, the approach outlined in this chapter can be completed in a single day.

Your Starting Condition

There are essentially three potential starting conditions for rolling out Scrumban:

- You're working with a team or organization for which both Scrum and Scrumban represent new ways of working.
- You're working with an existing Scrum team or organization that will use Scrumban to improve its mastery of the responsibilities and ceremonies associated with the Scrum framework.
- You're working with an existing Scrum team or organization that will use Scrumban to monitor performance, diagnose issues, and adapt existing practices to the form best suited for their context.

It's best if all teams participating in a formal kickstart program share the same origin, but it won't necessarily be fatal if they don't.

When You're New to Scrum

Scrum can be difficult to master, even though it is a relatively simple framework. Recognizing this reality, we've made Scrumban our chosen framework for introducing Scrum to teams and organizations for the first time.

Because Scrumban seeks to minimize the disruptions associated with imposing new definitions and responsibilities upon employees, rolling out Scrum under this framework is substantially different from traditional approaches. Rather than starting out with Scrum-specific orientation and training, we emphasize discovery of existing systems and processes, then use the framework to gradually introduce elements of Scrum as warranted by the context.

This gradual introduction can be both role based and process based. For instance, the "daily scrum" is a process-based change the team can begin to employ within the context of a Scrumban framework, just as new Scrum masters can be eased into their responsibilities one element at a time.[1]

The Kickstart Process

Coaching Tip!

Prefer to bypass the background detail provided in this section? Check out our quick Kickstart reference in the Appendix.

The kickstart process covered here is particularly effective when you're faced with limited time or resources—in other words, when teams or organizations need to better manage workflow, but don't have sufficient resources to develop those better ways. Naturally, this is not the only way to introduce Scrumban to teams.[2] Always use your understanding of Scrumban principles to modify the process to fit your context.

Incidentally, this process is modeled after a Kanban kickstart process developed by Christophe Achouiantz, a Lean/Agile coach, and Johan Nordin, development support manager at Sandvik IT. Sandvik needed a way to empower its company's teams to begin a process of continuous improvement that wouldn't involve a significant initial investment of time or effort. Achouiantz and Nordin have documented this process and made it available to the public as a reference guide. While the particulars

---

1. In some contexts, the role of Scrum master may even remain optional. In working with a variety of organizations over the years, Frank Vega notes that one of his earliest efforts to help a team move toward more iterative and incremental ways of working dispensed with this role altogether. It remains one of the most effective teams he's ever worked with. I don't necessarily consider this an ideal approach, but mention it only to underscore the importance of contextual discovery and decision making.

2. For example, the approach taken by Siemens Health Services (see the Appendix for the full case study) would not have called for individual teams to engage in a process of systems discovery and definition.

may not apply directly to your needs, it's an outstanding summary of the key points and objectives relevant to any process.

Preparation

As systems thinkers, it's critical to first understand the context of the environment before attempting to kickstart anything. At a minimum, preliminary preparation should include the following steps:

- Identifying the current conditions and organizational priorities (e.g., increased quality, productivity, predictability)
- Developing working relationships with key managers and team leads
- Ascertaining areas of desired change
- Introducing Kanban/Scrumban as a framework for evolutionary change
- Starting to educate staff on Scrumban's core principles and practices
- Identifying any risks and potential impediments to introducing Scrumban to targeted teams

Regarding that last item, it's important to recognize that some teams or contexts may not benefit from introducing Scrumban until certain conditions or impediments are addressed. These can include teams in an active state of reorganization, teams with serious internal conflicts, and so forth. Your context will determine how you address these situations. For example, Sandvik's needs dictated that such teams be bypassed until circumstances changed.

Though it's possible for teams to initiate Scrumban adoption without organizational buy-in, as previous chapters indicate, broader engagement is necessary to achieve the full breadth of desired outcomes and to sustain them over time. As such, Scrumban is not substantially different from a pure Scrum context.

PMO/Program Managers:

If you're overseeing a pilot program or broad-based transformation effort, we strongly encourage you to consider the recommendations outlined here. The choices you make in the early stages will greatly influence your ultimate success.

In his book *Succeeding with Agile: Software Development Using Scrum* (Boston: Addison-Wesley, 2009), Mike Cohn addresses a variety of considerations that apply when you're selecting the project context in which to roll out a new process (these considerations are made with an eye toward building off demonstrated success). Though less critical in a context where the Scrumban or Kanban framework is employed, they nonetheless represent worthy

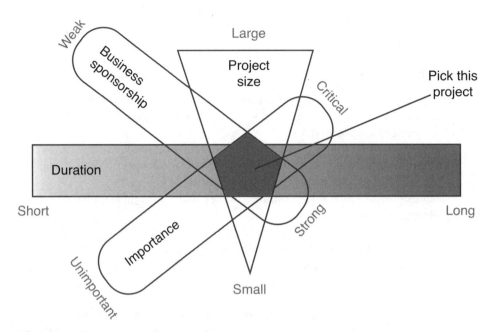

FIGURE 5.1   The convergence of key considerations in selecting a pilot project for introducing Scrum. These same considerations apply to Scrumban.

Source: Michael Cohn. *Succeeding with Agile: Software Development Using Scrum* (Boston: Addison-Wesley, 2009).

considerations (see Figure 5.1 for a graphical illustration of the convergence of these considerations):

- *Project size*: For Scrum pilots, Mike suggests selecting a project that will not grow to more than five teams, and limiting initial efforts to just one or two of those teams. Coordinating work among more Scrum teams represents more work than you can effectively tackle.

  For Scrumban rollouts, there's substantially more leeway. With fewer concepts to learn and master (again, we start out respecting current roles and processes), working with a slightly larger number of teams is feasible.

- *Project duration*: Select a pilot project of average duration for your organization, ideally around 3–4 months. This is plenty of time for teams to begin mastering the framework and seeing benefits. It's usually also sufficient for demonstrating that your new approach will lead to similar success in other contexts.

- *Project importance*: Mike suggests that with Scrum pilots, it's critical to select high-profile projects. Unimportant projects will not get the organizational attention necessary to make Scrum successful, and team members may be disinclined to do all the hard things Scrum requires.

There's slightly more leeway with Scrumban. Building momentum and trust through success is still an important objective, but the framework's service-oriented agenda and active management of psychological barriers to change represent additional capabilities that can be leveraged to ultimately satisfy these needs.

> ### Executives:
>
> Your efforts to educate your organization's nontechnical employees about how this undertaking is important to the business, and encouraging their active engagement in the process, will go a long way toward creating long-term success.

- *Business owner's level of engagement*: As previously mentioned, Scrum and Scrumban ultimately require changes in the way both the business and the technology sides of the house approach things. Having an engaged player on the business side can be invaluable for overcoming challenges and evangelizing success across the organization.

Scrumban modifies the weight of this factor substantially. To function properly, Scrum requires active engagement on the business side—its prioritization and feedback functions depend on it. Scrumban won't function well without business engagement, but it does afford teams the ability to create positive changes by allowing knowledge discovery to "stand in" for disengaged business players.

In a similar vein, Scrumban is ultimately designed to respond to business demands. If the business isn't demanding change, then Scrumban's pragmatic "response" is to reflect the absence of any need to change (although a culture of continuous improvement will continue to spawn incremental changes to make what you're already doing well even better).

Initial Considerations

Many topics can be addressed during a kickstart. What constitutes "information overload" for a particular group will vary from context to context, and must always be judged against the level of ongoing support available following the kickstart (for example, you will likely cover more material if teams will have coaching support following the kickstart than if they will have none at all).

With these considerations in mind, incorporating themes that reinforce the service-oriented philosophy and the organization's core values will go a long way toward positioning teams to evolve more effectively. There are many ways to do this, and it's one area where an experienced practitioner or coach will really add value to the process.[3]

One special consideration for existing Scrum teams may be to introduce the concept of Sprint 0 (if this tactic is employed within the involved team or organization). There's much debate about the "appropriateness" of Sprint 0 in Scrum circles. These special sprints are often described as necessary vehicles for managing what needs to be done before a Scrum project can start. For example, the team may need to be assembled, hardware acquired and set up, and initial product backlogs developed. Purists' feathers may be ruffled by the notion of differentiating sprints by type and, more importantly, by the idea that any sprint would be structured in a way that fails to deliver value.

The Scrumban framework obviates the need for debate on these issues. The tasks associated with ramping up a new project can be easily accommodated and managed within the Scrumban framework as a special work type. If it's important for your environment to ensure Scrum ceremonies hold true to their Agile objectives, then Scrumban provides a ready solution.

It also makes sense to assess existing Scrum practices with an eye toward understanding their impact on performance. Larry Maccherone and his former colleagues at Rally Software have analyzed data from thousands of Scrum teams in an effort to assess how differences in the way Scrum is practiced affect various elements of performance. This data mining exposed some interesting realities about how our choices involving Scrum practices can influence various facets of performance. Incidentally, Maccherone's analysis is consistent with data mined from hundreds of teams using my own Scrum project management platform (ScrumDo.com).

Maccherone elected to adopt a "Software Development Performance Index" as a mode of measuring the impact of specific practices. The index is composed of measurements for the following aspects:

- *Productivity*: Average throughput—the number of stories completed in a given period of time
- *Predictability*: The stability of throughput over time—how much throughput values varied from the average over time for a given team
- *Responsiveness*: The average amount of time work on each user story is "in process"
- *Quality*: Measured as defect density

---

3. As previously noted, the Siemens Health Group case study (see the Appendix) represents a great example of how expert assistance played a critical role in contributing to the depth of the company's success.

How You Choose to Organize Makes a Difference

| Especially For: |
| Managers & Executives |

As noted, Larry Maccherone's analysis reflects a definite correlation between certain choices and software development performance. Although correlation does not necessarily mean causation, we can use these relationships as a guide for tailoring a kickstart process to address specific factors relevant to a particular implementation. Teams can be guided to position their visualizations and practices to better understand and discover which choices regarding Scrum practices are likely to work best for their desired outcomes.[4]

Determining Team Size

Humans are the slowest-moving parts in any complex organization. Teams can help us counteract this reality by making us smarter and faster. However, this outcome is possible only if we get teams right. Team dynamics is Scrum's strong suit—and an arena Kanban addresses only tangentially, if at all. In fact, providing a framework that helps us improve team dynamics is a great example of how Scrum boosts Kanban's capabilities.

To this end, size stands out as the most significant predictor of team success. There's a right size for every team, and like so many other aspects of managing systems, that size should be dictated by overall context. Even so, having guidelines doesn't hurt.

The military is a great starting point for gaining perspective on ideal team size. The basic unit in the U.S. Army's Special Forces is the 12-person team. The army arrived at this number after recognizing there are certain dynamics that arise only in small teams. For example, when a team is made up of 12 or fewer people, its members are more likely to care about one another. They're more likely to share information, and far more likely to come to each other's assistance. If the mission is important enough, they'll even sacrifice themselves for the good of the team. This happens in business, too.

The founders of Scrum understood these dynamics. Ask anyone in the Scrum community about ideal team size, and you'll hear 7 members plus or minus 2.

The reasons for maintaining small team sizes are valid, but not every 12-person military unit is right for a particular assignment. Likewise, not every 9-person Scrum team is right for a given environment. Your system ultimately will dictate your needs, and it may very well require expanding your teams to incorporate a larger number of specialists or address some other need.

---

4. In sharing this data, Maccherone has been diligent in emphasizing that there is no such thing as "best practices" relevant to all contexts. Each team and organization must discover what works best at any given point in time.

Scrumban supports this flexibility through its enhanced information sharing and visualization capabilities. Even the cadence of daily stand-ups is different: We've seen daily stand-ups in a Scrumban environment involving almost 100 individuals that are both effective in addressing organizational needs and capable of being completed within 15 minutes. This would be impossible in a Scrum context.

Iteration Length

Many organizations seek to establish uniform iteration lengths because they mistakenly believe this is a good approach for aligning different systems to the same cadence. Yet for many years, the general consensus among Scrum practitioners has been to recommend two-week iterations. What does the data tell us?

Rally Software's data shows that almost 60% of the software development teams using its tool adopt two-week sprints, and I've seen similar patterns among users of ScrumDo. The data also suggests a team's overall performance tends to be greatest at this cadence (Figure 5.2).

Dig more deeply, however, and differences begin to show up among the various components of the index. Throughput, for example, tends to be greatest among teams adopting one-week iterations (Figure 5.3).

Quality, in contrast, trends highest among teams adopting four-week cadences (Figure 5.4).

PERFORMANCE

Iteration length relationship to performance

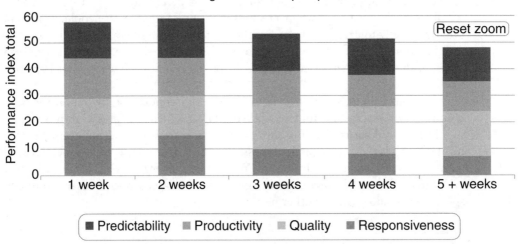

FIGURE 5.2   A view into the relationship between iteration length and team performance.

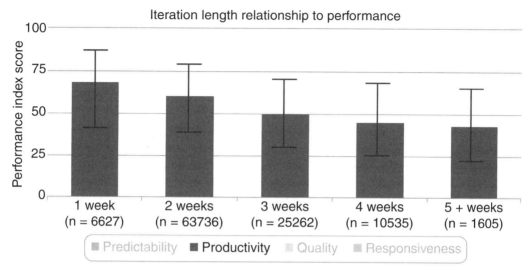

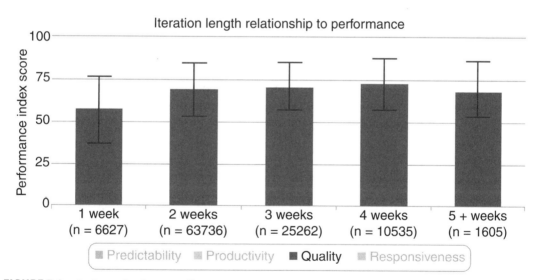

Every organization possesses characteristics that drive different outcomes, which is where Scrumban's visualization and added metrics can help teams discover what's best for their unique circumstances. The higher throughput typically associated with two-week cadences won't magically materialize if the historical lead time for most of your completed work items is three weeks. Similarly, delivering completed work every two weeks won't magically produce better outcomes if the customers can't accept it at that rate.

Also, be wary of inferences drawn from data associated with teams that have adopted longer iterations. For example, Frank Vega recently made an interesting observation on this topic, recounting instances where teams chose longer iteration periods as a means of opposing (consciously or subconsciously) Agile transformation efforts because agreeing to a shorter iteration cycle would counteract their position that nothing of any real value could be delivered in such a short time period.

Estimating Story Points

Scrum prescribes the Sprint Planning ceremony as an event that determines which specific stories can be delivered in the upcoming sprint and how that work will be achieved.

Although Scrum itself doesn't prescribe a particular approach or method that teams should use to assist with this decision making (other than expecting it to be based on experience), most Scrum teams use story points and team estimation techniques as components of this process.

Another process that teams use to aid their estimation efforts is Planning Poker—a consensus-based technique developed by Mike Cohn. With this approach, which is used primarily to forecast effort or relative size, team members offer estimates by placing numbered cards face-down on the table (rather than speaking them aloud). Once everyone has "played," the cards are revealed and estimates discussed. This technique helps a group avoid the cognitive bias associated with anchoring, where the first suggestion sets a precedent for subsequent estimates.

Scrumban enables teams to begin measuring the correlation between story point estimates and the actual time spent completing development, measured from the time work on a story begins until the story is completed. Some teams reflect a strong correlation between their estimates and actual work time. Others are more sporadic, especially as the estimated "size" of stories grows. Teams using exponentially based story size schemes tend to be more precise with their estimates. Comparing the two charts in Figure 5.5 and Figure 5.6, it's fairly evident that exponential estimation reflects a tighter band of variability in lead time—especially among smaller stories. The spectrum of variability is much wider across the Fibonacci series.

As with the data on sprint length, the way teams estimate the size and effort of work tends to correlate with overall performance (Figure 5.7).

It is not uncommon to find a lack of correlation between a team's velocity, the average number of story points completed during a sprint, and actual throughput. Nonetheless, there are many instances when the estimating process works well for

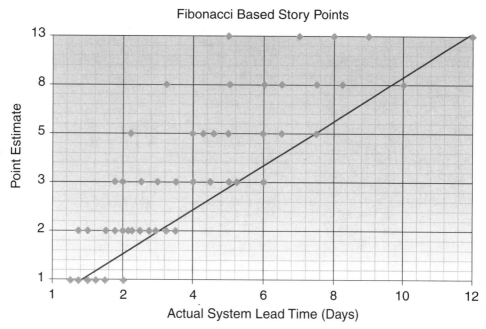

FIGURE 5.5   There tends to be only a loose correlation (if any at all) between esti-mated story points and actual lead time.

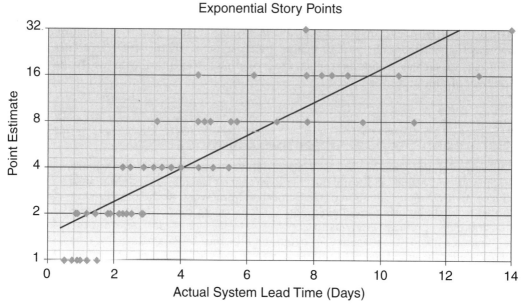

FIGURE 5.6   The correlation is slightly better in an exponential points scheme.

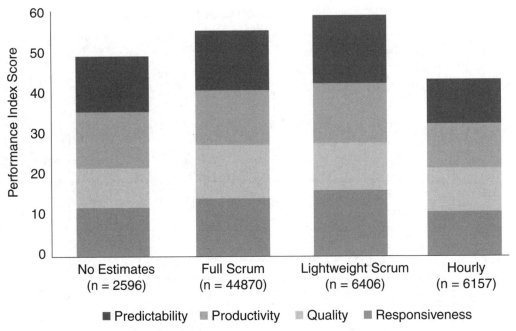

FIGURE 5.7   The relationship between team performance and estimation schemes.

individual teams. As mentioned previously, it's more challenging to work with this metric on a portfolio level involving multiple teams. Calculating relative correlation is one way that Scrumban helps teams gain a better sense of whether the ceremonies they engage in, such as estimation events, are providing sufficient value to justify the investment of time and effort.

Scrumban Stories: Objective Solutions

Objective Solutions' teams showed a lack of correlation between their story point estimates and actual lead time, but this discrepancy wasn't noticed until after the company's implementation of the Scrumban framework. As the organization opted to continue using team estimates for forecasting purposes, its solution for improving predictability was to apply a "velocity factor" derived from the difference between these values. To avoid the influence of Parkinson's law (the tendency for the time needed to complete work to expand to the time allowed for it), these velocity factors were not communicated to the team members, and only used by the product owners and Scrum masters engaged in planning.

Read the full story of Objective Solutions in the Appendix.

Contextual Responsibilities

As teams begin to employ Scrumban, members will assume a range of new "responsibilities."

First and foremost, team members must be groomed to challenge and question their team's policies, facilitating team interest in and ownership of how they work. Fortunately, this basic concept should not be foreign to people already used to a Scrum context. A great way to promote and support this mindset is through the establishment of "working agreements."[5]

Not surprisingly, Scrum's existing ceremonies and artifacts implicitly support the notion of working agreements. Scrumban's framework goes one step further, calling for the team to make such agreements explicit and to visualize them on their boards as appropriate. In many respects, they are akin to establishing an internal service level agreement between team members.

Ultimately, we want to develop leaders who help all team members acquire the ability to see and understand concepts like waste, blockers, and bottlenecks. Good leaders also ensure teams don't get stuck in a comfort zone, by prodding team members to always seek out ways to improve.

As previously mentioned, although teams will experience work improvements simply from employing Scrumban independently, an active management layer is essential to realizing benefits at scale. Systemic improvements are less likely to occur without a manager who maintains contact, helps resolve issues outside the team's domain, and oversees the extent to which teams devote time and effort on pursuing discovered opportunities for improvement. Setting expectations for this need at the kickstart helps ensure a more sustainable implementation.

Scrumban Stories: Objective Solutions

Like Siemens Health Services, Objective Solutions had successfully adopted Scrum/XP practices in its development operations but was struggling with a number of challenges at scale. The company adopted elements of Scrumban to address these challenges. Not surprisingly, this journey allowed the organization to improve many of its Scrum and pair programming practices that had been negatively influencing throughput and quality.

For example, Objective Solutions was experiencing challenges with managing the pair programming process: Keyboard work was not balanced, the time required to complete work unnecessarily expanded, and mentoring benefits were not being fully realized. Scrumban allowed this company to recognize specific problems, and to implement processes for managing its pair programming practices in the course of managing its regular workflow.

Read the full story of Objective Solutions in the Appendix.

---

5. See, for example, http://tiny.cc/AgileTeamAgreements.

The Kickstart Event

> **Coaching Tip!**
>
> This overview was prepared for initiative leaders, and covers broad, general guidelines. Adjust to your context as warranted.

As with any initiative, adoption of Scrumban should start with some type of "formal" event. Though simpler to launch than a direct transformation to Scrum, some elements of "education" and setting expectations are still necessary to ensure a smooth start. All team members should be physically present for any kick-off meeting. This is obviously more of a challenge with distributed teams, so some consideration must be given to communications and visualization. The topics that the agenda for a good kick-off event should, at a minimum, address are covered in the following sections.

Introductory Remarks

The kick-off event is an opportunity to set the stage for what follows. Remarks should reinforce at least two key concepts.

First, you want to underscore that this effort is solely about introducing and employing Scrumban in the context of your current ways of working, and represents little to no change in existing work roles or responsibilities. It's important to address this point up front to minimize the potential barriers to effective learning caused by fear or resistance to change.

Second, you should reinforce the fact that this event has just one achievable outcome—each team walking away with a clear visualization of how it works. As with threatened change, epic objectives create unnecessary psychological barriers. Communicating an achievable outcome up front will help engage participants early on and make the kickstart process considerably more meaningful. We define our "definition of done" for this step as follows:

- Each team member has a clear understanding of his or her team's purpose.
- Each team has created a visual representation of its ongoing work and current workflow.
- All team members agree on their most important and relevant work policies.

Current Concerns

Service orientation lies at the core of the Scrumban framework, so it's critical for teams to begin with a clear identification of their stakeholders and any dissatisfaction they might have. Getting stakeholders to work with you, instead of against you, is one of your greatest tools for achieving continuous improvement.

Though adjustments should always be made based on the context of your environment, Klaus Leopold recently articulated one approach for visualizing stakeholder relationships that seems particularly informative and useful for introducing Scrumban to an organization.[6] Among the suggestions he offers are the following:

- Visualizing the power and influence of each stakeholder using different size cards.
- Visualizing the degree to which stakeholders support your initiative through a spatial reference point: The closer to the point they're positioned, the stronger their level of support. Although Leopold's article specifically speaks to stakeholder relationships relative to undertaking a change initiative in general, there's no reason this approach can't be undertaken for any initiative.
- Visualizing the frequency of the relationships among stakeholders with different style lines (e.g., dotted for infrequent or tenuous connections, other styles for different grades).
- Visualizing the quality of the relationship with special symbols (e.g., friendly or adversarial, healthy and strong or tenuous and weak).

Why engage in this evaluation of stakeholders? Because you need to understand your stakeholders' sources of dissatisfaction, and find the most effective ways to work with them toward resolving those issues. In fact, teams should change their work policies and work visualizations only if doing so will help resolve areas of dissatisfaction.

Visualizing the dynamics associated with key relationships also creates a clear view of who holds the most power, the current state of each relationship, and the steps that must be taken to move closer to a solution. It helps prioritize an approach to resolving dissatisfaction.

Next-Level Learning:

Evolving to More Advanced Practices

If you're looking to apply an even greater level of calibration to the process, this arena is ripe for applying a model like the Cynefin framework to provide information on how best to manage a given relationship.

In most circumstances, it is appropriate to facilitate discussions around current issues. Simply invite members to identify the top three to five issues that represent irritants or impediments to their work. Any issues that relate to how work is done or how the team interacts with other groups can be set aside for possible discussion, as

---

6. See http://tiny.cc/StakeholderDissatisfact.

these represent way-of-working or policy matters the team will be addressing during the kickstart. Any others should be tabled, as they don't relate to issues relevant to the workshop.

Defining Purpose and Success Criteria

Teams and organizations that lack a common purpose typically cannot achieve or sustain high levels of performance. Any exercise that moves them toward a common understanding of purpose and criteria for success is all that matters. I like to have teams answer the question, "Why does our team exist?"

You should skip this step only when you're sure everyone agrees they're on a common journey to pursue incremental change toward working more effectively.

Identifying How Work Is Done

The goal for this segment is to have teams gain a realistic understanding of their current situation—in other words, how they actually perform work versus how they *think* they perform work. We get to this point by introducing a systems perspective—by asking the team to visualize itself as a closed system having several basic components (Figure 5.8). This exercise may be the first time many teams acquire a realistic sense

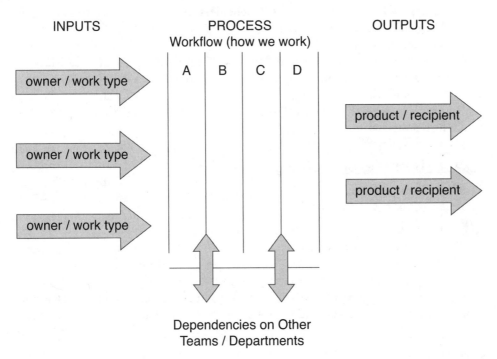

FIGURE 5.8   Visualizing a closed system.

of the complexity of how work flows in and out of their domain, plus the full scope of what they're responsible for producing on an ongoing basis.

The team's articulation of upstream demand represents which work they're asked to perform, who makes those demands (internal customers, external customers, or a combination of both), how those demands are communicated, and what their relative frequency and quantity are. These understandings are used to categorize work types later in the workshop.

Defining the downstream end reinforces the notion of recipients as consumers or partners in a process, thereby reinforcing Kanban's concept of knowledge work as service delivery. These initial definitions of system boundaries clarify the scope of the team's responsibility—where their work begins and ends.

Articulating how the team performs its work should command most of the team's attention. Teams should be guided to creating a simple, high-level visualization of the stages that each type of work must pass through before completion; this will be the foundation upon which their working board is built. Simple and abstract is the key—no more than 2–3 different kinds of workflows and no more than 7–10 stages in each.

Focusing on Work Types

A good kickstart process will incorporate activities that ensure team members acquire a common understanding of work types and their significance. It may be relevant to your organizational context to have teams identify and manage their work using pre-defined types, but in any case it's important for the team to understand the nature of the demands placed upon them. Naturally, this is an ongoing process. Common modes of approaching this include assessing which work types meet the following criteria:

- Have the most value for their customers or partners
- Are demanded the most and the least (in terms of quantity)
- Are usually more urgent than others
- Are best aligned with the team's purpose (the kind of work the team should do to a greater extent)
- Are least aligned with the team's purpose (the kind of work the team should do to a lesser extent)

It may be relevant to your organizational context to have teams identify and manage their work using predefined types. Nevertheless, regardless of how you elect to proceed, it's ultimately most important that they understand the nature of the demands being placed upon them. Naturally, this is an ongoing process. Common categorizations include the following:

- By source (e.g., retail banking, product X, maintenance items)
- By size (e.g., in terms of effort)
- By outcome (e.g., production release, analysis report)

- By type of flow (e.g., development, maintenance, analysis)
- By risk profile (e.g., standard work, urgent work, regulatory compliance)
- By relevance (how closely the work is aligned with team purpose)

Whatever scheme you choose, categorization provides a frame of reference against which an appropriate balance of work in progress can be created and managed.

Basic Management

It's one thing to have teams begin visualizing how they work; it's another thing to provide them with a framework for using these visualizations to discover better ways of managing it. I recommend using the GetScrumban game (Figure 5.9) to introduce teams to the basic principles behind managing their workflow. (Full disclosure: I designed this game.) It's usually employed in tandem with other "classroom" exercises to illustrate and emphasize key principles and practices.

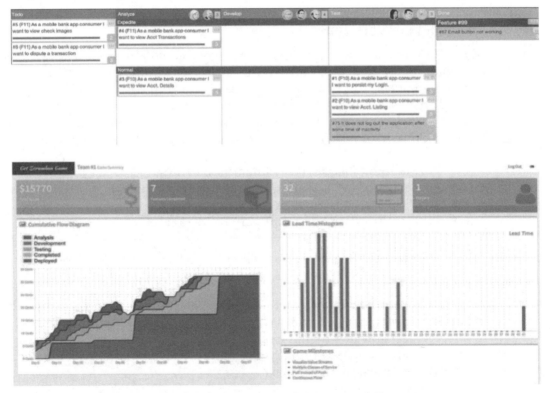

FIGURE 5.9   The GetScrumban game lets players experience the typical evolution of Scrum teams after introducing the Scrumban framework into their way of working.

Source: GetScrumban.com.

The GetScrumban game simulates how a software development team that employs Scrum as its chosen framework can use Scrumban's core principles and practices to amplify its current capabilities, overcome common challenges, or forge new paths to improved agility. The game allows players to experiment with and experience the impact of these principles and practices:

- Expanded visualizations
  - Value streams
  - Types of work
  - Risk profiles
- Pulling work versus assigning work
- Evolutionary adjustments versus radical change
- Cost of delay versus subjective prioritization
- Distinct classes of service versus a single workflow
- Continuous flow versus time-boxed iterations
- Value of options

Whether you use an interactive tool like GetScrumban or employ some other mode of instruction, your teams should walk away with an understanding of the following:

- **Concepts Already Familiar to Scrum Teams**
  - *Work items/cards (user stories)*: These are typically visualized on physical boards in the form of a sticky.
  - *Work size estimate (story points)*: As most Scrum teams already engage in some form of estimation, the concept of estimating (and the notion of breaking larger stories down into more manageable sizes) should be very familiar.
  - *Definition of done*: A short checklist of standards that must be present for a work item to move from one column to another.
  - *Daily stand-ups*: Scrumban stand-ups tend to eliminate declarations of status (what each team member completed, what the team member is committing to complete, and the identification of impediments) because all of that information is already visualized on the board. Instead, stand-ups evolve to focus on how well work is flowing and which actions the team can take to improve overall flow and delivery of value.
- **New Concepts**
  - *Work type*: Often represented by the color of a work card; reflects the mix of work in progress. Visualizing and actively managing the mix of work (i.e., standard user story, bug fix, maintenance item, estimations) is usually a novel concept for Scrum teams.

- *Workflow*: Columns on a work board represent the value-adding stages work passes through to completion. These usually start with "Ready" and conclude with "Done," "Ready to Deploy," or some similar terminology. Scrum teams often welcome this change because story progress and individual contributions toward it are made more visible.
- *Pull*: Though some Scrum teams may be familiar with pull-based systems, many others are new to this mechanism. Pull mechanisms avoid clogging the system with too much work. Rather than work being "pushed" onto a team by those with a demand, the team selects work to pull into their work stream when they have the capacity to handle it.
- *Ready for pull*: These "holding" areas are visualized as columns within a column. Typically used when a handover occurs (such as from a development phase to a test phase), they help manage bottlenecks.
- *Definition of ready*: A short checklist at the bottom of a "Ready" column that visualizes the relationship a team has with those requesting work. The definition should specify the information or resources a team needs to effectively begin working on an item. Though many Scrum teams may employ definitions of ready in their work, they are rarely explicitly defined and visualized within a working framework.
- *Blockers*: Flags that indicate when work on an item is suspended because of dependencies on others. Blockers are usually visualized as an additional sticky or magnet (pink or red) on a work item. The purpose is to call attention to such items so the team attends to removing the impediment. Some Scrum teams may already visualize blockers on their task boards.
- *Classes of service*: Different "swim lanes" used to call out different risk profiles associated with given work items. We can choose to visualize separate classes of service to reflect and manage risk better (e.g., helping to ensure higher risk profiles attract more attention from the team than lower risk profiles. Similarly, you may want to help the team recognize it's okay to take longer to complete lower-risk items.
- *Explicit WIP limits*: Teams should limit the amount of work in progress at any given time. We can do this by establishing explicit WIP limits across the board, within each column (preferred), within each swim lane/class of service, by work type, by team member, or any combination. Limiting WIP improves flow efficiency (by reducing or eliminating the cost of context-switching, among other things).

Common Language (Optional)

If you're looking to align Scrumban practices across a large number of teams, it's usually beneficial to establish a "common language" around common concepts. It's possible to borrow some terms from Scrum (for example, teams might all carry a "backlog" or items that are ready to be worked on). Similarly, it may make sense for teams working on different aspects of the same program to use the same visualization scheme and share common policies.

Visualization Policies

One of Scrumban's core practices is to ensure that all work policies are explicit. We do so to ensure that everyone is on the same page, and that the work policies can be easily remembered and shared with others. Common practices include the following:

- *Work items*: Most practices will be natural carry-overs from Scrum:
  - Due date (if any).
  - External reference (e.g., from a management/tracking tool).
  - Size of work (e.g., story points or person-hour estimates).
  - Start date (important to track for measurement purposes).
  - End date (date work was fully completed—some metrics can be impacted by how you measure this, but any agreed-upon policy is sufficient when starting out).
- *Workflow*: The basic elements should already be incorporated in the systems diagram the team developed earlier. Some columns may be adjusted and rows added, however, as the team's understanding develops.
  - Pull Criteria: Scrum practitioners familiar with Definition of Done can optionally break it up into more granular lightweight "Pull criteria" visualized as a combination of mandatory and optional conditions before which a pull can be made.
- *What* not *to visualize*: Cluttering up your visualization with unnecessary items defeats the objective of bringing greater clarity and understanding to how you work. Although teams should capture as much of their work as possible, there can be legitimate omissions, as in the following examples:
  - Administrative activities (such as meetings unrelated to ongoing work). However, there may be great value to capturing how much time meetings are taking away from actual work, or whether certain resources are more encumbered than others.
  - Short, ad hoc work (5- to 10-minute requests or incidents). As with administrative activities, there can be value in capturing these items. Measuring the number of such work items in the course of a day or week could reveal a significant and ongoing demand that would otherwise fly beneath the radar.

Frequency of Synchronization

Daily meetings are as much a ceremony with Scrumban as they are with Scrum. Unlike in Scrum, however, teams can move beyond sharing status and making commitments to collaborating on impediments to workflow and recognizing opportunities for improvement. This requires the team's visual board to be in sync with reality. Some development teams may be able to get by with once-a-day synchronization, whereas others will need real-time updates. Decisions made in this context can impact tool choices and other related factors.

Create a Working Board

The kickstart session is an ideal time to assist teams with setting up their working boards. The sooner a team starts to see and work with actual items, the more relevant the process becomes. This effort typically involves the following steps:

- *Drawing the workflow*: Creating columns that represent the value stream of the team's work process.
- *Creating the board*: I recommend that the teams create the board together, whether it's an electronic tool or physical board. This accelerates team learning and ownership.
- *Ticket design*: The information to incorporate on a work ticket will vary from team to team. We discuss these considerations in more detail in Chapter 7.
- *Adding current work* (self-explanatory).

This is also an ideal time for teams to establish their definition of ready and definition of done for work items and lanes. Ready definitions can be easy to neglect, but they help avoid potential blockages once work begins. Teams might also discuss prioritization, but in a Scrum context this issue should have been already addressed by product owners.

Way of Working Policies

It's critical that all team members agree how work will be handled in their visual boards so that it is done in a consistent manner. Areas to address include the following:

- Which individual(s) will be responsible for managing the ready buffer (placing new work items in the buffer and prioritizing them for the team to address as capacity allows). This topic is not relevant for teams that continue to use time-boxed sprints.
- When and how the ready buffer will be replenished. For teams that continue practicing Scrum, this usually coincides with the sprint planning process. In complex environments, developing policies could become quite involved. The immediate objective is simply to have a workable starting point.
- Which individual(s) will be responsible for managing completed work (especially important when work is to be forwarded to downstream partners).

- How ad hoc work or requests from outside normal channels should be managed. Consideration must be given to the needs of the system making the request.
- When work should be pulled from the ready buffer (typically whenever a team member has capacity and can't contribute to any ongoing work). Consideration should be included for managing WIP limits and what should occur if exceptions are to be made.

Most of these considerations involve assessing risk (addressed further in Chapter 6). Having teams explicitly address risk as part of the kickstart process is the best way of ensuring more considered management as they mature. At a minimum, teams should be encouraged to explicitly articulate how work will be prioritized and which considerations are expected to be addressed as part of this process (i.e., is prioritization based exclusively on market/business risks, or should the decision incorporate an assessment of risks associated with the underlying technology, the complexity of the work, the team's familiarity with the domain, and other factors).

Limiting WIP

Coaching Tip!

This is an especially important topic.

Setting explicit limits on work in progress will be a new concept for Scrum teams, and the science behind this mandate can be counterintuitive. For teams already practicing Scrum, it may be beneficial to point out how the Sprint ceremony is an implicit WIP-limiting mechanic. The idea is not to dive into detail, but rather to provide enough of an overview so the team understands why limiting work in progress matters.

"Stop starting and start finishing" should become every team's mantra. Pull mechanisms are one way to ensure new work items are started only when a team member has capacity to do the work, thereby enabling the team to eventually attain a stable WIP level that matches its total capacity. Explicit WIP limits are another strategy (but should really be reserved for more mature teams, as they require a more complete understanding and practice of many core concepts).

To help ensure system agility, it's essential to maximize your options. The more tightly work is packed within a system, the less agile you become (tightly packed work reduces your available options to respond to changes in circumstances). Limiting WIP is one mechanism for maintaining a sufficient amount of slack to ensure a smoother flow through the system.

A commonly used approach when introducing teams to the concept of explicit WIP limits is to establish them based on available resources or some other factor that's not associated with actual demand and capacity. As with most things, the best approach will be dictated by the team's specific context.

As the team performs work, circumstances may call for violating WIP limits. These are learning opportunities, and should always trigger a discussion. Perhaps current limits are too low and should be raised. Or perhaps circumstances are such that the need constitutes a one-time exception. Regardless of the context, WIP limits represent an essential constraint that forces teams to improve their process and way of working.

Practice Tip

The amount of work a system should have in progress at any given time is a matter of balance. Just as tightly packed work can impede flow, so carrying too many options can represent waste. The proper balance is achieved over time, and is not something to target when starting off. Nonetheless, understanding what proper balance is expected to resemble is important to establishing any "proto" constraints with which you elect to begin.

Teams will confront some common challenges with regard to establishing and abiding by WIP limits (we address these in greater detail in Chapter 7). These include the following issues:

- *Variability*: In the form of demand, the work, the risks, and numerous other factors.
- *Constraints*: Constraints ultimately determine system capacity. In knowledge work, they tend to move around, making them difficult to identify and manage. This makes discovering and establishing the right WIP limits very challenging.
- *Human nature*: People are funny. They often mask their true desires and intentions in less than obvious ways.

Planning and Feedback Loops

Scrum practitioners are already used to daily check-ins. Employing Scrumban, however, presents the opportunity to shift the meeting's focus from status and commitment to more proactive planning. The kanban board already provides status information and should detail who is working on what. Impediments should also be visualized. Consequently, the focus of the team's discussion can shift to a collaborative effort geared toward identifying potential impediments, dealing with requested exceptions to policies, and otherwise addressing discoveries about how work is being performed.

If your Scrum teams are made up of inexperienced practitioners, it's possible they don't know whether their existing stand-ups are even effective. If the teams to which you're about to introduce Scrumban fall into this category, the kickstart is an opportunity to help them improve.

Jason Yip, a principal consultant at the firm Thoughtworks, has effectively summarized patterns to establish for a good stand-up (easily remembered using the mnemonic GIFTS):

- *Good start*: Good stand-ups should be energizing, not demotivating.
- *Improvement*: The primary purpose of the meeting is to support improvement, not to discuss status.[7]
- *Focus*: Stay focused on the right things, which should be to move work through the system (rather than dwelling on pointless activities).
- *Team*: Good stand-ups foster effective communication and collaboration. If people aren't helping one another during stand-ups, something is awry.
- *Status*: Stand-ups should communicate a basic sense of what's going on. As previously noted, the actual conversations move away from this information in Scrumban (i.e., this information should be communicated through the kanban board).

Scrum's time-boxed Sprint remains the main vehicle for coordinating the delivery of completed work and replenishing the team with new work. Over time, teams can opt to modify the process for replenishment and commitment to delivery (and even de-couple these cadences) to adopt approaches more focused on actual demand and capacity.

Sprint Reviews and Retrospectives are existing feedback loops within the Scrum framework that we tweak in some measure when practicing Scrumban. For example, whereas Sprint Reviews are focused on soliciting customer feedback on the delivery of completed product, in Scrumban we incorporate the concept of reviewing overall service delivery (borrowing from the Kanban Method's Service Delivery and Risk Review cadences). Similarly, the Sprint Retrospective takes on more of the flavor of the Kanban Method's Operations Review.

It is also important to mention the importance of conducting organizational level feedback loops, such as the Strategy Review cadence integrated within the Kanban Method.

Individual Flow (Optional)

Some of the concepts and techniques Scrumban employs to give teams greater control over their collective focus and workflow are not obvious and are sometimes

---

7. To this end, helping team members learn how to effectively engage in difficult conversations can be immensely beneficial. See our references in the Appendix for additional guidance in this area.

counterintuitive. Devoting a portion of your kickstart program to techniques for managing personal workflow is one way to enhance appreciation of their effectiveness. Topics of particular relevance include the following:

- Managing energy and not time (introduced via the Pomodoro technique, for example)
- The power of habits in knowledge work (by way of a brief introduction to disciplined approaches in problem solving such as A3 Thinking, for example)

Wrapping Up

Kickstart workshops should always be closed with a summary of what the teams achieved and the next steps that will be taken moving forward. In all instances, some degree of continued coaching and guidance is necessary for teams to optimize their understanding and practice.

Some Final Thoughts

> **Coaching Tip!**
>
> Important Concept Ahead

We've encountered a common misconception among Agile consultants and coaches regarding Scrumban implementations—the notion that because kanban systems are grounded in queuing and systems theories, there is no value in implementing them until the systems in which they're used are stabilized.[8]

Key Take-Away

As Deming recognized decades ago, systems should be stabilized before undertaking efforts to improve them. Unfortunately, many Agile experts fail to recognize that kanban systems provide a path to stability in and of themselves (from which we can apply scientific principles in pursuit of more considered improvements).

For example, WIP limits should ultimately be established based on the characteristics of the stable system to which they apply. However, initial-WIP limits can be used to bring a system into stability. I've pursued this path in many contexts, and

---

8. This mindset was recently communicated by a leading consultant in the Boston Agile community during a regular monthly gathering.

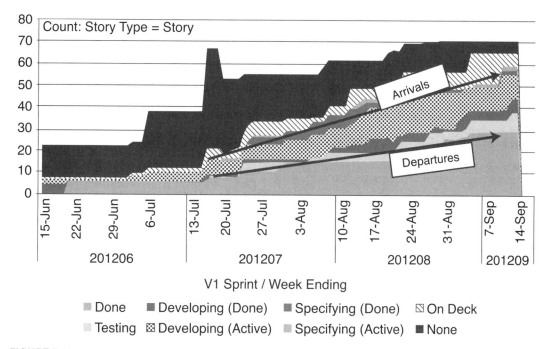

FIGURE 5.10   A cumulative flow diagram showing effort being committed to new work increasing faster than existing work can be completed.

this approach is specifically cited in the Siemens Health Services Scrumban story. It's worthy to call out some of the particulars here.

By way of background, the Siemens group elected to refrain from imposing WIP limits on their initial rollout. They soon discovered that the absence of WIP limits did nothing to stabilize or reverse their existing trend of ever-increasing cycle times. A cumulative flow diagram generated from their data showed the system was out of balance, with teams accepting new work faster than they were delivering completed work (Figure 5.10). Past patterns of increasing cycle times had not been influenced.

Upon establishing initial-WIP limits, the teams immediately began to see a stabilization in both system lead times[9] and overall system performance (Figure 5.11 and Figure 5.12).

The moral of the story is clear: Yes, systems need to be stable before we can improve them, but they also afford us mechanisms to achieve the stabilization needed to undertake our true journey.

---

9. Depicted here as cycle time. The terminology in the industry can be quite confusing. Cycle time here is the time taken to complete a work item. Refer to Chapter 7 for more precise definitions.

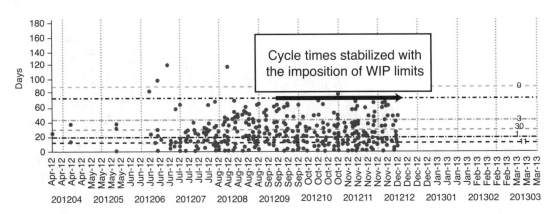

FIGURE 5.11 System lead times being stabilized.

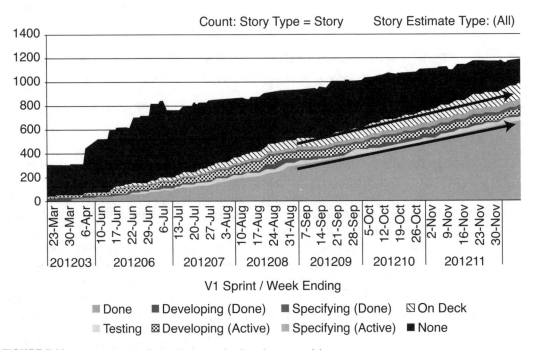

FIGURE 5.12 Cumulative flow diagram indicating a stable system.

Tying It All Together

This chapter outlines one approach for introducing Scrumban to a team or organization. Though not explicitly called out, it assumes the rollout is taking place in a midsize or larger organization with an objective of catalyzing change to key outcomes across the enterprise.

Software engineers, project and product managers, and the other professionals with whom they interact are generally intelligent and capable people. While this chapter has provided enough detail for the uninitiated to begin introducing Scrumban on their own, don't discount the value of calling in outside experts, especially those who have seasoned systems thinking capabilities and a deep understanding of the Kanban Method. Indeed, the folks at Siemens Health Services made a point to call this out in the case study of their own experience.

Chapter 6

METHOD: WORKING UNDER THE HOOD

IN THIS CHAPTER

- Better Decisions through Improved Risk Recognition and Management
- Improving Release and Sprint Management with Scrumban
- Tactical Design Choices That Improve Understanding and Collaboration

This chapter and the two that follow are all about getting our hands dirty and acquiring a deeper understanding of the mechanics for executing Scrumban. That said, I will still relate these mechanics back to the foundational principles that make them work.

The first major mechanic is tangentially related to Lean thinking. Lean principles view any activity that doesn't generate value for the end customer as "waste." Therefore, efforts to eliminate waste are generally beneficial—especially as teams see their performance plateau.

With knowledge work, it's not so easy to separate truly "wasteful" activities from those that actually lead to valuable information discovery. Risk management represents an alternative path to the same outcome. Good risk management techniques lead to the delivery of higher value, the ultimate objective of eliminating waste.

Managing Uncertainty and Risk

Learning Levels:

Risk is relevant to all levels of learning but can escalate to more advanced concepts quickly.

In today's highly competitive world, it's increasingly important to make the right decisions: decisions about which projects to start; decisions about which tasks to complete first; decisions about what to abandon. Unfortunately, traditional approaches to decision making rarely take a complete inventory of uncertainty into consideration. More significantly, factors that are difficult to assess are either ignored or assigned arbitrary values. When we improve the management of risk, however, we also improve our decision making.

Software development inherently involves a high degree of uncertainty. Much of this work involves creating something for the first time (or at least the first time for a given team). The process involves a great deal of discovery and imagination, which leads to high levels of variability. Other uncertainties include a team's size, skills, and stability (such as unplanned attrition). These uncertainties combine to make it difficult to accurately forecast staff requirements and delivery dates.

One of the more powerful capabilities Scrumban brings to the traditional Scrum context is the integration of enhanced risk management mechanics. Although these capabilities represent a significant addition of value for teams and organizations, they are not typically targeted for immediate introduction. That said, I don't delay their introduction very long, either. Let's ease into the subject by examining the distinction between uncertainty and risk.

Although conceptually related, uncertainty and risk are actually two different things. Risk arises from uncertainty and is composed of two dimensions:

- The likelihood that an event will take place at some future time
- The consequences of that event once it occurs

Identifying and managing risk in a disciplined and scientific way is particularly powerful because it enables us to enjoy three benefits:

- Better understand the likelihood of a risk occurring
- Better understand the probability of different outcomes associated with a risk
- Better understand the costs associated both with reducing the likelihood of a risk occurring and with mitigating the consequences associated with a risk

With this additional knowledge, we can plan our work by making intelligent decisions about whether to reduce the likelihood of risk, to mitigate the consequences associated with a risk, or both. These decisions ultimately maximize the ROI of our work.

Types of Uncertainty and Risk

Many different types of uncertainty exist, but they can generally be divided into two categories: aleatory and epistemic (Figure 6.1). Let's forget about these fancy labels, however, and instead focus on understanding the relevant differences by their essential characteristics.

From a pragmatic standpoint, it's useful to categorize uncertainties to better understand the extent to which they can be managed. Generally speaking, aleatory uncertainties cannot be made more certain, whereas epistemic uncertainties can potentially be reduced by gathering more data or undertaking other actions.

A good example of aleatory uncertainty in business is the loss of inventory through events other than sales, such as theft or breakage; this loss is commonly

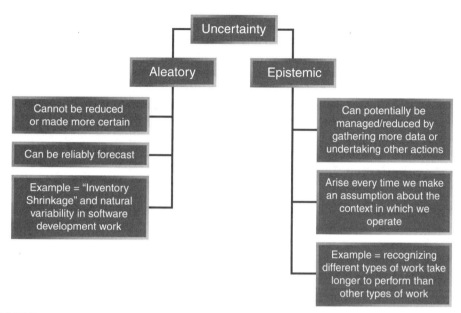

FIGURE 6.1   Categorizing risks helps us understand how best to manage them.

known as "shrinkage." Retail stores can't be certain as to exactly what will drive shrinkage, but they can reliably forecast the amount over a given time period.

Examples in the software development context might include natural variabilities in work effort and productivity as well as the recognition of quality issues that necessitate rework. We can't be certain as to exactly how they will manifest, but we know these factors will crop up on a regular basis. Such issues can rarely be eliminated because they essentially represent natural variations. Much of the "common cause variation" that Deming references arises from these kinds of uncertainties.

Risks arise when we fail to account for uncertainties in our planning, or when we fail to incorporate a sufficient buffer to protect against them. For example, retail operations can measure their average annual loss of inventory to shrinkage. They put their operations at risk when they set prices without accounting for these losses. Rather than trying to manage these kinds of risk out of the system (i.e., totally eliminate them), we simply need to recognize and account for them in a workable fashion. Scrumban allows us to manage these risks through metrics that help us understand the natural range of these uncertainties and through mechanics like buffer columns that help us account for them.

The second type of uncertainties that Scrumban helps us address are epistemic risks—that is, risks we can reduce or eliminate through increased knowledge. These uncertainties arise every time we make an assumption about the context in which our systems operate.

Risks arise from epistemic uncertainties when we don't use data to quantify them, when we neglect certain effects from their occurrence, or when we have insufficient or inaccurate measures of relevant factors. Scrumban enables us to manage these kinds of risks by providing new data that helps us better evaluate their probability, by providing means to quantify and visualize undesirable consequences, and by providing a variety of risk-handling techniques to account for and actively manage them (the integration of risk profiles and distinct classes of service represent a few specific examples).

How Scrumban Boosts Scrum's Capabilities

Both Scrum and Scrumban have mechanisms that help reduce the impact of natural variations in software development work. One of these is their mutual bias toward small items.

The Scrumban framework adds significantly more robust mechanisms for managing risk at many levels. Flow-based management techniques bring empirical measurements that clarify the natural variations in our work in more detail. I'll highlight the particulars as we discuss specific mechanisms in this and subsequent chapters.

Scrumban is particularly enabling when it comes to providing additional tools for managing epistemic risk. This framework minimizes the risk resulting from lack of data by applying metrics that aren't gathered in a traditional Scrum context. It allows teams to employ robust probabilistic forecasting models and enables us to visualize risk throughout our workflow, empowering collective and adaptive management.

How Scrumban Improves Management of Risk

Risk resides in essentially three arenas that are relevant to technology work:

- Market-based risk
- Environmental risk
- Work-related risk

In a typical Scrum context, the product owner is charged with managing market-based risks. These efforts are commonly integrated into the development process in the form of backlog prioritization.

The Scrum team is responsible for addressing environmental (e.g., external dependencies, staff availability) and work-related (e.g., technology) risks. These efforts are commonly integrated into the development process in the form of story point or similar estimates.

The first step to improving decision making is strategic in nature. It calls for organizations to move away from efforts to optimize efficiency and costs. Instead, organizations are encouraged to invest time and effort in activities that improve speed and value. Changing to this mindset is not easy.

The second step is more tactical in nature. It calls for the active evaluation and management of risk through a variety of mechanisms. Two impediments to effecting tactical change in this manner are often observed.

At one end of the spectrum, the mindset of business managers and executives must change. The good news is that these individuals are accustomed to incorporating considerations of risk and value into their daily work. Unfortunately, their assessments tend to be subjectively based.

At the other end of the spectrum, IT employees must embrace a new vision of risk. Unlike their business counterparts, they rarely incorporate considerations of risk and value into their daily work. However, when they do address risk, their approaches tend to be more comprehensive and empirical. Scrumban excels at bringing these mindsets together, and integrating common approaches into everyone's ongoing work processes.

How Scrumban Boosts Scrum's Capabilities

Most development frameworks (including Scrum) are not structured to help us determine which tasks to start first, or when to stop work and move on to something else, or how to determine which work carries the greatest value. In most of these contexts, Scrum defers to product owners' knowledge, which is presumed to drive the proper prioritization of work items. Just as Planning Poker has become a de facto technique for team estimation, so schemes have emerged to help teams understand appropriate prioritizations. The MoSCoW approach is one such example.[1]

Scrumban can change this landscape. It is biased toward establishing scientific approaches to risk assessment and prioritization. It enables teams and organizations to easily incorporate sophisticated prioritization functions into their visualization and management frameworks.

Enabling teams to visualize the impact of failing to complete an item of work allows them to continually adjust their local choices to complete work based on changing values of delivery at every phase of the development cycle. More importantly, economic-based schemes are a great way to reinforce the notion that delivering business value is the team's real bottom-line objective.

---

1. The MoSCoW technique puts stories into one of four categories: Must have, Should have, Could have, and Won't have.

Improved Flow through WIP Limits and Buffers

One of the ways Scrumban helps teams and organizations reduce uncertainty lies in its provision of new mechanisms for managing workflow. In today's highly dynamic environment, we're overloaded with information and expectations in both our personal and professional worlds. We're constantly interrupted, and we're constantly complicating the lives of those around us by asking them to do things without any real understanding of the scope of their existing workload.

When individuals, teams, and organizations take on more work than they can sustainably handle, that overloaded status heightens distractions and decreases focus. Trying to work on several things simultaneously decreases efficiency. Moreover, work goes unfinished and both quality and attention to detail suffer. Deadlines are missed, and when we have to hand off work to others, it's rarely efficient. All of these consequences create even more work and uncertainty.

Limiting work in progress (WIP) may not eliminate these consequences, but it will make them far less likely to happen. However, failing to limit WIP makes it certain you will be experiencing all these bad consequences more frequently (Figure 6.2).

Healthy systems require healthy constraints. When we limit WIP, we're essentially filtering out distraction, information overload, and complexity. This is why limiting WIP goes hand-in-hand with better risk management and improved prioritization. Limiting our focus allows us to become more aware of what we're doing,

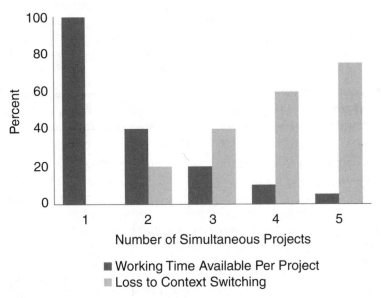

FIGURE 6.2   The cost of context switching.

Source: Gerald Weinberg. *Quality Software Management: Systems Thinking Vol. 1* (John Wiley & Sons, 1992).

what we're not doing, and why we've made those choices. As we make more informed choices, we increase the value of our efforts. Consequently, introducing this constraint means teams will be constantly reinforced to adopt behaviors that achieve the following aims:

- Improve attentiveness
- Become aware of and engage in a constant, dynamic reprioritization of work (reinforcing the concept of delivering value)
- Actively manage risk
- Strive to continuously improve

Managing WIP[2] also enables us to understand the effects of individual actions on the system as a whole. Ideally, we want to align work in process with our system's overall capacity to ensure a consistent flow. To do so, we need to consider how starting new work influences downstream processes.

For example, when we optimize individual efficiency, it's easy to inadvertently create "downstream" bottlenecks that reduce the output of the entire system. Similarly, certain functions can process work too quickly, resulting in "starvation" as they wait for additional work to perform. Because our primary goal should be to deliver value, we may sometimes need to establish WIP limits that ensure we don't introduce new work into the system. This may create situations where individual team members are *not* working at 100% of their capacity. This is counterintuitive, as we've been conditioned to equate personal utilization with productivity for most of our lives.

Coaching Tip!

Take advantage of this insight when introducing WIP limits in your context.

There are two key aspects to consider when introducing WIP limits— how to deal with the psychological factors and how to pragmatically manage it. In each arena, we have three different perspectives to consider: personal, team, and organizational. A common trap lies in assuming the same approach for managing WIP limits will be effective at all three levels.

The Individual

The more comfortable individuals are with the idea of limiting their personal WIP, the more receptive they'll be to limiting WIP at higher levels. If indicators of early psychological barriers to understanding the relevance of WIP limits appear, introducing

---

2. The players of the GetScrumban game can experience the impact of WIP limits in action.

the concept at an individual level first can be helpful. I like introducing individuals to Personal Kanban for just this reason.

The Team

At the team level, we primarily limit WIP to ensure a smooth flow of work, reducing the amount of time it takes for the customer to receive value. A number of challenges are associated with creating and sustaining WIP limits at this level. Two of particular note are as follows:

- There is a great deal of variability in software development—for example, in the nature of demands, the nature and complexity of the work, economic and other risks, the availability of different skills, and the extent to which the team is dependent upon others. Identifying all of these individual components is challenging. Understanding the combined effect of these elements requires patience and perseverance.
- Goldratt's theory of constraints tells us that the natural constraints in our systems dictate overall capacity. Unlike in manufacturing, however, the variability associated with knowledge work typically prevents us from stabilizing these constraints. This, in turn, makes it challenging to determine the capacity of our system with any degree of confidence. That explains why we must constantly measure and adjust to our system's changing capacities.

The Organization

At an organizational level, the primary objective should be to identify the work that delivers the most value. Consequently, limiting WIP at this level is more about establishing a clear focus and direction than about controlling the flow of work. Specific examples include limiting the number of active projects or the number of features under development.

Most organizations struggle with managing the number of options available to them. If individuals can recognize the personal and team-level costs of context switching, there's a better chance they'll have a sense of its immensity at an organizational level.

Unfortunately, management groups often struggle with limiting strategic focus, perhaps because of the fear of losing out on opportunities. If the leadership team first identifies the best opportunities and then ensures its pursuit of opportunities matches its capacity for execution, it will go a long way toward creating the kind of focus and alignment needed for sustained high performance.

Visualizing Risk

Another way Scrumban can be effectively leveraged to help individuals and teams is by integrating risk-based visualizations into their workflow. Although there are many ways to accomplish this, one of the simplest is through the adoption of risk profiles. Essentially, teams should be encouraged to consciously recognize the reasons why some work is more important to complete sooner than other work.

Kanban practitioners have identified four common risk profiles associated with knowledge work. These profiles are by no means exhaustive, nor are they necessarily applicable to all environments. They can be summarized as follows:

- *Urgent/emergency cost profile*: Represents the highest risk and greatest immediate impact (Figure 6.3). In such a case, the team's typical lead time will not result in delivery of the work before the impact can be realized. This is why teams typically establish policies that call for all members to immediately stop other work and expedite these items. This corresponds to a priority discipline in queuing theory.
- *Fixed cost profile*: Represents medium to high risk, with an immediate impact if not completed by the required delivery date. Legal commitments to customers or suppliers and regulatory requirements are good examples of this kind of work (e.g., if work *x* isn't completed by a certain date, the company will be fined $*y*).

  Teams have a variety of options for handling work falling under this profile. Fixed date items may need to be prioritized over standard work. If work is started too late, these work items can transform to emergency profiles. Pragmatically, the only difference between the two is that the latter affords the opportunity to plan. If work is performed too early, however, you may be deferring other, more valuable, work, resulting in a greater overall cost of delay to the business (Figure 6.4).
- *Standard cost profile*: Represents medium risk with a shallow and immediate impact (Figure 6.5). The typical policy is to process such items on a first-in-first-out basis. This particular scheme is referenced as a queuing discipline in queuing theory. Standard work items can become more or less urgent over time, transforming into different risk profiles as warranted.

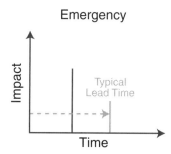

FIGURE 6.3   Urgent or emergency work would not be completed within the typical lead time absent special treatment.

■ *Intangible/investment cost profile*: Represents almost no risk with a low to moderate impact on the organization. Intangible or Investment work typically has no measurable cost of delay in the near future (Figure 6.6), and is performed as needed so the team may continue developing with high quality and speed. Examples of such work include dealing with technical debt, emergent architectural issues, and general improvements.

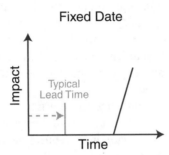

FIGURE 6.4   Completing fixed date items too early can defer more valuable work unnecessarily.

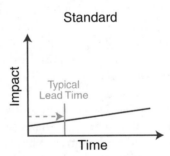

FIGURE 6.5   The cost of delay for standard work items typically grows over time.

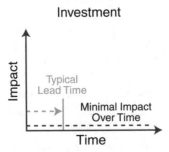

FIGURE 6.6   Investment or intangible risk profiles have a minimal cost of delay that remains fairly static over time.

Quantifying Cost or Value

It's one thing to talk about value or impact abstractly; it's another thing to arrive at an objective calculation. For the concept of cost or value to be useful, its measurement can't be subjective. Does this sound familiar? It should. It's the same challenge organizations face when seeking to leverage velocity metrics for Scrum teams.

While it's important for teams to both understand and appreciate the value placed upon work by the marketplace (and have some idea of why the organization or market prioritizes some types of work over other types), development teams are rarely in a position to discover this information on their own. The responsibilities for quantification of value and prioritization of work appropriately lie with those in the business arena. Consequently, if an organization truly wishes to maximize its ability to respond to the marketplace, it's critical to integrate improvement efforts across functions.

Scrum calls for the product owner to perform the function of prioritizing work. But what if your organization is transitioning to Scrum, and the individuals serving in these capacities bring varying degrees of capabilities to the table? What are the implications of their developing different approaches to quantifying value and prioritizing work? It's easy to defer paying attention to these considerations, but scaling Agility becomes significantly more challenging when the organization predominately focuses its attention on the technology realm. For this reason, I encourage teams and organizations to think through these considerations as early as possible, and try to ensure that they "attack" the product owner function in a meaningful way.

To this end, I like introducing a framework the good folks at Black Swan Farming have put forth as a suggested starting point for standardizing the consideration of value and prioritization across teams. This approach seeks to more objectively quantify the value of completed work by evaluating its worth to the market or organization across four general categories:[3]

- Work that will increase revenue (more sales)
- Work that will protect existing revenue (improvements or innovation that sustains market share)
- Work that will reduce costs (greater efficiency)
- Work that will avoid cost (costs not currently being incurred but are likely to be in the future)

We can use this framework to employ a more objective, data-based approach to assessing value and the relative importance of work.

Employing Cost of Delay

Because humans have an innate sense of prioritization that is aligned with delay, calculating the economic costs associated with delays in completing work is a natural

---

3. http://tiny.cc/UnderstandingValue.

starting point for adopting an approach that can be universally understood. Unfortunately, few organizations prioritize development work with regard to these natural understandings.

In simple terms, we want to understand the financial impact to our business for every hour, day, and week our work is not complete and available to end users. Associating a cost of delay to individual work items typically involves considering each item's value, urgency, and duration (smaller, short-duration tasks should receive higher priority). One approach gaining favor among Lean and Agile teams is cost of delay divided by duration (CD3). In a typical Scrum context, the product owner manages this factor, with assistance from the Scrum master.

CD3 is effectively a form of the weighted shortest job first queuing method. While it's possible to weight work by other factors, CD3 uses cost of delay (Figure 6.7). The idea is to prioritize the order of features or projects by dividing the estimated cost of delay for that work by the estimated duration it will take to complete it; the higher the resulting score, the more urgent the work.

A function like CD3 enables teams to utilize a common measure that compares work choices associated with different values, urgency levels, and anticipated durations. Because CD3 uses duration as the denominator, it offers the additional advantage of encouraging breaking down work into smaller batches, which is one of the easiest and most effective ways to improve flow, quality, and delivery of value.

Note the formula calls for *estimated* duration—a value the product owner, the team, or some combination of designated individuals must provide. Using an estimate for this value is not ideal, but it's a good compromise in exchange for simplifying the process of getting started, especially as most individuals and teams adopting this approach will be used to estimating work.

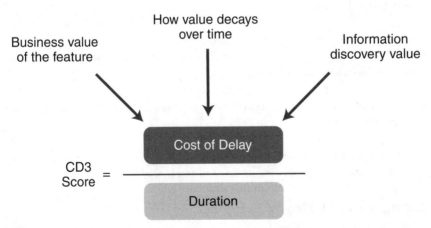

FIGURE 6.7   CD3 represents a prioritization scheme built on natural human understandings.

Source: Black Swan Farming (http://blackswanfarming.com/cost-of-delay-divided-by-duration).

TABLE 6.1   Proposed Backlog of Work

Feature	Duration	Cost of Delay	CD3 Score
1	6 weeks	$3000/week	500
2	2 weeks	$4000/week	2000
3	2 weeks	$5000/week	2500

The most common implementations of CD3 treat the resulting score as a static value. In other words, the CD3 value is calculated once and assumed to remain constant until the work is delivered. While this process is easy to manage, it doesn't account for potential changes in value or urgency. Again, we're willing to compromise on precision in return for simplicity. Let's walk through an example of a very basic implementation.

First, assume we have three proposed product features in our work backlog (Table 6.1).

Now let's calculate the financial impact to the organization if the development team completed work without any consideration of the cost of delay. We'll assume these three features are worked on in the order they appear.

For the six weeks it takes to complete work on feature 1, the business would incur the cost of delay associated with all three features:

$$\$3000 \ (feature \ 1) + \$4000 \ (feature \ 2) + \$5000 \ (feature \ 3) = \$12{,}000/week$$
$$\$12{,}000/week \times 6 \ weeks \ (duration \ to \ complete \ feature \ 1) = \$72{,}000$$

For the next two weeks that work is performed on feature 2, the business would incur the cost of delay associated with the remaining two features:

$$\$4000 \ (feature \ 2) + \$5000 \ (feature \ 3) = \$9000/week$$
$$\$9000/week \times 2 \ weeks \ (duration \ to \ complete \ feature \ 2) = \$18{,}000$$

For the final two weeks that work is performed on feature 3, the cost of delay would be

$$\$5000 \ (feature \ 3) \times 2 \ weeks \ (duration \ to \ complete \ feature \ 3) = \$10{,}000$$

The total cost incurred over the time required to complete all three features would be

$$\$72{,}000 + \$18{,}000 + \$10{,}000 = \$100{,}000$$

Now that we know the cost incurred by the business until all work is complete under our first scenario, let's examine the impact to the organization if the development team prioritized its completion of work by cost of delay. Under this approach, the same work is now prioritized based on CD3 calculations. Here, the team begins work on feature 3 first because it was assigned the highest CD3 value. The business would still incur the cost of delay associated with all three incomplete features while work is performed on feature 3, but this cost would be incurred for only two weeks versus six weeks in our original scenario:

$3000 (feature 1) + $4000 (feature 2) + $5000 (feature 3) = $12,000/week

$12,000/week × 2 weeks (duration to complete feature 3) = $24,000

Feature 2 would be worked on next, as that has the next highest cost of delay associated with it:

$3000 (feature 1) + $4000 (feature 2) = $7000/week

$7000/week × 2 weeks (duration to complete feature 2) = $14,000

Finally, feature 1, with the lowest cost of delay, would be completed:

$3000 (feature 1) × 6 weeks (duration to complete feature 1) = $18,000

Having prioritized work based on the CD3 calculations, the total cost of delay incurred by the business under this scenario is $44,000 lower than in the original scenario—a marked improvement:

$24,000 + $14,000 + $18,000 = $56,000

Next-Level Learning:

Evolving to More Advanced Practices

We alluded earlier to shortcomings in the simplified approach—static valuations and reliance upon duration estimates in particular. As individuals and teams expand their mastery of Scrumban principles and practices, they can improve their application of this approach.

A first evolution might be to substitute actual lead-time data for estimated duration when making CD3 calculations. We'll see how Scrumban enables probabilistic forecasting techniques based on lead time later in this chapter, and there's no reason why similar techniques can't be applied in this context.

Similarly, Scrumban makes it relatively simple for CD3 calculations to be continuously updated as work items progress through the value stream. More significantly, these recalculations can take into account data generated as work progresses. This knowledge enables team members to make informed "just-in-time" choices about which work to pull first. This kind of robust management, however, represents a capability that most teams and organizations may never need to pursue.

CD3 represents just one approach an organization can take to improve its risk awareness and management. It's still just a proxy for improving work choice priorities, and it's not entirely reliable because it tends to trivialize risk and subjectively forecasts market value. Considering that most organizations don't incorporate any kind of risk assessment into their prioritization schemes, however, it's a great model for fostering more sophisticated approaches over time.[4]

How Scrumban Boosts Scrum's Capabilities

Assessing a work item's cost of delay dynamically and at a local (team) level—ideally as work cards are available to be pulled—represents an opportunity to optimize value generation for the business. Scrum does not inherently provide for such assessments during sprints. In fact, the framework can actually hinder risk management because of the constraints created by time-boxed iterations.

Additionally, Scrum's point estimate doesn't capture risk in a disciplined fashion. It's true that larger work items tend to be riskier, but how do we compare two items with the same relative size? Their associated risks can often be dissimilar. A clearly visible and commonly understood risk profile that brings additional intelligence into the decision-making process provides a significant advantage.

Using Classes of Service

When we establish and visualize different risk profiles in Scrumban, we're essentially identifying and proactively managing risk across our work items by continuously evaluating work based on scientific approaches and separately measuring our performance against different profiles. As teams mature their virtual kanban systems, it's not unusual to see the establishment of separate swim lanes for different "classes of service" based on cost of delay risk profiles. Later in this chapter, we'll consider how measuring across classes of service can be used to better inform both release and iteration planning.

Continuing to Emphasize Proper Work Breakdown

There's a lot to be said for user stories as work items of choice. They emphasize verbal communication across the team and with the product owner, allowing details

---

4. The players of the GetScrumban game can experience the cost of delay concept in action.

to be worked out to far greater precision than is possible with a lengthy set of written requirements. It's easier to estimate how much time and effort will be required to develop them as opposed to estimating from use cases and other modes of scope definitions.

Although Scrum emphasizes smaller user stories primarily for planning and comprehension, it also minimizes risk. Scrumban enables further capabilities here by allowing us to consciously approach story development with an eye toward improved flow.

User stories that require many decisions to be saved up and passed from one person to another lead to larger "batch sizes" being associated with the hand-off. Goldratt's theory of constraints and other models demonstrate that larger batch sizes almost always produce negative consequences. Natural variations in work speed—no matter how small—produce unpredictable delays. Thus even well-designed systems can be unpredictable. Reduced batch sizes, however, generate smoother flow and improved predictability.

Theories are great, but nothing beats the impact of actually observing the smoother flow and improved predictability provided by proper story development (reduced batch sizes). Scrumban's visualizations and metrics make this possible in ways that are readily understandable by people in both the business and technology units.

So how do we continue helping teams develop optimally sized user stories in Scrumban? The same way we would in traditional Scrum—by emphasizing the characteristics of a good user story. But there is one small difference. Rather than having to home in on the size of the estimated effort, we need only ensure our stories are both "small enough" and "big enough." Bill Wake's "INVEST" principles remain a gold standard for guidance:

- *I—Independent*: We want to be able to move stories around, taking into account their relative priority. Taking this preference into consideration, stories are easiest to work with when they are independent. Although independent stories are important for reasons beyond ensuring a smooth flow of work, Scrumban enables us to more effectively manage dependencies, so this factor is less critical to overall performance than in a traditional Scrum context.
- *N—Negotiable*: Stories are not an explicit commitment to produce certain features, but rather a framework for ultimately defining what to produce for the end user.
- *V—Valuable*: A story needs to be valuable to the end user. Development issues should be framed in a way that illustrates their importance to the end user.
- *E—Estimable*: In a pure Scrum environment, we want stories to be estimable; otherwise, they're not likely to be tasked for development. Whether a story is estimable depends on its ability to be negotiated (you can't estimate what you don't understand), which is a function of its size and the team's experience. Although the importance of estimation is reduced under a Scrumban

framework, factors that allow for estimation also support higher confidence in the probabilistic forecasting methods Scrumban employs.

- *S—Small*: Stories should be small—with Scrum, no more than a few person-days of work. Stories greater than this size make it almost impossible to know the full scope. Knowing the full scope of a story in a continuous flow framework is not as critical, but smaller sizes do result in improved flow.
- *T—Testable*: Finally, we want stories to be testable. If a story isn't testable, you can't really determine when it's done. Test-driven development has shown us how actually writing the tests early helps us know whether the business goal is being met.

Facilitating Transitions with Evolving Roles

Especially For:

Managers & Executives

As teams and organizations seek to adopt Lean and Agile practices, the evolving roles of existing workers represent a significant environmental risk. We've highlighted how Scrumban's core practices respect existing roles and responsibilities. This characteristic makes for a particularly powerful capability in almost any context.

If you're seeking to adopt Scrum "by the book," the only roles with titles are those of the product owner and the Scrum master. While there are good reasons for prescribing this kind of flat structure, most organizations either maintain a variety of "holdover" roles for a host of business reasons (not the least of which is the identification and sense of validation people associate with their job titles) or simply "reassign" existing staff with little consideration as to whether the individuals involved possess the characteristics and capabilities needed to effectively change their way of working so as to fulfill the essential functions of their new roles. As noted earlier, the product owner role often falls victim to the organization's failure to holistically address changing needs.

While their traditional work may no longer be relevant to "new" processes that exist within a Scrum context, individuals who held traditional roles will not necessarily immediately adapt to the nascent environment and start delivering value to newly defined work processes. Scrumban can ease the transition to fulfilling the essential purposes as envisioned in a more traditional Scrum framework. We discuss some of the particulars in Chapter 8, but mention this factor here as an important capability that is closely connected with many of the mechanics discussed in this chapter.

Releases and Sprints

Because most Scrum teams will have to manage releases and sprints in the course of performing their work, it's particularly relevant to call out how a Scrumban framework can be advantageously leveraged.

Thinking Differently about Commitment

One of the most important thought evolutions to evoke when Scrum teams begin applying Scrumban lies with the notion of commitment. Scrum's Sprint Planning ceremony represents the point of commitment for the team: Once a story is selected for inclusion in a sprint backlog, the team has committed to completing all work on that story within the duration of the sprint.

Kanban emphasizes a two-phased commit. The first point of commitment occurs when a work item is first pulled into the queue. The second point of commitment occurs when completed work is actually delivered to the customer. We encourage Scrum teams to think of a sprint as a single instance of Kanban's two-phase framework, where the start of the sprint represents the first point of commitment and the end of the sprint represents the second. Why is this distinction important? Because such a mindset allows management and workers to assume more control over the constraints they place on themselves rather than simply following a prescribed process.

The most common constraint that management and workers place on themselves is synchronizing both commitment points, or believing that new work must be accepted at the same cadence with which finished work is delivered. In fact, the time-boxed sprint reflects this mindset exactly. The Scrumban framework, however, offers multiple options.

One option is to establish different acceptance and delivery cadences (such as accepting new work every two weeks, but delivering completed work every four weeks). Another option is to have no acceptance cadence (continuous flow) while maintaining a delivery cadence such as every three weeks. Scrumban emphasizes that business needs, rather than process methodology, should dictate whether to synchronize acceptance and delivery cadences.

Scrum's "mandated" cadences often have a cascading impact. For example, one of the most common sources of dissatisfaction among organizations adopting Scrum is the perception that this framework imposes an onerous routine of meetings around the sprint cadence. These meetings can be especially demoralizing when you consider that teams miss making their sprint commitments on a fairly regular basis, up to 30% to 50% of the time for many Scrum teams.

The stress "roller coaster" experienced by many teams during every sprint is an important psychological consideration that impacts sustainability. Scrum team members almost always experience high levels of stress during the latter portion of a sprint, reinforced by frequent fire drills and quality issues leading up to the demo (sprint review). It's not uncommon for team members to work late and over weekends to make their sprint commitments, and these patterns exact a psychological toll that needs to be recognized and managed. Scrum does not predict these outcomes, but they represent the real-world effects of changing how an organization works.

These challenges, among others, are why many suggest moving away from time-boxed iterations altogether and adopting a model of continuous flow. This is the evolution Corey Ladas promoted when he introduced the first Scrumban system in 2008.

Continuous Flow versus Time-Boxed Iterations

Practicing Scrumban often sparks a renewed investigation of sprint duration, and sometimes a debate over whether to maintain time-boxed sprints at all.

Scrum prescribes a sprint duration that's short enough to be tolerated by the organization, yet long enough to complete the above-average-size piece of work. Because Scrum views cadence as important, it strongly recommends against changing established sprint durations. Unfortunately, sprint cadences are rarely established based on systemic understandings. As system understanding improves, teams and organizations develop a benchmark against which to evaluate their practices.

Scrumban always takes a pragmatic approach based on what makes sense from a systems point of view. Strict adherence to time-boxed cadences, for example, may not make sense for your system.

Perhaps the kind of work is highly complex and can't be broken down into batches that can be completed within a two-week sprint. Perhaps your customers prefer a steady stream of deliveries rather than a burst of releases that coincides with the end of your sprints. Whatever the reason, a continuous flow model such as the one that gave birth to Scrumban (reviewed in Chapter 4) may be more appropriate for your context. If the purpose of the time-box is being fulfilled through other mechanisms and your organization is realizing its business objectives, then does it really matter if you're no longer practicing the prescribed version of Scrum?

At the same time, Scrum has been purposely designed. Its events and artifacts serve multiple purposes, some of which address basic truths about human systems and behavior. The rhythms associated with successful deliveries breed enthusiasm and trust. Forced interactions within a defined framework improve understandings and capabilities. Synchronized cadences may be a necessary discipline for external dependencies to perform satisfactorily.

For these reasons, the most common form of Scrumban implementation is *not* the more radical, continuous flow paradigm advocated by Corey Ladas. Rather, this version focuses on the creation of kanban systems within the Scrum framework and their use to manage flow within the context of a sprint.

Scrumban systems recognize the realities of most environments. They account for and provide a framework for managing urgent or emergency work requests outside the context of a sprint backlog. They incorporate nonstandard work like technical debt into a consolidated management framework. They enable teams and organizations to function under structures that conflict with Scrum's prescribed practices that we may not have the ability to change, such as specialized teams and external dependencies. Scrumban systems don't care which flavor of the framework an organization adopts; they simply seek to ensure the business is being served in the process.

Additional Dimensions for Managing Releases and Sprints

At the beginning of the chapter, we discussed the benefits of quantifying the cost of delay as a means of prioritizing work order, and "assigning" risk profiles to improve our management of that work. Scrum teams don't need Scrumban to adopt similar techniques, but the Scrumban framework provides a robust tool for easing that adoption and improving shared understandings among the team and across the organization. These same mechanisms can be leveraged to ease management of releases and individual sprints.

For example, in larger organizations it's not uncommon for Scrum teams to perform work across multiple product backlogs. These backlogs rarely have a common product owner or even overlapping stakeholders. As a consequence, work is often prioritized on a rotating basis without regard to value or based on political horse-trading. Neither approach maximizes ROI. Adopting disciplined approaches and visualizing the additional information they provide expands shared understandings and provides a data-based foundation for moving toward real Agility.

Another example relates to visualizing dependencies at the program or portfolio level. In a Scrum context, this often relates to cards representing epics, which are ultimately broken down into features and user stories. Progress of the epic is ultimately a function of its child components, which may be spread across multiple teams.

Traditionally, PERT charts and Gantt charts have been used to visualize and manage the complex dependencies that typically arise under large programs and projects. Each of these devices has significant limitations for providing visual and actionable information, not to mention significant management overhead. These traditional tools stand in contrast to layered kanban boards, which can seamlessly link information together (Figure 6.8). With the kanban boards, real-time views of progress and impediments are obvious and transparent to all.

Similarly, the simple act of visualizing when a work item is "done," and providing mechanisms that help enforce more granular definitions of "done" along every phase of the value stream, have proved to reduce rework and bug fixes—even among teams considered to be highly mature in Scrum and Agile practices.[5] Figure 6.9 depicts such a visualization system.

Improved Planning and Forecasting

While Scrumban can support pragmatic deviations from Scrum, some of its most powerful attributes derive from how it enhances core Scrum practices. One area where this is most evident is in coordinated planning and forecasting.

In a Scrum environment, the workflow typically consists of user stories that represent some measure of independent business value. Projects or product releases represent a collection of work items from among the overall flow. In this context, planning takes place on two primary levels—release planning and sprint planning.

---

5. The Siemens Health Group documented these improvements most convincingly. Read its case study in the Appendix.

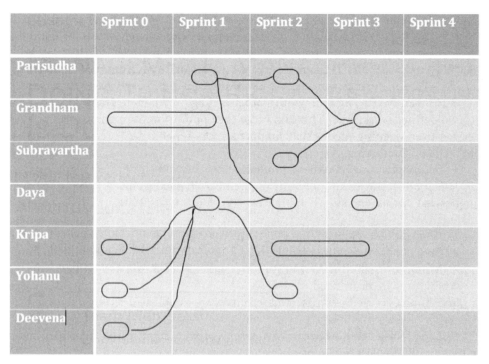

FIGURE 6.8   An example visualizing dependencies across epics and sprints.

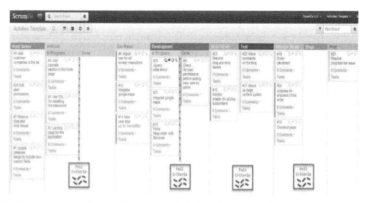

FIGURE 6.9   Representation of how explicit "definition of done" policies across the value stream help minimize the frequency of rework and improve quality.

Scrum teams employ team estimation, story point velocity metrics, and other mechanisms to provide clarity when planning their releases and sprints. While these mechanisms are superior to many other options, they remain limited in terms of both reliability and scalability. Perhaps the greatest limitation stems from the fact that team velocity—Scrum's primary metric—is a subjective prediction relative to each team.

Scrumban systems measure both a broader range and a more granular set of data around defined workflows. This allows for the application of mathematical models derived from queuing theory that support a more reliable and precise approach—probabilistic forecasting.

In release planning, in either a product release planning or project planning context, the product owner and senior team members typically engage in a process that progresses like this:

1. Concept is developed
2. Project parameters are established
3. Minimum viable product/minimum marketable features are defined
4. Features are prioritized
5. Estimates of required time and resources are established

This section focuses on how Scrumban systems provide significantly expanded capabilities around the last two steps.

Release planning usually involves reviewing broadly defined features versus specifically defined user stories. Beyond helping the IT unit engage in a necessary level of architectural and resource planning, these longer-range forecasts are often used by the business to coordinate related efforts (such as marketing and sales) as well as to inform basic financial planning. The high-level nature of feature descriptions means the team's estimates will contain substantial variability.

Similarly, the prioritization of features directly influences total ROI. The product owner often exercises subjective judgment to establish a perceived business value for application features and then prioritizes them accordingly. Scrum is silent regarding these decisions, and it does not enable the product owner to address risk factors in a disciplined or scientific manner. ROI potential is only as good as the person prioritizing the work and his or her techniques allow.

In sprint planning, the primary objective is to reliably identify the number of stories that can be completed within the iteration. Frequent failures at meeting sprint commitments erode trust and confidence, creating high levels of stress and anxiety. Work is not fun. At the other end of the spectrum, excess capacity is wasteful and indicates employees may be limiting their professional growth and earning potential.

The completeness of workflow visualization dictates the degree to which a team or organization gains additional capabilities from better forecasting—the amount of time required to complete a given release or project (provided certain variables are known quantities), the number of user stories to be included within a sprint backlog, and so forth. Even the most rudimentary kanban system will allow teams to produce more reliable forecasts than Scrum's estimation techniques alone.

Early Planning

> ### PMO/Program Managers/ Product Owners:
>
> These next few sections are most relevant to your roles. While it's good for team members to be involved with planning and forecasting functions, they do not need to be proficient with these concepts.

Estimation is a risk mitigation mechanic we use to help prioritize options and manage the expectations of others. Unfortunately, reliable estimations are difficult to produce, especially when a wide degree of variability is evident in the work to be performed. Many folks artificially or superficially account for this factor by randomly "padding" projects and sprints rather than managing variation more scientifically. The business is provided with a forecast, but its precision is generally suspect.

Sprint 0 is another technique some folks use to manage expectations. This mechanism enables teams and product owners to better understand the full extent of the work that needs to be done for a given project, and it is even used to finalize resource needs and budgets. From the perspective of managing expectations, Sprint 0 is yet another way to reduce business and technical risk, and represents a crude form of early demand shaping. Sprint 0 is undertaken at the start of a new project, however; thus its improved understandings come too late to prioritize it against other alternatives.

In the Scrum context, numerous other techniques have been introduced to address strategic planning needs. For example, we use epics to define projects before their full scope is truly understood, then we employ epic breakdown techniques and vertical slicing to better understand the work that needs to be done and plan more granularly. It's unreasonable, however, to expect that all epics can be broken into stories before work begins, especially on large projects. So how can we set expectations in a more scientific way that isn't wasteful?

Randomized Batch Sampling

Randomized batch sampling (RBS) is derived from a mathematical technique first proposed by Raymond Jessen[6] as a means to efficiently estimate the total number of

---

6. R. Jessen. "Determining the Fruit Count on a Tree by Randomized Branch Sampling." *Biometrics* 1955;11:99–109.

fruits found within the canopy of a given tree. Called, appropriately enough, randomized branch sampling, this technique allows an individual to count only the number of fruits on a limited number of branches to arrive at a highly reliable estimate of the actual number of fruits for the entire tree. Dimitar Bakardzhiev has outlined a manner in which this same technique can be applied to forecasting user stories and tasks (or scenarios for those using ATDD [acceptance test-driven development] or BDD [behavior-driven development] practices) across a range of proposed epics.

In applying this technique to a Scrum context, it's helpful to think of the release or product as representing the trunk of a tree, epics as representing major branches, user stories as representing terminal shoots, and story points as representing the actual fruit (Figure 6.10). Rather than counting the number of fruit on a branch to

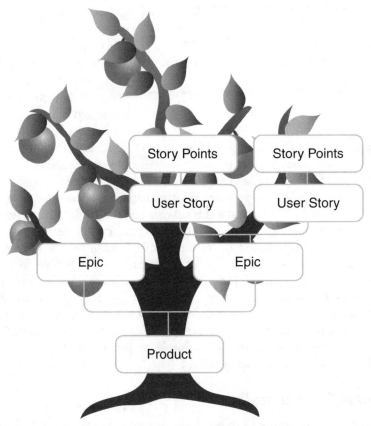

FIGURE 6.10   How to think of a project when applying random branch sampling to estimate its scope.

establish our initial data, however, we elaborate on a given epic to calculate an initial set of user stories and story points. The actual steps to follow are as follows:

1. If not already done, break your project into epics.
2. Randomly sample one of the epics.
3. Record the number of stories in your chosen epic.
4. Randomly sample one of the stories.
5. Estimate the number of story points for your chosen story.
6. Calculate the story points for the project using this formula:

$$Estimated\ number\ of\ story\ points = \frac{Story\ points\ of\ sampled\ user\ story}{(1\ /\ number\ of\ epics\ in\ project) \times (1\ /\ number\ of\ user\ stories\ in\ sampled\ epic)}$$

7. Repeat steps 2 through 6 between 7 and 11 times.
8. Calculate the distribution of total story points for the project.

I teamed up with Dimitar to test RBS estimates against the actual delivery times of real project data from ScrumDo.[7] We wanted to determine the degree of correlation between RBS size estimates and actual performance, and following is a recap of some of the amazing results from our experiments. In conducting our experiments, we randomly selected projects that met the following criteria:

1. The project possessed clear epic, user story, and task breakdowns.
2. The project reflected a successful release history.
3. The project was undertaken by stable teams (systems).
4. The project was commercial in nature (i.e., paid teams working on a project that either served the internal needs of an existing business or was sold in the open market).
5. The project included at least 12 epics or other features.
6. Projects had an active coach or Scrum master.

Table 6.2 shows our actual RBS calculation based on data from one project.

Calculating the mean, median, mode, and distribution of values from your data provides a reliable set of information upon which to estimate the actual number of story points represented by your project. Table 6.3 shows these results for the ScrumDo data.

---

7. ScrumDo is the online project management and collaboration tool I co-developed with Marc Hughes (http://ScrumDo.com).

TABLE 6.2   Randomized Batch Sampling Results for ScrumDo Data

Epic Number	Story Number	Number of Story Points	Task Count
1	569934	0.5	1
2	570772	0.5	3
3	569581	3	15
3	569604	2	15
3	570941	0.5	3
4	569573	13	13
4	569599	5	4
4	569602	0.5	12
5	569574	2	3
6	569579	1	4
6	569584	8	11
6	570149	1	11
6	570425	8	13
7	569592	8	1
7	570935	0.5	8
8	569595	2	14
8	570102	1	4
8	570426	0.5	13
9	569591	5	3
9	569596	8	3
9	569597	2	0
9	569601	1	5
9	570427	1	2
9	570938	0.5	7
10	569594	8	12
10	569598	3	4
11	569580	3	5
11	569593	3	3
11	570104	0.5	14
12	570928	0.5	4
Totals		92.5	210

TABLE 6.3   Estimated Project Size

Estimated project size	94
Number of RBS paths	7
Standard deviation	65
Median story points	6
Mode of story points	6

At this point, it can be very tempting to simply apply a team's historical velocity against the forecast story points to predict the number of sprints needed to complete this project. But story points are estimates of the effort required to complete a story, and are only loosely correlated with the size of the work at hand. Also, the data we've used is only representative of one project. Although we did not do so in these experiments, it's possible to enhance our estimation by applying correlation data from other projects (which would provide a systems-context understanding that is otherwise less developed).

Table 6.4 summarizes the raw data from our experiments comparing RBS estimates against actual performance. As reflected in these raw numbers and the scatterplot shown in Figure 6.11, there is a high correlation between the estimates and actual numbers.

This forecasting technique is a prime example of Scrumban's emphasis on the scientific method as a means of bringing meaningful perspectives and capabilities to Scrum teams. Next we'll explore how the introduction of kanban systems can be leveraged for similar outcomes.

Planning with Little's Law

Because Scrumban systems are queuing systems, they enable the application of Little's law to statistical data measured through their kanban systems. Specifically, teams are afforded the ability to define a mathematical relationship between their average lead time for work items processed through their systems and the finite time at which they

TABLE 6.4 Comparison of Actual Project Size and RBS Estimations

ScrumDo Project	Estimated Project Size Using RBS	Actual Project Size upon Completion	Point Variance	Percent Variance
1	902.5	1246.5	−344	−27.60%
2	133.57	177	−43.43	−24.54%
3	173.64	188.5	−14.86	−7.88%
4	243.29	411	−167.71	−40.81%
5	1954.29	3423	−1468.71	−42.91%
6	252.86	313	−60.14	−19.21%
7	209.14	265.5	−56.36	−21.23%
8	716.57	1590	−873.43	−54.93%
9	500	573.5	−73.5	−12.82%
10	254	297	−43	−14.48%
11	531.14	752	−220.86	−29.37%
12	791.29	1578	−786.71	−49.85%
13	91.29	92.5	−1.21	−1.31%

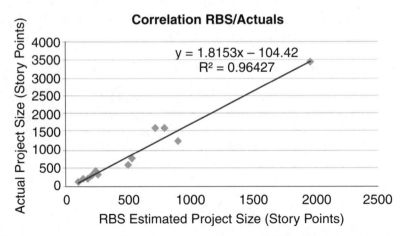

Correlation RBS/Actuals

$y = 1.8153x − 104.42$
$R^2 = 0.96427$

FIGURE 6.11 Scatterplot of the correlation between RBS estimates and actual points.

$$\begin{array}{c} \text{average output} \\ \text{(per time period)} \end{array} = \frac{\begin{array}{c} \text{average inventory} \\ \text{of work} \\ \text{(per time period)} \end{array}}{\begin{array}{c} \text{average lead time} \\ \text{of work} \\ \text{(per time period)} \end{array}}$$

FIGURE 6.12   A mathematical expression of Little's law.

deliver a particular project. At its most basic level, this relationship deals with averages and is expressed mathematically as shown in Figure 6.12.

In the equation in Figure 6.12, "lead time" is also called flow time or throughput time. The "average inventory of work" is nothing more than the average number of user stories between the starting and ending points of a production process for a given period of time, or work in progress. The "average lead time of work" is the average amount of time it takes for a work item to move from the first stage of a production process to the end of that process.

Little's law provides Scrumban teams with another reliable forecasting technique that can be used to influence expectations. One of its more powerful features lies in the fact it scales seamlessly from single to multiple teams. This capability has tremendous implications for forecasting at the program and portfolio management levels. It is also a feature that Scrum's native capabilities lack, since velocity is a subjective measurement.

Little's law cannot be applied indiscriminately. Rather, a system unit must demonstrate two important conditions to apply it with confidence. First, the system being measured must possess a "conservation of flow." In other words, the amount of work entering the system must, on average, be equal to the amount of work leaving the system. Second, all work items that enter the system must exit as some form of output. Put another way, no work can be lost or remain in the system indefinitely. These conditions represent a mathematical application of Deming's notion that systems must be stabilized before they can be improved.[8] As you define your kanban systems, measuring conservation of flow and conservation of work is a great way to verify stability.

Beyond the conditions cited previously, some other assumptions are made when we apply Little's law to systems-based knowledge work. These are drawn from areas ranging from queuing theory to probability distributions. Though it's not necessary to master these underlying assumptions to begin pragmatically applying these

---

8. Sufficient "stability" can be confirmed in many ways. Most simply, the presence of conservation of flow and the absence of significant churn in personnel and other system parts are sufficient. We've seen many Agile consultants avoid applying Little's law for no good reason (other than their own discomfort), relying on feigned concerns about stability or complexity as convenient excuses.

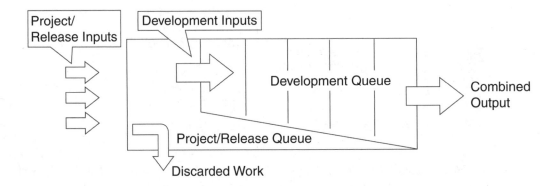

The project/release queue (system) processes the full project/release scope (any number of work items), and represents the total period of time required to complete the project.

The development queue (system) processes work items selected for actual development (work items entering and leaving the system are equal, and the total number of work items passing through the development system must be either equal to or less than the total number of work items processed by the project queue).

FIGURE 6.13   A visualization of a project system in which conservation of flow is ensured.

techniques, a better understanding of the underlying fundamentals will give you a greater ability to identify patterns, achieve more meaningful interpretations, and generate more precise models.

Diving into the Particulars

Dimitar Bakardzhiev has outlined a means by which we can ensure the applicability of Little's law by defining a system within a system against which to apply it.[9] In his model, the containing system shares the same delivery outcome as its subsystem, but allows work items to be abandoned or remain within the system indefinitely. The contained system provides the full conservation of flow needed for a valid application of Little's law. Bakardzhiev's example was provided in the context of project planning (Figure 6.13).

As noted earlier, the development subsystem possesses a full conservation of flow and work. Because the two systems share the same output, flow calculations derived from the subsystem are applicable to the project system as a whole.

---

9. In fairness, Dimitar's work is built upon a foundation that was first laid out by David J. Anderson in his book *Agile Management for Software Engineering: Applying the Theory of Constraints for Business Results* (2003).

Release Planning with Little's Law

Learning Level Tip:

This application represents a very basic and introductory approach. More refined applications are detailed in later chapters.

The project queue in this example contains a quantity of work items represented by the release backlog. Work items entering the release backlog are typically expressed in terms of minimum viable product definitions or minimum marketable features. Their individual sizing is irrelevant; we'll see how variations in size and complexity are handled shortly.

This model offers two different planning approaches. The first is to plan for future projects based on data measurements obtained from prior work. The second is to refine existing forecasts based on data developed as the project or release is being developed.

With the latter approach, work entering the project queue is broken down into epics and user stories, prioritized and ultimately passed through to the development queue in batches such as sprint backlogs. As work is performed in the development queue, we begin acquiring data related to the project, to which we can then apply Little's law. This data should be the most relevant gauge of performance.

The project's lead time is defined as the interval between when a request is accepted into the system for processing and when it is delivered to the customer. For the development system, we measure lead time as the interval between when a commitment to produce the work item is made (when it enters the queue) and when the work item is delivered to the customer.

While we will not provide a full proof of the mathematics involved,[10] the formula in Figure 6.14 can be derived for this system.

Other relationships can be derived from the base formula (Figure 6.15).

A few words about the relationship between average WIP and "resources" are in order. We don't like talking about human beings as interchangeable "resources," but in the context of forecasting and planning it's an appropriate label. Average WIP represents the inventory of work under active development at any given point in time.

$$\text{Average WIP} \begin{bmatrix} \text{The amount of resources} \\ \text{(developers, etc.) needed} \end{bmatrix} = \text{Average Lead Time} \left[\frac{\text{\# of User Stories}}{\text{Total Project Time}} \right]$$

FIGURE 6.14   A mathematical expression of Little's law.

---

10. See Dimitar Bakardzhiev's paper at http://tiny.cc/ProjectPlanningLL.

$$\text{# of User Stories} \left[\frac{\text{Average Lead Time}}{\text{Average WIP}} \right]$$

$$- OR -$$

$$\begin{matrix} \text{(Project/Release)} \\ \text{Lead Time} \end{matrix} = \left[\frac{\text{# of User Stories}}{\text{Average Throughput}} \right]$$

$$- OR -$$

$$\text{# of User Stories x Average Takt Time}$$

FIGURE 6.15   Little's law recast in different formulas.

Consequently, this value directly relates to the average number of people performing that work.

Let's now address our first wrinkle in this release planning process. In a Scrum context, work items processed in the development queue arrive in the form of user stories. The performance data we acquire thus relates to the user story as a unit. The work units addressed in the release planning process, however, are normally defined at a feature level. Consequently, it's important to design our kanban systems so we can acquire historical data that we can then use to calculate the average number of user stories associated with a defined feature. This last point raises a couple of key considerations.

First, many of the variables in the formulas above are "average" values. Readers with a more statistical bent will immediately recognize some of the inherent issues associated with average, and even median, values. For one thing, they can misrepresent actual performance if the items being measured have dense, "long-tail" distributions. The more sophisticated modeling described in later chapters addresses this imprecision. Those discussions will introduce applications of probabilistic frequencies utilizing Weibull distribution patterns, game theory, and probabilistic modeling with Monte Carlo simulations. Many teams and organizations will never need these more complex models. The fact all of these models are available, however, is a testament to the capabilities Scrumban adds to your management toolbox!

Second, don't let the use of mathematical formulas and proofs mislead you into believing that Scrumban will magically make your planning and forecasting perfect. At the end of the day, we're still making assumptions and we're still applying probabilistic methods. These approaches don't provide an absolute answer—just a more informed one.

Now, let's explore these formulas in action. We'll start with an example of using Little's law to enhance release planning, and then apply similar approaches to sprint planning.

Project/Release Planning Example

The backdrop for this example is the development of a mobile banking application by the RAD group at Mammoth Bank.[11] When this project was scheduled, two development teams were assigned to work on it exclusively. These two teams had been using kanban systems within their Scrum process for several months.

Historically, both teams maintained policies that resulted in each team member averaging 2 items of work in progress at any given time. Combined performance data for the teams reflected an *average* completion of 28 user stories per 2-week sprint, or approximately 14 stories per week. They also reflected an *average* lead time of 0.9 week per user story.

The primary product owner (Julie) had been investigating how to use historical performance data to better inform future planning. Consequently, she made a point of having teams track the *original* number of user stories created as each feature in a release backlog was broken down. This data was pulled from multiple projects, and reflected an historical average density of 13.5 user stories per feature.[12] Though an RBS calculation of user stories would be more reliable, this estimate represents the initial approach undertaken in this example.

Working with the business unit, Julie defined a total of 50 features for the mobile app. Applying RAD's historical data to the number of user stories per feature, she calculated the release backlog would translate to approximately 675 user stories. With this information, she could conduct a probabilistic forecast of the time and resources needed to complete the project through a simple application of Little's law.

Let's consider a scenario where Julie was informed the entire release had to be completed within 26 weeks. Applying Little's law, she would be able to initially estimate whether the two RAD teams assigned to the project represented sufficient resources to complete the work within that time frame:

$$Average\ WIP = average\ lead\ time \times (number\ of\ stories\ /\ duration)$$
$$Average\ WIP = 0.9 \times (675\ /\ 26) = 23.36$$

As RAD's work policies resulted in an average WIP of 2 items per team member, this value indicates the assigned teams would have to consist of approximately 12 members (6 on each team) for the project release to be completed within the requested time frame. This matched the teams' actual make-up.

---

11. Mammoth Bank is a fictional entity created to provide a meaningful context for a number of actual case study outcomes. Client confidentiality commitments preclude more transparent disclosure.

12. Again, this particular approach relies on the use of many "averages." We underscore that this application simply represents a gateway to learning more advanced (and reliable) approaches.

What if Julie had been informed the project must be completed in 18 weeks? She could use the same formula to estimate the number of additional members required to meet the new deadline:

Average WIP = 0.9 × (675 / 18) = 33.75 [round up to 34]

34 / 2 WIP per resource = 17 resources [approximately 9 people per team]

This result *may* signal another team is needed, because the system data from which this forecast was derived involved two 6-person teams; adding team members to these existing systems would not necessarily produce the same results as adding a third 6-person team.

Now let's use this same approach to forecast the project scope from a different perspective. What if Julie had only two teams to work on the release? This approach would better enable her to set realistic expectations for a delivery date:

Duration = number of stories × (average lead time / average WIP)

Duration = 675 × [0.9 / (12 resources × 2 items each)] = 25.3 weeks

If Julie could finagle an extra team, forecasting the impact on the delivery date can be similarly approached:

Duration = 675 × [0.9 / (18 resources × 2 items each)] = 16.9 weeks

Wait a Minute: Accounting for Inherent Uncertainty

We began this chapter by talking about uncertainty and risk. Fortunately for Mammoth Bank, Julie was paying close attention to team performance across releases. She recognized that work delivery rates across releases and projects were not uniform, but rather tended to follow a fairly predictable Z-curve (Figure 6.16).[13] With this type of curve, work flows more slowly during the early stage of new projects as understandings are refined, and it also flows more slowly toward the end of project cycles because of testing overhead, bug fixes, and regression effects. For these reasons, Julie understands that Little's law can be applied with high confidence to only the middle portion of most projects (approximately 60% of total project duration).

Moreover, Julie noticed that other things influence overall project duration—things like dark matter, the expansion of work as we learn more about the true requirements, and failure demand customer demand that might have been avoided by delivering higher quality earlier. Addressing technical debt is a prime example of failure demand.

---

13. The concepts outlined here were recognized by David J. Anderson in *Agile Management for Software Engineering: Applying the Theory of Constraints for Business Results* (2003).

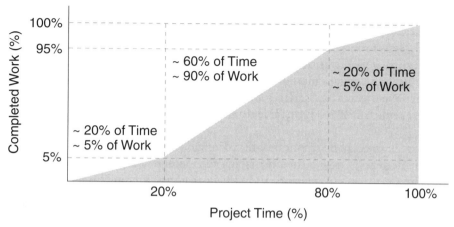

FIGURE 6.16   Typical project Z-curve.

So how can Julie extend the high confidence gleaned from an application of Little's law to both these uncertainties as well as the remaining 40% of the release cycle?

Julie applied an approach based on a model created by Dimitar Bakardzhiev. This model calculates an appropriate "project buffer" based on three calibrated estimates.[14] Beyond assisting with forecasting, the project buffer can be actively monitored and managed to proactively address issues before they become problematic. The formula for calculating the project buffer as follows:

$$Project\ Buffer = Z\text{-}curve\ coefficient \times$$
$$[(1 + average\ failure\ demand + average\ dark\ matter)$$
$$\times (number\ of\ stories\ /\ average\ throughput)]$$

Most of the variables utilized in this model remain best estimates based on an historical observation of team performance. Breaking them down and applying them in a correlated fashion, however, brings more calibration to the process:

- *Z-curve coefficient*: Expressed as a percentage. This factor accounts for uncertainty associated with the slower first and third legs of the Z-curve. The teams' historical performance suggests applying values between 25% and 50%. Every system will be different.

---

14. Dimitar's approach uses a project buffer for planning and forecasting purposes only, and is not something he has visualized on a Kanban board or other mechanism. In other contexts, project buffer consumption has been visualized through the use of "fever charts." (See, for example, the approach described by Steve Tendon in *Tame the Flow.*)

- *Average failure demand*: Expressed as a percentage. This factor accounts for the typical rate of failures the system experiences across development efforts (defects, rework, and technical debt, among others).
- *Average dark matter*: Expressed as a percentage. This factor accounts for the typical rate of dark matter (work expansion on knowledge discovery) the system experiences across development efforts. This value can range from 20% to as much as 100% for novice teams.

The rates associated with both failure demand and dark matter vary based on a variety of factors, including the underlying technologies, the amount of innovation involved in the work, team maturity, and the underlying architecture. Identifying the core variables that influence these ranges is part of the art of applying probabilistic forecasting models, and something a good manager or analyst will perfect over time.

Next-Level Learning:

Evolving to More
Advanced Practices

From a learning standpoint, it's beneficial for new practitioners to begin working with Little's law by capturing new data, calculating averages from that data, and applying the formulas as outlined in this chapter. Once individuals gain basic understanding in this manner, they should move toward more probabilistic forecasting methods. One of the best ways to ease into this exploration is by using a probabilistic "guesstimate" of the lead time value as a substitute for the average value calculation (Figure 6.17).

How do you create a probabilistic "guesstimate"? By referencing a lead time histogram of data from your system (metrics and histograms are addressed in more detail in Chapter 7). The chart in Figure 6.17 represents the distribution of lead times for user stories in a Scrumban system, where the *y*-axis represents the number of user stories completed and the *x*-axis reflects the number of days required to complete those stories. Although most user stories required between 2 and 7 days to complete, there are a significant number of outliers, including many user stories that took 30 days or longer.

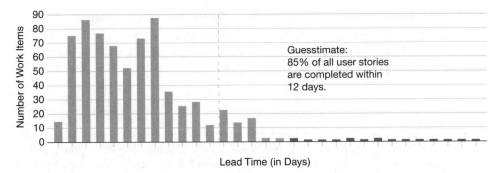

FIGURE 6.17   Guesstimating lead time based on a distribution of historical values can be a first step toward more probabilistic forecasting.

Outliers skew average values to a considerable extent. An average value calculation of lead time from the data reflected in this chart might equal 18 days. Visualizing the actual distribution helps us recognize that 85% of all stories are completed within 12 days. The latter is a better number use for forecasting, especially given that we're accounting for many of the factors creating our "outliers" in our Z-curve accounting.

The Project Buffer as a Management Tool

This approach for calculating a buffer that accounts for the variability introduced by dark matter, failure demand, and the first and third legs of the Z-curve is a good start. Unfortunately, short of tracking our forecasts against reality, we can't really measure the effectiveness of our risk mitigation measures. In other words, we have no way of evaluating the accuracy of our allowances for dark matter or failure demand.

One way to improve future forecasting is by creating a mechanism for gathering baseline data for these risk factors into the board. You can do this by incorporating "optional" work item cards into your project/release backlog that represent the primary factors covered by the buffer:

- Dark matter
- Failure demand

Dark matter and failure demand represent the kind of statistical (natural variances) and systemic (measurable) uncertainties discussed at the beginning of this chapter.

These cards are pulled into the work queue only if these work expansions are realized. The actual time required to complete this additional work is measured, therefore, and provides hard data for future forecasts. A similar approach can be taken when measuring scope creep against the release backlog. Note that this process just entails calling out and measuring identifiable components of user stories during the course of a sprint; it does not mean accepting new work into a sprint.[15]

Our Forecast

Applying the formula for project buffer calculation to the mobile app project, Julie calculated the following buffer for the original two team allocation:

Project buffer = 40% [(1 + 27% + 80%) × (675 / 26)] = 11.2 weeks [12 weeks]

---

15. We used a similar technique to create iteration-specific story point buffers in a Scrum context where relative estimation was working well. Read more at http://codegenesys.com/scrumban/scope-buffer.

Julie elected to apply a *Z*-curve coefficient that is on the lower range of typical experience. She made this choice because the two teams initially assigned to the release were two of RAD's best teams. These considerations also drove her choices related to failure demand and dark matter. Even so, the project buffer is almost as large as her time calculation for the middle of the *Z*-curve.

When you take time to reflect on the realities of software development, this outcome makes sense. Moreover, this reality reflects what Mammoth Bank implicitly understood: All of the RAD teams would need to be assigned to this project if work had to be completed within 26 weeks. Perhaps even that plan was an aggressive schedule. This example is intended to show how even a simplistic approach to applying Little's law can quantify this understanding far more precisely.

Adaptive Buffer Management

As work is executed, it's possible to monitor and manage the project buffer to identify and proactively address potential problems more quickly than traditional project management techniques allow. If an item takes longer to complete than anticipated, for example, it consumes at least part of the project buffer. As items are delivered, we can compare the consumption rate of the buffer against the rate of progress on the project as a whole. These are the two essential measurements of project performance from a buffer management perspective.

As long as some predetermined proportion of our buffer remains, it is reasonable to assume project progress is sound. If project work consumes more than a certain amount of the project buffer, however, that event should be considered a warning signal. If your buffer consumption is so high that you will consume the entire buffer before completing the project, you know you need to take corrective action.

Let's approach this issue from the context of the Mammoth Bank. Assume 14 weeks have passed since the project's first sprint was scheduled (so we're at the end of Sprint 7), 85 user stories have been delivered, and the two RAD teams working on the project were staffed as originally forecast (12 team members).

Percentage of project complete = 85 stories delivered / 675 backlog = 12.6%

Projected lead time = (average lead time / average WIP)
× (number of stories) (0.9 / 24 × 85 = 3.2 weeks

Percentage of buffer consumed = (actual lead time − projected lead time)
/ buffer (14 weeks − 3.2 weeks) / 12 weeks = 90%

With slightly less than 13% of the project complete, 90% of the buffer has been consumed. Is that a comfortable ratio given where the project likely resides along the *Z*-curve?

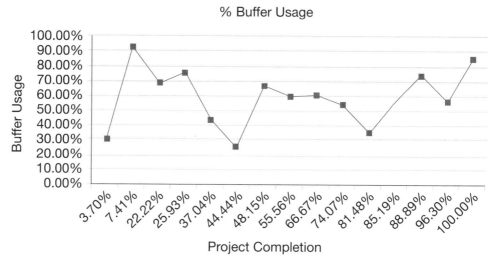

FIGURE 6.18   Visualizing buffer usage.

You should expect to see fluctuations in your project buffer consumption, with higher percentages of the buffer consumed during the beginning and end stages of your project. A healthy visualization might look like the chart depicted in Figure 6.18.

This scientifically based approach represents a significant shift in the way organizations and their Scrum teams can conduct release planning and manage ongoing work. Capabilities like this are what make Scrumban such a powerful tool for practicing Scrum more effectively.

A More Disciplined Approach to Sprint Planning

Similar techniques to those applied in release planning can be employed at the sprint planning level, where the focus shifts to selecting user stories upon which to work.

For teams that still find benefit in using story point estimation techniques, Little's law provides a check on the correlation between velocity and actual throughput. More significantly, however, teams that actively manage risk through cost of delay and class of service mechanisms are able to engage in more granular forecasting processes.

Scrumban Stories: Mammoth Bank

Scrum teams can evolve their practices in many ways toward more robust sprint planning. The path followed by the Scrum teams at Mammoth Bank represents one such journey. Like many other teams, Mammoth's teams had been using story points and team estimation techniques for sprint planning. Shortly

after adopting Scrumban and evaluating new metrics (such as lead time) from
the company's virtual kanban systems, data showed there was little correlation
between the estimates and actual performance.

One team elected to begin using, visualizing, and measuring performance
around general categories of risk profiles. These distinct evolutions occurred
over the course of several months, and ultimately led to adoption of a technique similar to that described in this section.

Read the full story of Mammoth Bank in the Appendix.

Returning to our Mammoth Bank example, the RAD teams had been visualizing work items based on rudimentary risk profiles—a simple grading scheme (low/
medium/high) associated with technology/skills-based risks according to the following factors:

- Complexity of work to be undertaken
- Past experience of team in completing similar work
- Amount of effort involved

Regardless of the specific mechanisms used to visualize these risk assessments,
Scrumban enabled the teams to capture average lead times across each distinct
risk type (most virtual tools have reporting capabilities that automatically generate
this information). Let's assume the most recent data reflected average lead times as
follows:

- High-risk items = 1.6 weeks
- Medium-risk items = 1.0 weeks
- Low-risk items = 0.4 week
- All types = 0.9 week

Now imagine you're participating in the planning session for the teams' next
sprint. The product owner has prioritized the top 70 stories remaining in the release
backlog as follows (for ease of illustration, we assume the remaining work items are
independent stories and don't rely on other work being completed):

- High risk: 20 stories
- Medium risk: 36 stories
- Low risk: 14 stories

At the release/project planning level, we're typically limited to forecasting based
on a general description of features. Consequently, while some risk assessments can

be applied at the release/project level, in most instances those forecasts will be based on data related to all risk profiles and classes of service.

At the sprint planning level, we're working with more precise evaluations of the underlying work. Consequently, we can make more informed decisions about which stories to commit to our sprint backlog.

From Little's law, we know:

$$Duration = (number\ of\ stories) \times (average\ lead\ time\ /\ average\ WIP)$$

$$Number\ of\ stories = duration \times (average\ WIP\ /\ average\ lead\ time)$$

The combined lead time across all risk types allows us to ascertain a general number of user stories to incorporate in a sprint backlog:

$$Number\ of\ stories = 2\ weeks \times (12\ resources \times 2\ stories\ each\ /\ 0.9\ week)$$
$$= 53.33\ user\ stories$$

Let's consider how the total number of user stories available for a given sprint might vary based on the risk profiles:

$$All\ high\text{-}risk\ stories = 2\ weeks\ (12 \times 2\ /\ 1.6\ weeks) = 30\ stories$$
$$All\ medium\text{-}risk\ stories = 2\ weeks\ (12 \times 2\ /\ 1\ week) = 48\ stories$$
$$All\ low\text{-}risk\ stories = 2\ weeks\ (12 \times 2\ /\ 0.4\ week) = 120\ stories$$

These estimations aren't entirely realistic, because the historical data doesn't likely represent a scenario where every team member worked on all risk types (or the number of work items sharing the same risk type may not have remained consistent over time). Nonetheless, it's a starting point for recognizing and accounting for the impact of risk on overall variability.

Next-Level Learning:

Evolving to More Advanced Practices

If it makes sense for your context, you could create subteams and visualize them on your board, acquiring actual performance data for teams assigned to work within specific swim lanes. In such a scenario, applying horizontal WIP (by lane or class of service) may make sense. Historical data derived from this type of setup can provide a more accurate reflection of real capacity, which teams can then use as a guide in their backlog selection.

In any event, for most sprints, the combination of risk profile and lead time data provides additional information we can use to improve our backlog selection. Point estimates alone rarely incorporate these additional dimensions in a useful fashion.

This is just one example of how Scrumban can provide added insight for story selection. As previously mentioned in other contexts, the level of sophistication that a team or organization ultimately elects to apply should be driven by its unique needs.

Feedback Loops

As with most Lean and Agile frameworks, feedback loops play a critical role in Scrumban. Let's explore some of the ways Scrumban seeks to expand existing functions.

Feedback Mechanisms: Scrum versus Kanban versus Scrumban

As a process framework, Scrum provides a number of feedback mechanisms. Daily stand-ups, for example, represent a limited feedback loop that focuses on the rate at which work is progressing. Sprint reviews offer an opportunity to review whether the team is producing the right product. Retrospectives address general process improvements. These ceremonies (and their timing) don't have to change under Scrumban, but the framework opens up a variety of alternatives that require less overhead, such as adopting specific continuous improvement katas on a less frequent basis.

As of this writing, the Kanban Method recognizes seven explicit feedback mechanisms that serve to drive continuous improvement:

- The daily stand-up
- The service delivery review (also referred to as the systems capability review, and recommended as a weekly cadence)
- The operations review (recommended as a monthly cadence)
- The risk review (recommended as a monthly cadence)
- The strategy review (recommended as a quarterly cadence)
- The replenishment/commitment meeting
- Release/delivery planning

In a Scrumban framework, we seek to take advantage of existing ceremonies and introduce additional mechanisms only as necessary. For example, existing sprint and release planning mechanisms serve the same essential purpose of the Kanban Method's replenishment and delivery planning feedback loops. The additional feedback mechanisms we seek to ensure are in place are summarized in Table 6.5.

Potential Hazards of Feedback Loops

Regardless of the context in which you view feedback loops, Scrumban practices help you manage a number of potential traps associated with them more effectively.

TABLE 6.5   Scrumban Feedback Mechanisms

Feedback Loop	Frequency	Essential Characteristics
Team stand-up	Daily	A walk-through of the kanban board from right to left to evaluate the flow of work. Focus on blockers, defects, and higher classes of service (a delivery of value emphasis). Discuss priorities and team member assignments. Facilitate discussions that explore opportunities to improve flow.
Service delivery	Weekly	A focused discussion between a more senior manager and the individual responsible for system operation (the Scrum master, in most instances). Review fitness criteria metrics and discuss shortfalls against customer expectations. Discuss options for risk mitigation and system design changes.
Operations review	Monthly	A systems of systems perspective with multiple teams represented. Monthly cadence ensures enough time and data to show trends, but not too much time elapsing so that memories of significant events fade. Some financial measures should be reviewed here to reinforce alignment between present work and financial outcomes.
Strategy review	Quarterly	Attended by senior executives and members from strategic planning, sales, marketing, portfolio management, risk management, service delivery, and customer care. Assess current markets, strategic position, go-to-market strategies, KPIs, capabilities, and more.

Role Binding

Role binding occurs when team members limit their contributions based on perceptions of their job role (e.g., "I'm a QA engineer, so I just have to concern myself with testing"). Continuous improvement and value delivery should be owned by the whole team, not distributed in layers based on what how team members contribute.

Although we desire collective ownership of the outcome, we can't ignore the innate human desire to recognize individual contributions. Scrumban's visualization of work by value stream (contrasted with the "To Do," "Doing," and "Done" columns on a typical Scrum board) acknowledges this psychological need by conveying individual contributions; completed work is reflected by actual movement of the card through the value stream.

At the same time, Scrumban's mechanics provide additional means of reinforcing collective ownership and responsibility. It does so by visually emphasizing flow (and the speed of flow). Also, the conversations in daily stand-ups move away from topics of status and toward a greater collective focus on delivery of work.

For example, a typical Scrum stand-up format calls for team members to report on what they accomplished the previous day, what they're committing to accomplish for the current day, and any impediments to completing the work. This emphasis on individual reporting does not encourage a mindset of looking to contribute beyond the person's current role. While the team can acquire a sense of flow from these meetings, the actual state of flow is not as apparent as when visual cues are available.

Implementing Scrumban allows teams to change the "flavor" of their stand-ups. Because the board is more granular, it shows everyone what individuals have completed and what they're planning to work on. It makes slow or blocked flow painfully obvious, and encourages the team to spend its time discussing why work isn't being delivered.

Can role binding be broken down through traditional Scrum? Absolutely. Scrumban certainly provides additional mechanisms that facilitate a faster outcome.

Tampering

Tampering relates to the tendency to adjust processes unnecessarily, often resulting in real problems and inefficiencies. In the context of a two-week retrospective, it can be easy to fall into the trap of trying to identify and eliminate the cause of every performance variation. We tend to see every variation as being due to a special cause rather than simply being normal variability. Scrumban's bias toward disciplined katas and empirical decision making helps teams and organizations develop a natural resistance to such behavior.

For example, Scrumban frameworks encourage us to recognize characteristics that help to understand variation more completely. Though assigning more points to a story containing high degrees of risk may capture some of the natural variation, it's an imprecise mechanic at best. With Scrumban, we can actually segregate our measurement of different risk profiles and work types to develop a greater understanding of their natural variation, thereby making it easier to recognize when variation is truly extreme and worthy of further investigation.

Applying the Wrong Solution

In a similar vein as tampering, application of the wrong solution can occur when we fail to identify the root cause of a problem, and treat symptoms rather than origins. This results in both unnecessary churn and a delayed resolution.

Though we don't need Scrumban to adopt disciplined approaches to problem solving, the framework's additional values of empiricism, humility, and constructive interaction certainly help foster a greater recognition of the need for one. Similarly, while both Scrum and Scrumban emphasize an "inspect and adapt" approach (or Deming's "plan, do, check, act" cycle), Scrumban enables us to easily integrate specific models and practices into our management framework. For example, the visual characteristics shared by the Scrumban and A3 problem-solving methods help teams execute a disciplined path toward resolving root causes.

Deferring to Management

A distant cousin of role binding, deferring problems to management occurs when team members are inclined to abdicate responsibility for improvement efforts to management rather than assuming ownership of the process and service to the customer. Scrumban helps teams see that they can influence and control some things independently; it shows them that the team doesn't need managerial action or authority to improve their way of working.

As an example, consider incoming requests. Many teams have to contend with a variety of ad hoc requests outside of their "standard" work. These include requests to estimate the scope of a proposed project or respond to a customer emergency. Scrum doesn't provide clear mechanics for managing such nonstandard work. By comparison, Scrumban emphasizes the importance of capturing, defining, visualizing, and measuring all work. The objective data gained from the framework enables teams to negotiate changes that might be impossible to achieve without managerial intervention.

At the end of the day, all of Scrumban's principles and practices provide teams with an enhanced framework that enables them to concentrate their ongoing improvement efforts in a more effective fashion. Note that I don't claim Scrum teams, or teams working under any framework, need these additional capabilities to achieve the same outcomes; rather, I'm simply highlighting their availability.

Design Thinking

Next-Level Learning:

Evolving to More Advanced Practices

As noted earlier, A3 Thinking's disciplined approach to problem solving supports Kanban's agenda of sustained improvement by providing a common model of problem solving throughout an organization. As individuals, teams, and organizations grow in their mastery of core principles and practices, design thinking represents another model Scrumban can easily integrate within its management framework.

Whereas A3 Thinking represents an analytical approach to solving a specific problem, design thinking comprises a formal method for creatively resolving problems with the intention of producing an improved future result. It is a form of solution-based thinking that starts with a future goal instead focusing on a specific problem, emphasizing human-centered design processes and methods to add a new perspective on the situation.

Consider Kanban's core principles of visualizing work and explicitly defining policies. These practices can become very involved, and they have the potential to make the very tools we're using so complex that they become meaningless. Design thinking methods and processes can help ensure our efforts don't become self-defeating.

"Design methods" and "design process" are terms that are often used interchangeably, but there is a significant difference between the two. Design methods are the techniques, rules, or ways of doing things employed by a design discipline. Some of the methods of design thinking include creating profiles, creating prototypes, and mind-mapping.

The design process, in contrast, is the way the methods come together through a series of actions, events, or steps. There is no solitary process that can define design thinking. Indeed, there are as many different design processes as there are designers multiplied by design problems. A fairly typical design thinking process might have these stages:

1. Define
2. Research
3. Ideate
4. Prototype
5. Choose
6. Implement
7. Learn

Although these stages bear resemblance to the plan–do–check–act cycle of A3 problem solving, they don't have to proceed in a linear fashion in design thinking. In fact, these stages are often undertaken simultaneously and repeated as necessary. Within these seven steps, however, problems can be framed, the right questions asked, ideas created, and the best answers chosen.

Visual analogies in design thinking provide a two-way mapping that iterates between the source and the target. Image manipulations in the reasoning process provide feedback regarding both, enabling us to more easily visualize relationships associated with ideas or concepts, especially when different levels of expertise are evident among the people working on the issue. Design thinking techniques are particularly effective in areas such as visualizing problems on A3 worksheets, designing boards, designing work cards, determining how to best visualize the results of our metrics, and designing tool interfaces.

To this end, it's important to remember that effective visualization practices follow the Five U's:

- Uncluttered
- Up-to-date
- Universal
- Uniform
- Useful

A quick comment on uniformity: While I encourage teams to visualize relationships in ways that work best for them, from a scaling perspective it's helpful to enforce some degree of uniformity across visualizations. This helps minimize miscommunication based on differences that may not be immediately recognized by others familiar with other approaches. It also helps ease the transition of members between systems.

Ticket Design

Just as board designs can take on different shapes and forms, so should the tickets representing work items. Again, design thinking principles come into play here, with a focus on incorporating the most relevant information for your environment (Figure 6.19).

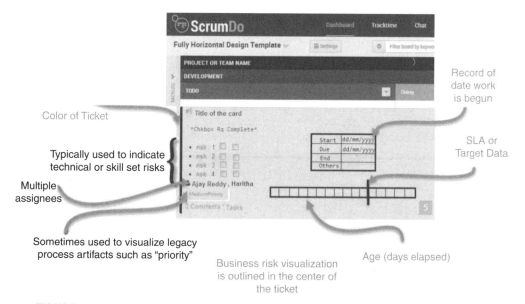

FIGURE 6.19   Enough information to make a good pull decision.

Source: ScrumDo.com.

Board Design

Teams can visualize their work in many different ways. The best visualization is the one that makes the most sense for you and your teams at any given point in time. As each team's understanding improves, team members will naturally improve their visualizations. Helping teams create effective visualizations is another area where seasoned practitioners and coaches can add value to Kanban adoptions. Figure 6.20, Figure 6.21, and Figure 6.22 are examples of board designs from a variety of contexts. Additional samples are included in the Appendix.

Not all work has the same value as it moves through workflow systems. Moreover, varying levels of time pressure may be exerted on different items at different points in time. Planning and coordinating all the possible impacts would be very difficult. Establishing classes of service for different work profiles is a simple and transparent approach that enables teams to self-organize around pending work in a way that best meets the needs of the business.

Using rows to visualize different classes of service is particularly useful when you are looking to reserve some specific resource or other capacity to the class of service. It's also easier to establish specific WIP limit policies (for example, allowing for a work item to exceed the column WIP limit could reflect that there is a maximum of a particular class of service, or require a minimum of a class of service).

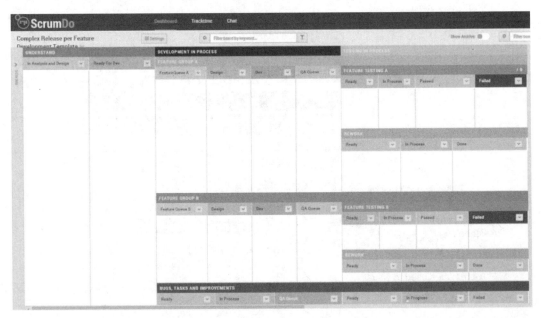

FIGURE 6.20   Representation of how swim lanes are delineated for features (capacity allocated horizontally by lane).

Source: ScrumDo.com.

FIGURE 6.21   Representation of swim lanes delineating work types (capacity allocated horizontally by lane).

Source: ScrumDo.com.

FIGURE 6.22   Representation of card color signifying class of service (capacity allocated by color across the board).

Source: ScrumDo.com.

On a board that uses card color to distinguish classes of service, teams might elect to include a policy or other indication of WIP limits for each card type on the board. For example:

Gold cards = 10 (50% capacity)

Orange cards = 4 (20% capacity)

Blue cards = 6 (30% capacity)

Black cards = 1 (5% capacity)

Teams can also elect to establish other policies around classes of service (Figure 6.23). Consider, for example, this example policy around "urgent" work types:

Urgent work requests will be immediately pulled by a qualified resource, with all other work put on hold to expedite the request.

Teams can elect to establish pull and/or exit criteria for vertical columns (value stages) in their work process. Explicit policies help to ensure work quality is maintained throughout the development process, even when teams think they're already implicitly following those policies (see, for example, the Siemens Health Systems case study).

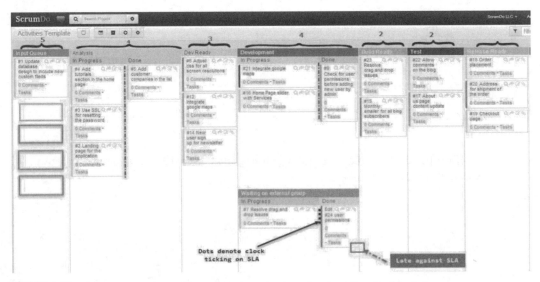

FIGURE 6.23   Representation of how local cycle time is visualized with dots.

Source: ScrumDo.com.

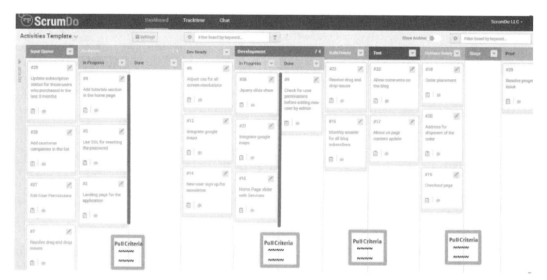

FIGURE 6.24 Representation of how caption pull criteria policies encourage a focus on quality and progress (with imperfect information).

Source: ScrumDo.com.

In the board in Figure 6.24, pull criteria for the "Test" column could include the requirement that completed development work demonstrate that functional acceptance criteria have been met.

Tying It All Together

This chapter began with an exploration of uncertainty and risk. At the end of the day, the work processes we create all represent an effort to exert control over uncertainty.

There's no way around it. The principles and practices explored in this chapter are very dense. If you're a new practitioner (a Shu level student), don't get lost in the forest. Select a single concrete practice with which to begin working. Once you've mastered this technique, then return to this chapter and begin anew.

Unfortunately, there's no simple way to provide a holistic sense of how all the capabilities of a Scrumban framework can interact without running the risk of having new practitioners feel like they're drinking water from a fire hose. Rest assured, the interaction of all these components will become more understandable as your familiarity with the framework grows through actual practice.

Chapter 7

MEASUREMENTS: GAINING INSIGHTS AND TRACKING PROGRESS

IN THIS CHAPTER

- Why Measuring Is Important
- Measuring What Matters
- Common and Advanced Scrumban Metrics

Our problem is not that we aim too high and miss, but that we aim too low and hit.

—Aristotle

The plan–do–check–act cycle is central to both Scrum and Scrumban, and being able to measure the right things is central to the cycle. This chapter is dedicated to laying the foundation as to why metrics are necessary, how different measurements help us understand different things, and which measurements the Scrumban frameworks can make available.

Why Measure?

Measurements are important for a number of reasons. One of the most important is to ensure we have an effective way to evaluate past outcomes so that we can make better decisions in the present. After all, not all decisions result in meaningful outcomes, so finding ways to measure them provides insight into the effectiveness of our efforts. Additional reasons include the following:

- Measuring against common benchmarks as an indicator of relative health (healthy/warning/danger)
- Measuring things to help diagnose a problem or condition
- Measuring performance data upon which to base forecasts of future results
- Using metrics as a lever to influence the behavior of individuals

Two common organizational pitfalls of metrics revolve around measuring the wrong things and using measurement systems that aren't clearly connected to our real goals. For example, the real goal for most business organizations is to make money. However, indirect measurements of related functions such as customer satisfaction are often used in this goal's place. To be sure, customer satisfaction is a necessary condition for making money. It is not, however, a sufficient condition in and of itself for making money.

Proper measurements help us understand the health of our undertakings and give us relevant data to make intelligent choices. Larry Maccherone, formerly Rally Software's Agile guru, summed up the relevancy of proper metrics as follows:

Better Measurements → Better Insight → Better Decisions → Better Outcomes

At the end of the day, we want to identify metrics that clearly represent our ultimate objectives, and we want to use them to intelligently guide our decisions.[1]

A Few Words about Measuring the Wrong Things

> **Especially For:**
>
> Managers & Executives

Executives and managers tend to hyper-focus on system outputs. A prime example is their propensity to monitor monthly or quarterly key performance indicators (KPIs) without any real understanding of the system inputs driving those outcomes. Measuring outputs in isolation doesn't tell us anything about the dynamic factors that produce those outcomes. If we want to pursue different outcomes, this data provides little insight into what we should do differently.

Another common example of leaders failing to pay attention to system inputs is the pointless target setting used as a misguided strategy to influence systems toward desired outcomes. Unfortunately, over time such programs tend to be counterproductive and create dysfunctional behaviors, such as "manipulating the numbers," that then become "hidden" systemic influences. Instead of creating these programs, leaders should look for ways to empower the people working within their systems to figure out better approaches that will produce better results for the organization.

Managing by numbers alone—especially measuring performance against a target—usually leads to higher costs, worse service, and lower morale. To avoid these unwanted outcomes, leaders need to determine how the numbers they use add value to decision making, and then communicate these relationships to employees. The journey toward high performance thus begins with learning how to distinguish between traditional approaches and more effective ones. Table 7.1 provides examples.

---

1. Eric Ries, pioneer of the Lean startup movement, suggests all good metrics are actionable, accessible, and auditable [*The Lean Startup* (Penguin Books, 2009)].

TABLE 7.1   Adopting a Lean–Agile Mindset around Measurements

Traditional	More Effective
A top-down perspective	An outside-in perspective
Measure targets and standards related to budgets and schedule	Measure value, process, and flow related to purpose
Decision making is separate from work	Decision making is part of the work process

Here's a short list of common pitfalls managers should look out for:[2]

- Beware of proxy measurements—numbers that may correlate to a desired result but are not directly representative of it. For example, story points are proxy measurements for both team throughput and time to market. Some proxies *may* be better than the absence of measurements in some instances, but it's important that the people in your systems understand them for what they are.
- View measurements derived from an aggregation of data across systems with some degree of skepticism. For example, team velocities theoretically measure the same things, but the measurement standards are unique to each team.
- Don't neglect to consider the cost of measurement. You don't need exact measures to make better decisions. Barring some manner of simplification, the amount of work needed to solve a set of equations increases with the square of the number of the equations (Gerald Weinberg, *Quality Software Management*).
- Be wary of all temptations to resist gathering measurements. Probe further when you hear objections because:
  - Your problem is not as unique as you think.
  - You have more data than you think.
  - You need less data than you think.
  - An adequate amount of new data is more accessible than you think.

Effectiveness is ultimately dictated by how well management can integrate purpose, measures, and methods. Scrumban provides an ideal foundation to make this happen, but the individuals throughout the system are ultimately responsible for seeing it through its execution.

---

2. Douglas Hubbard. *How to Measure Anything* (Wiley & Sons, 2007).

Hallmarks of Good Metrics

Practically speaking, good metrics possess most, if not all, of the following characteristics:

- Objectively comparative (able to be compared to other time periods and/or groups)
- Easily understandable (changes in data can't become a change in process or culture unless people at all levels can internalize and discuss the information)
- Preferably quantitative (because quantitative data is usually more scientific and easier to understand—but qualitative data has its uses, and often helps to answer "why" questions)
- Either reporting (inform us about what's happening) or speculative (help us discover new insights)
- Either leading (trends or predictors of future outcomes) or lagging (illuminate actual conditions and outcomes)

We should "mix and match" our metrics to achieve the following aims:

- Verify what we know we know (perceived truths should always be checked against data to confirm their veracity)
- Answer questions to which we know we don't currently have an answer (discoverable knowledge—information we can typically glean from reporting metrics)
- Expose things we don't know that we know (all too often we ignore available data that can better inform our intuitions)
- Discover things we don't know we don't know (this is the area where we can uncover unfair advantages and epiphanies)

How to Measure

PMO/Program Managers/ Project Managers:

Although all team members can certainly benefit from understanding metrics more completely, how to measure and what to measure represent topics that are most relevant to your roles.

Scrumban systems support organizational objectives when they're operating as designed and producing predictable outcomes. These conditions usually mean there's a focus on flow and continuous improvement within the system. Similarly, Scrumban systems are reliably predictable when they perform well against their commitments (such as service level agreements). The Scrumban framework provides a variety of metrics we can use to monitor these outcomes and gauge our overall level of performance.

For every performance indicator we select, it's important to identify both overall trends and the spread of distribution. The latter is particularly meaningful, as it reflects the degree of variability in the results (whether they are highly concentrated or span a wide range).

Practice Tip

If your system is effectively engaged in continuous improvement, the mean of the distribution of your measurements should improve over time (either increase or decrease, depending on your indicator). For example, if your system is improving its predictability, the spread of most distributions should decrease over time.

Selecting the right measurements is one aspect of high performance; another is visualizing those measurements in meaningful way. Scrumban employs a variety of tools to better visualize our measurements, and one of the first tools you need to master is the histogram.

A histogram is a vertical bar chart that reflects how a set of data is distributed. These graphics make it particularly easy to visualize where the majority of values lie on a measurement scale. Figure 7.1 shows an example of a histogram.

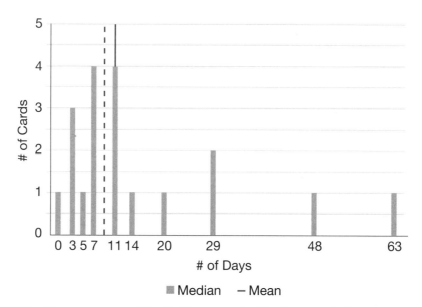

FIGURE 7.1   Histograms graphically illustrate the distribution of data across a continuum of measurement.

Source: Scrumdo.com.

A histogram that is widely employed in Kanban/Scrumban is the lead time histogram. This chart displays the distribution of how long it takes for work to be completed once it enters the development system. Wider distributions of data typically signal greater variability and lower predictability. More tightly concentrated distributions, by comparison, typically reflect higher-performing systems. They also indicate the specific expectations we should establish in negotiating probabilistic-based service level agreements with our customers.

Histograms can also be used to diagnose potential issues, as the "shape" (Figure 7.2) associated with specific distribution patterns can signal common conditions. For example, histograms with multiple peaks are often observed with mixed data sources. In a kanban system, this may signal an opportunity to recognize different work types or create separate classes of service leading to better management of work flow. Other visualizations illustrate the probability density of our distributions, raising the confidence level in our understandings even further.

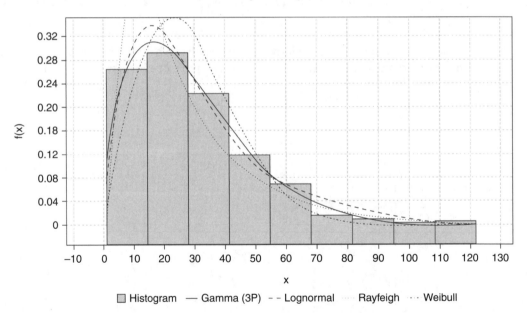

FIGURE 7.2 The "shape" of lead time distributions can signal underlying conditions that warrant attention.

Source: Wikipedia (http://en.wikipedia.org/wiki/Rayleigh_distribution).

Constructing Histograms

There are many different ways to organize data and build histograms. Most Kanban management tools create them automatically across common data points. When you are first beginning to work with different sets of data collection, however, you can gain a better appreciation of the data that histograms visualize (and recognize key patterns more adeptly) by first creating them manually.

You can safely organize and build histograms by following some basic rules. I recommend starting with a nine-step approach:[3]

1. Count the data points in your set.
2. Summarize your data points on a tally sheet.
3. Compute the range of your data (largest – smallest).
4. Determine the number of intervals you'll use to visualize the distribution spread.
5. Compute your interval "width."
6. Determine your interval "starting points."
7. Count data points within each defined interval.
8. Plot the data.
9. Add your title and legends to the chart.

Scrumban Measurements

In Chapter 6, we dealt extensively with how Scrumban can substantially enhance how we undertake release and sprint planning in a Scrum context. The metrics we relied upon to drive that process were basic measurements that can be derived from "kanbanized" systems. This chapter provides more specific information relating to each of these measurements.[4]

Naturally, Scrumban teams retain the ability to use all of the traditional metrics and reporting mechanisms employed under Scrum. However, as the purpose of this book is to detail what Scrumban *adds* to the Scrum context, a full review of traditional Scrum-based metrics is outside its scope.

Productivity Metrics

This section describes Scrumban metrics that teams and organizations can use to monitor overall performance.

---

3. See http://tiny.cc/histgram for a great overview.
4. A good portion of this material is derived from a presentation prepared for the 2013 Lean Kanban Netherlands Conference by Ajay Reddy and Dimitar Bakardzhiev.

Cumulative Flow Diagram

The cumulative flow diagram (CFD) is the heart and soul of basic kanban systems metrics. Though technically not a measurement in and of itself, the CFD reflects the quantity of work in progress (WIP) at each value stage of a defined system. When the system is operating correctly, the bands of the diagram will be smooth and their height stable (Figure 7.3). Variations signal potentially troublesome areas requiring attention.

Conceptually, CFDs represent a collection of snapshots of your visual board over time. Let's start with an example of a simple Scrum task board (Figure 7.4). The CFD captures the number of work items in progress within each column. It combines these slices of information over time to produce the chart shown in Figure 7.4.

This single visualization provides a plethora of information, providing insight into burn-up, cycle time, WIP, and bottlenecks. For example, vertical slices from the chart reflect the amount of WIP at any given time; horizontal slices reflect average cycle time. The wide bands shown in Figure 7.5 suggest too much WIP throughout

Cumulative Flow Diagram

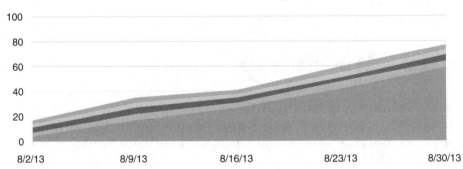

FIGURE 7.3   An example of a CFD from a high-performing system. Narrow bands reflect a good balance of demand and capacity across the system over time.

TO DO	IN PROGRESS	DONE
El ad	In bar In bar Mush on In bar Mush on El ad Mush on El ad	

FIGURE 7.4   A snapshot in time of a typical Scrum task board.

the measurement stream—either this team is having difficulty finishing work within those stages or the following stage doesn't have the capacity to take it on.

Uneven slopes (Figure 7.6) can indicate delays in delivering or handing off work, obtaining approvals, receiving dependent work, and similar events. In a kanban system, we strive for laminar flow (smooth delivery over time)—the kind of flow reflected in the CFD reproduced in Figure 7.3.

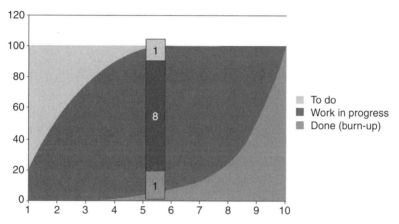

FIGURE 7.5 This CFD reflects a large amount of work in progress that grew in volume during the majority of the measured time frame.

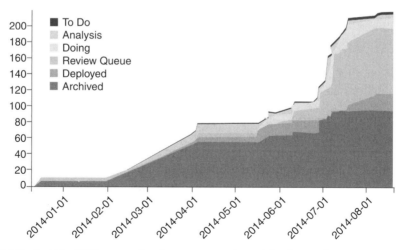

FIGURE 7.6 In this CFD example, the amount of work in the review queue grows significantly toward the end of the time frame (suggesting a major bottleneck).

Source: Scrumdo.com.

Two notable Scrumban variations of the CFD relate to sprints and releases. A sprint CFD displays the rolled-up state of scheduled stories or work items for the sprint. In these charts, the *y*-axis represents the total work increments (points/hours) for the sprint. A release CFD would display the same relationships across an entire release. As with a traditional CFD, teams can use these diagrams to identify bottlenecks, forecast progress, and manage scope.

CFD/Burn-up Overlay

The CFD is central to visualizing the performance of our kanban systems. The burn-up chart, in turn, is central to visualizing progress in the context of a release or sprint. Integrating these two tools enables Scrumban teams to derive additional information that can substantially expand our options for managing outcomes and expectations (Figure 7.7).

Lead Time

Lead time is an indicator of business agility. We track it for each work item delivered to the customer, evaluating both the mean and the distribution across each class of

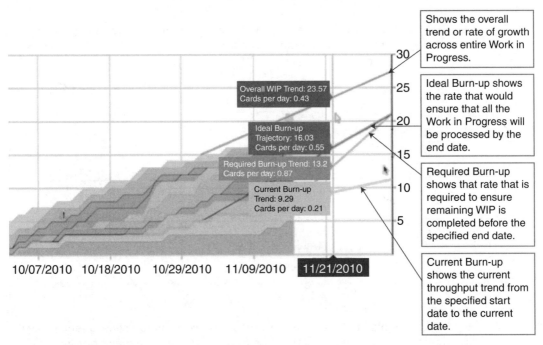

FIGURE 7.7   Example of a CFD/burn-up overlay.

Source: Leankit.

service. Comparing estimated versus actual lead times for a fixed delivery date class of service is especially important.

Several different types of lead time measurements are relevant to the health and agility of a system and organization. Steve Tendon has suggested the terms presented in Figure 7.8 for a variety of important lead time calculations.

Pragmatically, development teams are most concerned about lead time measurements tracked by the date/time a user story first enters their queue (denoted on a physical card by a date entry) and the date/time the same user story enters the final "done" column (or first infinite queue). The number of days between these dates represents the development system's lead time. This value can also be calculated using Little's law:

$$Average\ lead\ time = average\ WIP\ /\ average\ throughput$$

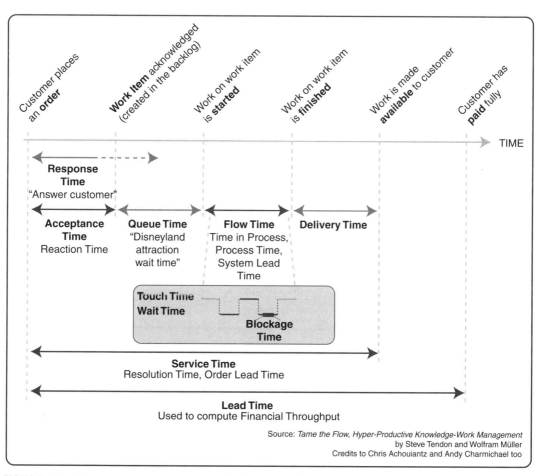

FIGURE 7.8   These measurements emphasize a service orientation.

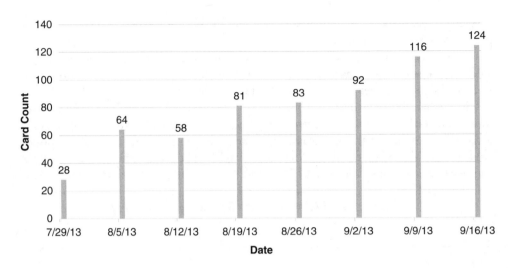

FIGURE 7.9   Trending increases in throughput confirm successful efforts at continuous improvement.

Source: Measurement of throughput for a CodeGenesys project using SwiftKanban.

Throughput

Throughput is the number of work items delivered in a given time period. The goal is usually to continuously increase this rate until you reach a pragmatic level of optimization. Figure 7.9 reflects a trending improvement typically associated with a team successfully engaged in continuous improvement.

Though seemingly related, throughput is different from Scrum velocity. Scrum's velocity measurements are based on the arbitrary length of a given sprint, and they depend on team estimates of time and effort. Throughput, by comparison, is a measurement of delivered work (not story points), which is typically more meaningful and can be consistently applied across multiple systems.

Aging of WIP

Lead times and their distributions are lagging indicators. They can be long in their own right, and the time required to collect data on their distribution may be even longer. When a process is stable, past performance can be a somewhat reliable indicator of future performance. Nevertheless, teams and organizations need a measurement to reflect whether flow is stable or stationary far in advance of lead time. Measuring the aging of WIP is one such way to assess this factor, as aging WIPs typically represent potential problems requiring attention.

There are two ways of measuring whether the WIP is aging. The first is to record the lead time for each card entering the "Done" column on a given day and then compute a daily average. Whenever the average lead time of the daily output is less than the nominal lead time for the system (the average predicted under Little's law), then the system's WIP is aging. If the reverse is true, the system's WIP is getting younger.

The other approach is to use "prisoner's metrics." Provided your workflow is not overly complex, you can simply use check marks to visualize the time a work item spends in your work queue adding a check mark to the card every day. You can then compare the lead time for the cards in your "Done" column with the number of check marks for the cards in progress. Stories and work items that have spent twice as much time as your average recorded lead time (this factor depends on the lead time distribution) should be viewed as aging. The presence of many aging work items indicates the WIP itself is aging.

Flow Efficiency

Flow efficiency is a Lean thinking metric and an important indicator of potential waste in a system. It is measured as the ratio of work time to lead time, and is calculated as follows:

$$Flow \; efficiency = [work \; time \; / \; (work \; time + wait \; time)] \times 100\%$$

Work time (or touch time) is essentially the lead time minus the waiting time. Waiting time includes the time a work item is blocked, the time it spends waiting in a "completed" or "ready" queue, and so on. The time a work item spends in an active work phase (such as "develop" or "test") is called touch time because of the difficulty of accurately measuring actual work activity.[5]

Flow efficiency is another tool for continuous improvement, showing the improvement a kanban system can realize simply by eliminating waste rather than changing engineering methods. With this measurement, 100% efficiency would mean a process loses no time to waiting or waste; 0% efficiency represents a condition of no work being performed.

Knowledge work tends to be very inefficient. In fact, studies have shown the average efficiency of knowledge work ranges between 5% and 40%. Consequently, you should seek to improve the flow efficiency of your system only in the context of that system. Common causes of poor flow efficiency include the following:

- *Variability*: Each user story and work item has different requirements, and the cycle time a particular item spends in each phase of the workflow will vary. We can manage this variability through use of buffers and other

---

5. As teams and organizations mature, we can envision efforts to track actual touch time more precisely, as there are many assumptions implicit in this approach that would benefit from further discovery and validation.

queuing mechanics. Although these mechanics help balance increased work demands against available capacity, they also increase wait time (which impacts flow efficiency). The alternative would be to impose significant amounts of idle time on workers (ensuring we always have available capacity to meet unexpected spikes in demand)—a strategy that results in low utilization (which is rarely economical).

- *Dependencies*: Teams have limited influence over factors like external decisions or waiting for others to finish work.
- *Staff liquidity/illiquidity*: Matching the right worker to the right work item requires having a greater amount of available work in the system. This has the effect of increasing wait time.
- Extra documentation requirements.
- Extreme backlog grooming.
- Report and status meetings.
- Unnecessary rework from lack of understanding, technical debt, and poor quality.

Takt Time

We know "lead time" is the time it takes to deliver a work item, as measured from the initial commitment through delivery into the first infinite queue. "Throughput" is the number of work items delivered per unit of time. *Takt time* represents the average time between successive deliveries or work items. Mathematically, it is the reciprocal of throughput.

In software development/IT organizations, we view takt time as "the cadence at which customers are comfortable receiving new versions [of software]." Consequently, it makes sense to try and align the cadence at which you release software to the cadence at which your users can use it (Figure 7.10).

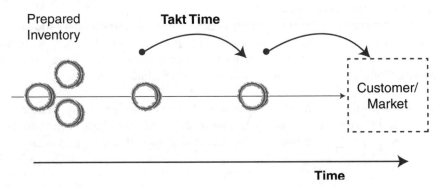

FIGURE 7.10 Takt time is a measurement of the amount of time between successive deliveries of work.

Source: Lean Kanban Netherlands, Metrics, 2013. Presentation by Ajay Reddy and Dimitar Bakardzhiev.

We align cycle time to takt time by managing WIP. These related measurements help us to define the maximum size of a work item (or aggregate) to incorporate within a planning horizon as part of commitments around responsiveness. They can also help us set up the harmonic cadences used for internal learning and feedback, and establish the most appropriate replenishment cadences needed at the program and portfolio levels in larger companies.

Quality Metrics

This section references Scrumban metrics that teams and organizations can use to monitor overall performance.

Failure Demand

Failure demand tracks how many work items the kanban system processes as a consequence of poor quality. This load includes production defects (bugs) in software as well as new features requested by users because the original work was not usable or failed to properly anticipate user needs. There are two core measurements in this arena of note: causes of defects and defect trends.

Causes of Defects

Defects represent opportunity cost and end up influencing both the lead time and the throughput of the kanban system. The change in the number of defects is a good indicator of whether the organization is improving.

I recommend developing a log system for production defects. In this system, the root cause of each defect should be logged.[6]

Visualizing root cause information can be very useful (Figure 7.11). For example, if the majority of defects are attributed to a "lack of testing," then the QA function may merit closer inspection. We can explore whether sufficient QA capacity is available, whether the testers know what to test, or whether introducing practices like ATDD is warranted.

Defect Trends

It can be very useful to track the accumulation of open defects over the life of a release (Figure 7.12). In addition to being another indicator of whether the team or organization is improving, visualizing the relative rates of new and closed defects provides insight regarding delivery date risk and related factors that static counts mask.

---

6. In some contexts, it may be more efficient to simply continue addressing the symptom rather than the root cause. Tracking of causes of defects is a path to making informed decisions about such issues.

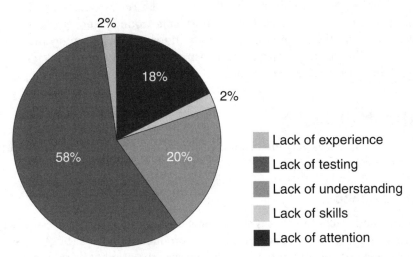

Cause of Failure Demand

- Lack of experience
- Lack of testing
- Lack of understanding
- Lack of skills
- Lack of attention

FIGURE 7.11 Tracking and visualizing the cause of failure often illuminates systemic causes we can improve.

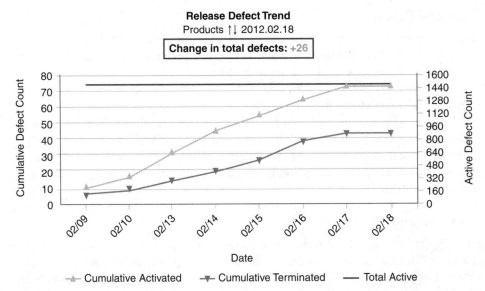

Release Defect Trend
Products ↑↓ 2012.02.18

Change in total defects: +26

Cumulative Activated — Cumulative Terminated — Total Active

FIGURE 7.12 Tracking defect trends helps illuminate delivery date risks and similar factors.

Source: Rally Software.

Blockers' Impact

Creating a prioritized list of blockers and their delay states can go a long way toward elucidating the nature of impediments in your system (Figure 7.13). Common examples of delay states might include descriptions such as the following:

- Waiting for an answer from the product owner
- Development environment down
- External system down

Whatever your list, it should be balanced to include your most frequent and biggest sources of delays.

With your list in place, order it by weighted impact of risks and delays using this formula:

$$Blocker\ impact = frequency\ of\ a\ blocker \times duration\ of\ the\ blockage$$

After visualizing your blockers in this fashion (Figure 7.14), you should be able to identify and remove the most significant delay combinations, thereby shrinking the area of your lead distribution (and creating the largest impact upon predictability).

The blockers CFD is another way to identify, report, and manage your blocking issues. It's an ideal chart for alerting senior management to impediments and their status.

Blocker	Frequency of Occurrence	Measured Impact [hours]
Broken environment	2	10
Waiting for feedback	6	48
Expedite request	1	10
Vacation/Sickness	1	40
Failure demand	3	21

FIGURE 7.13   Tracking the reasons for blocked work helps us discover and target systemic causes for improvement.

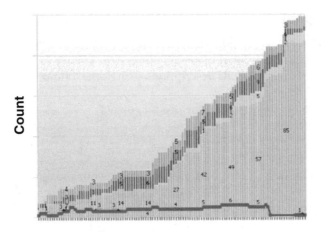

FIGURE 7.14   Another visualization of blocker impact.

Due Date Performance

For fixed date classes of service, it's important to know the dependency with which work items are delivered on time. The due date performance of fixed date work items is a key factor in determining the quality of your systems' initial estimates, and the accuracy of the estimate indicates how efficiently the system is working. This has implications for team performance: If the team doesn't believe in the accuracy of the estimate for fixed date work, items will be started early to ensure delivery, which does not represent optimal system performance. Figure 7.15 exemplifies this sort of analysis.

Arrival Rate Distribution and Service Rate Distribution

Measuring the rate at which work arrives in the system and is delivered is extremely useful when the system is suspected of being unstable. Whereas the aging of WIP is an indicator of instability, this data provides insight into what may be creating the instability.

Risk Metrics

As outlined in Chapter 6, risk consists of both uncertainty and cost. Theft is so common in large retail environments, for example, that it can be calculated as a fully anticipated cost rather than a risk that needs to be managed. Uncertainty, in contrast, implies the existence of more than one possible outcome. It doesn't rise to the

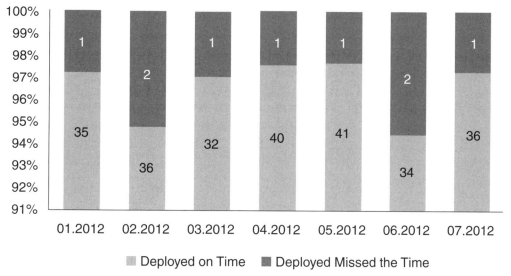

FIGURE 7.15   Visualizing due date performance.

level of a risk that should be managed unless it involves the possibility of a loss or injury (for example, a 30% chance that new features will sell fewer than 50 additional subscriptions).

High-performing systems manage real risks to more effectively influence and shape the demands placed on them. This often encompasses many aspects of system operation:

- Understanding and responding to market risks
- Improving direction and strategy
- Allocating responsibility for risks that materialize

As with any other aspect of our systems, we can't know whether our risk management efforts are effective unless we measure them. Objective measures of risk management should be based on how much risk is actually reduced (or whether certain risks are acceptable for a given benefit). To do so, risk management methods should incorporate an approach for properly assessing both the risks themselves and our efforts to manage them.

We introduced basic risk management concepts in Chapter 6. Managers should build upon these principles as the organization's practices mature. Risk evaluation measurement is a highly developed practice, with much to be learned from other industries (especially insurance and financial services).

Enhanced Burn-down Chart

In their book *Tame the Flow*, Steve Tendon and Wolfram Müller demonstrate how two characteristics from Goldratt's critical chain project management approach can be incorporated into Scrumban to enhance reliable management:

- Safeguarding the delivery date of a project or release by concentrating buffers at the end of the project
- Visualizing the project's status as progress on the critical chain and comparing it to cumulative buffer consumption in the form of a curve (Figure 7.16)

By comparing buffer consumption to project completion, teams and managers gain a ready visualization of how they're positioned to satisfy the delivery date established for the project or release.

Risk Burn-down Chart

Some work items are riskier than others, perhaps because of interactions with other systems, the use of new systems or technology, their relationship to new business domains, or any number of other reasons.

Developing an approach to quantify risk and tracking the degree to which it is reduced or eliminated over time is an excellent way to track the health of your release or project. If you didn't have an associated risk burn-down chart (Figure 7.17) for each of the projects depicted in Figure 7.18, you'd be inclined to believe the first project is

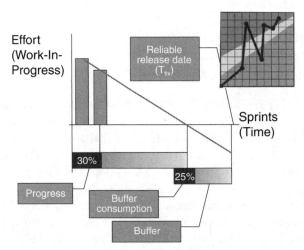

FIGURE 7.16 An example of visualizing a project timeline with a calculated buffer and superimposed "fever" chart reflecting project "health."

Source: Steve Tendon.

ID	Short Risk Name	Jan. Impact	Prob.	Sev.	Feb. Impact	Prob.	Sev.	Mar. Impact	Prob.	Sev.	Apr. Impact	Prob.	Sev.
1	JDBC driver performance	3	2	6	3	0	0	3	0	0	3	0	0
2	Calling Oracle stored procs. via web service	2	2	4	2	0	0	2	0	0	2	0	0
3	Remote app. Distribution to PDA's	3	2	6	3	1	3	3	0	0	3	0	0
4	Oracle Warehouse Builder stability	2	2	4	2	3	6	2	2	4	2	0	0
5	Legacy system stability	2	1	2	2	1	2	2	0	0	2	0	0
6	Access to user community	2	1	2	2	2	4	2	1	2	2	1	2
7	Availability of Architect	2	2	4	2	3	6	2	2	4	2	0	0
8	Server upgrade necessary	1	2	2	1	1	1	1	0	0	1	0	0
9	Oracle Handheld Warehouse browser launch	3	1	3	3	1	3	3	3	9	3	1	3
10	PST Changes for British Columbia	0	0	0	0	0	0	2	2	4	2	1	2
				33			25			23			7

Risk Burn Down

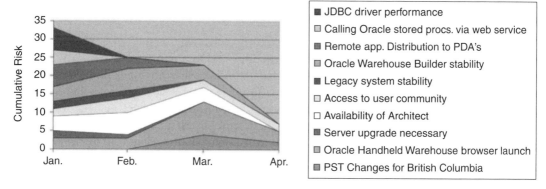

- JDBC driver performance
- Calling Oracle stored procs. via web service
- Remote app. Distribution to PDA's
- Oracle Warehouse Builder stability
- Legacy system stability
- Access to user community
- Availability of Architect
- Server upgrade necessary
- Oracle Handheld Warehouse browser launch
- PST Changes for British Columbia

FIGURE 7.17   This chart visualizes the reduction in project risk as identified risk factors are resolved.

Source: Dennis Stevens, Leading Agile, LLC.

in better shape because its feature burn-up chart indicates it's ahead of schedule. A quick glance at the cumulative risk associated with the remaining features, however, suggests this project could run into trouble.

Risk Index Chart

Another informative way to visualize risk is with a radar chart reflecting relative risk across a variety of domains (Figure 7.19). This graphic could be used during early-stage planning processes (conceptual or release planning) to improve prioritization.

For example, if two projects are projected to produce similar business value and require similar development time and effort, the less risky project should take priority. In another case, perhaps the business might be more capable of mitigating the specific profile of one project over another.

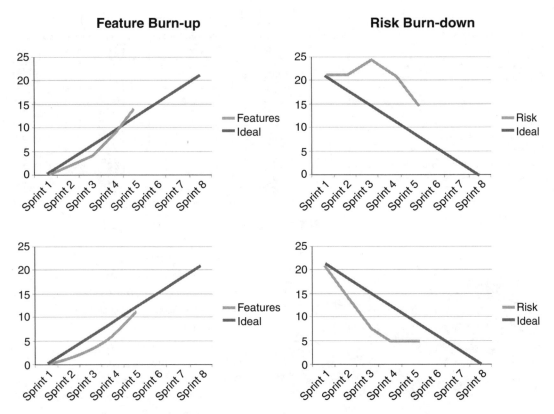

FIGURE 7.18   Having visualized metrics across multiple dimensions provides far greater insight into reality.

Source: Dennis Stevens, Leading Agile, LLC.

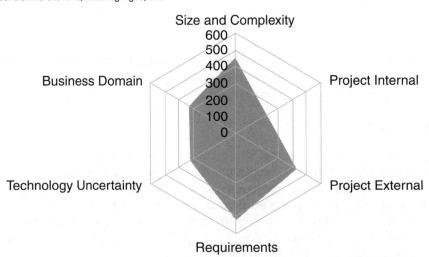

FIGURE 7.19   Visualizing project risk factors allows for better prioritization.

Source: Dennis Stevens, Leading Agile, LLC.

Improving Risk Metrics

Next-Level Learning:

Evolving to More
Advanced Practices

The pitfalls associated with subjective evaluations are why Scrumban generally stresses quantitative measurements over qualitative ones. However, most organizations evaluate risk subjectively. As your organization matures in its practices, there's no reason to be satisfied with subjective measures of risk.

Generally, we can consider four approaches for evaluating the effectiveness of risk management efforts:

- *Statistical inferences based on large samples*: Evaluating risk management efforts in this manner is challenging unless there's already research or data on the same process.
- *Direct evidence of cause and effect*: Great if you can find it, but is still likely to require statistical verification.
- *Component testing*: Using existing research on parts of the risk management method.
- *A "check of completeness"*: Simply comparing the items evaluated in a risk management system against a list of known risks can help determine whether risk management is too narrowly focused.

The first approach for measuring the effectiveness of risk management is not particularly pragmatic. Even if your efforts are having a significant effect on reducing losses from a variety of risks, a large number of samples are required to provide statistical confidence that your efforts are working. Given this challenge, I tend to emphasize other approaches.

Fortunately, risk management efforts can sometimes avert what would otherwise have been a disaster, such as IT security uncovering an elaborate embezzling scheme. In these cases, there is a very small likelihood that the organization would have discovered and addressed the risk without the use of that particular method. Of course, direct evidence of cause and effect is rarely that straightforward. Sometimes a risk management effort averts one risk but exacerbates another—a situation that is more difficult to detect. Thus you still need a way to check even apparently obvious instances of cause and effect against some other independent measure.

Enter "component testing." Though antithetical to systems thinking, this approach focuses on individual aspects of risk management. Examples include the following:

- If we rely on various scoring or classification methods (e.g., a scale of 1–5 or high/medium/low), we need to consider the results of research on how these methods are used and even misused by well-meaning analysts and account for these shortcomings accordingly.

■ If we use more quantitative models, we need to identify the most common known errors in such models, and check whether the sources of the data use methods that have proven track records of making realistic evaluations.

Finally, just a few words on the "completeness" of our efforts: Completeness is a matter of degree, and there's no guarantee that you will always identify relevant risks. All you can do is increase the completeness of your efforts by continual assessment of risks from several angles.

However you recognize and manage risk, applying these considerations fits naturally within Scrumban's measurement biases and will help ensure you're on a firm foundation for making better-informed decisions.

Extending Scrumban beyond IT: The Balanced Scorecard

Executives and PMO:

This section explores how Scrumban can integrate with and help inform non-IT initiatives to enhance alignment across the organization.

The balanced scorecard is a strategic planning and management system that is used to align business activities with the vision and strategy of the organization through the following activities:

■ Translating organizational vision into actionable strategy
■ Measuring and managing results
■ Creating better alignment across systems in the organization
■ Improving accountability
■ Communicating with clarity (both internal and external)

Looking ahead to Chapter 8 on management principles, the balanced scorecard supports the actions and values that leadership needs to employ to create high-performing organizations. It's an additional support framework that complements Scrumban and should be tackled at the senior management level.

Balanced scorecards are intended to present a mixture of both financial and non-financial measures in relation to target values. Such a report is not intended to replace traditional financial and operational reports, but rather to summarize the "most relevant" information for its intended audience according to structured design processes.

As a performance model, this report seeks to visualize the correlation between leading inputs (which can be human or physical in nature), the processes they go through, and the outputs (which lag in time). In this way, the balanced scorecard framework is yet another way to view systems more effectively, with an emphasis on incorporating key metrics into the visualization.

Finding the Right Measures

In balanced scorecard reporting, meaningful measures track outcomes, which tend to be less tangible than the things that organizations traditionally measure (such as how many units of a product were produced). So how do you capture robust measurements of intangible qualities such as employee morale or service quality?

First, we should understand the simplifying assumptions of a science—that is, the "objects of interest" and "well-defined conditions" that delimit the domain of application and magnify the power of prediction. As a framework grounded in systems thinking, Scrumban can help an organization simplify, idealize, and streamline the business world so that it can be understood by all employees. The first step in this direction involves finding the right measures.

As noted in earlier chapters, I favor beginning with the end in mind. In this context, then, the first step in deciding how to measure something is to articulate the difference you're trying to create. Once the end is clearly defined, using sensory language to describe the outcome as concretely as possible (i.e., describe what "efficiency" looks, feels, and sounds like) is generally the most effective way to ensure common understandings. It may be helpful to evaluate business objectives from the viewpoint shown in Figure 7.20.

FIGURE 7.20   A systems view of business strategy.

The next step is to consider the level of control you have in achieving the outcome you've described, and to be sure you understand the intended and unintended consequences of both the outcome and the act of measuring. This overall process is summarized in Figure 7.21.

> **Goal: Grow subscriber base from 5,000 to 20,000 users by year end.**

Resources: Current IT team of 10   Funds to add 1 member to
                     Current inside sales force of 2   an existing team or to pay
                     Current marketing team of 2   for 1 additional mktg
                                                         campaign

Strategies: Get desired functionality to market (Increase product
                     faster by hiring more IT staff   attractiveness, but
                                                          customer awareness not
                                                          impacted)

                     Acquire new customers more quickly   (Increase product
                     by spending on marketing campaign   awareness, but risk losing
                                                          new customers because
                                                          features are lacking)

Outputs: New functionality developed and deployed
                     Marketing campaigns completed
                     Sales efforts completed

Outcomes: Change in subscribers
                     Change in backlog of desired functionality

Performance   New subscribers added   Conversion rate—trial
Measures: Existing subscribers lost   subscriptions to paid
                     Conversion rate—prospects to trial   Change in conversion rates
                     subscriptions   with new feature deployment

FIGURE 7.21   An example of a discovery process you might go through to link individual or team performance measures to your organization's desired outcome.

Once you've identified the right outcomes and their general measurements, it's time to home in on what to count and make it happen. Balanced scorecards should be understandable and "owned" by everyone in the organization, so concise and simple metrics rule the day.

Measuring What Matters

In most cases, measuring what matters requires a combination of metrics relating to different aspects of your systems. Remember, you want to understand what's happening at the input level, what's happening within the work processes themselves, and which value is being delivered to your customers (Figure 7.22).

Cascading Strategic Objectives

We've previously alluded to the fact that high-performing organizations succeed in aligning work efforts with leadership's vision for success. Part of the art of effective management is "translating" organizational purpose into specific business unit and individual goals that align with desired outcomes. To achieve this, all management levels can contribute to clarifying the relationship between the work being performed and the organizational purpose it is helping to fulfill (Figure 7.23).

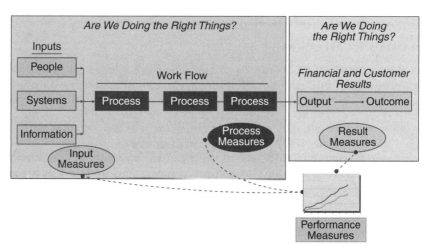

FIGURE 7.22   It's important to measure progress throughout your entire system.

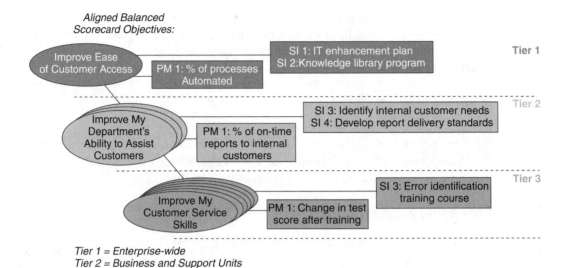

Aligned Balanced Scorecard Objectives:

Tier 1 = Enterprise-wide
Tier 2 = Business and Support Units
Tier 3 = Teams and Individuals

FIGURE 7.23   An example exercise of articulating "cascading" objectives that directly relate to units, teams, and individuals, but maintain a clear connection to furthering the organization's desired outcomes.

Scrumban Stories

Two of Mammoth Bank's overarching objectives were greater customer retention and sustained profitability. Unfortunately, Mammoth had made no effort to cascade the translation of its organizational objectives throughout the organization. The IT unit ended up measuring its success by how "Agile" it was becoming. These metrics were only an indirect assessment of how effectively IT was helping the organization achieve its intended objectives.

What difference would it have made if the bank had relied on balanced scorecard practices? Could the IT organization have measured how well it was delivering applications and products on time? Or controlled its operating costs through higher efficiencies? And how much more effectively could individual development teams have been aligned with the bank's overarching goals if their performance were being measured against the quality of work produced and metrics related to continuous improvement?

Tying It All Together

Scrumban enables us to track a wide range of metrics. More significantly, it enables us to integrate metrics from other frameworks and models, and visualize a wealth of information at the right times and places where it can be leveraged.

What's most important to recognize and embrace, however, is the notion that a single set of metrics can be relevant to all systems at all times. Though it's important to have some standardization of measured progress across the enterprise, it's equally important to continually assess where you're at, and to find metrics that will help you better understand and overcome current challenges. Sometimes this requires a narrower, more penetrating measure of team performance; at other times, it requires a broader measure of organizational outcomes.

PART IV

IMPROVING—ADVANCED TOPICS AND PRACTICES

Chapter 8

MANAGEMENT: MANAGEMENT IS DOING THINGS RIGHT—LEADERSHIP IS DOING THE RIGHT THINGS

IN THIS CHAPTER

- Principles of Convictional Intelligence and Leadership
- Reinforcing Leadership through Effective Management
- Facilitating Evolving Roles

Team Members:

Don't be deceived by the title of this chapter. The information it contains is as relevant to you and your function as it is to your managers and executives!

Although this chapter is ostensibly about the important roles that leadership and management play in achieving success, the information it conveys is intended for everyone. Scrumban encourages acts of leadership from all levels of the organization because no organization can *sustain* success without strong leadership and strong management. All employees should help their organization develop solid leadership and management capabilities if they wish to achieve the level of personal and professional satisfaction that comes with being a part of high-performing teams and organizations.

The first potential pitfall in this arena comes with the decision to adopt Agile practices. More often than not, when outside experts are brought in to assist with the transition, those in management forget they continue to own the process. Experts will do what they do best—focus on the mechanics of the process and help people begin to master it. Management, however, needs to remain actively involved in reminding people of their ultimate aim. Even more importantly, managers must continuously connect ongoing efforts to the organization's desired outcomes. When an organization's "official" managers neglect to do this, leadership from all levels is necessary to get the organization on track.

Scrumban, as mentioned repeatedly in this book, emphasizes systemic thinking. Though it provides a variety of ways for individual teams to enhance their understanding and performance from a systems viewpoint, it is not a substitute for the leadership required for scaling Agility across an enterprise.

As with individual teams, Scrumban provides a framework for more effective leadership at the executive level. In this chapter, we dive more deeply into the most important leadership and management principles that can be leveraged within a Scrumban framework to create and sustain high performance over time.

Convictional Leadership

One of the most important functions of business leadership is to articulate a clearly understood purpose across the organization. This is because focused work—not harder work—is the key to sustained success and market leadership. People work more intelligently when what they're doing serves a clear purpose. Leaders can ensure employees pursue a clear purpose by helping every working system understand how its outputs are relevant to the organization's desired business outcomes.

That said, leadership styles vary across a wide spectrum. At one extreme of this spectrum, leaders employ a pragmatic leadership style, one that's almost pure management. These folks are experts at techniques and strategies, but their actions are not driven by conviction. In other words, they're leading something, but you don't have any sense of what they really care about leading. At the other end of the spectrum are individuals who believe deeply in a particular vision, but are also blinded by that passion. They're so immersed in their beliefs that they end up trivializing some of the actual tasks and responsibilities of leadership. Effective convictional leadership falls between these two extremes.

With this spectrum of leadership in mind, let's consider a couple of great convictional leaders from the not too distant past—Ronald Reagan and Margaret Thatcher. People knew what they believed. People elected them because of what they believed. People elected them to accomplish outcomes that followed from their convictions. No one ever had to wonder what either of these two leaders believed on any major issue because they were identified by their conviction. Their leadership was completely saturated with their convictions.

Now consider Steve Jobs. No employee at Apple ever had to wonder about where Jobs would come down on most business issues. His convictional leadership became an extension of the man, and it saturated the Apple culture. In fact, it still does, even years after Jobs's death.

What if your organization doesn't have the equivalent of Steve Jobs, Ronald Reagan, or Maggie Thatcher? There are lots of successful companies that don't have charismatic leaders at the helm. Convictional leadership doesn't require a charismatic personality to be effective, nor does it have to emanate from the top (though it's very effective when it does). Many layers of leadership exist within an organization, and convictional leadership can be provided at all of these levels.

As important as clear convictions are to effective leadership, the communication of those convictions is perhaps even more important. Communication comes in many forms; we never make a decision, send a message, or take an action that is not filled with multiple levels of communication. It's the combination of our words and actions that matters, and this is where most managers need to develop greater awareness.

The power of convictional leadership runs deep through human history. Consider the Biblical story of Nehemiah.

Nehemiah was a layman who served the Persian king. He offered to lead a group of his fellow Jews back to Jerusalem to rebuild the city walls. Together with the priest Ezra—who led the spiritual revival of the people—he directed a political and religious restoration of the Jews in their homeland after many years of Babylonian captivity.

Nehemiah's life is a great portrait of convictional leadership. Consider all these actions in which Nehemiah engaged:

- He led by example, giving up a respected position in a palace for hard labor in a politically insignificant district.
- He collaborated with Ezra to solidify the political and spiritual foundations of the people.
- He never claimed glory for himself, always giving God the credit for his successes. This humility modeled the kind of behavior and attitude in others that sustained the Jews' ability to overcome adversity and achieve success after success.
- He managed risk in his strategy to use half the people to build the city walls, and the other half to keep watch for the Samaritans who threatened attack.
- As governor, he negotiated peace among the Jews who were unhappy with Persian taxes.
- He exhibited an unwavering focus and determination to complete his goals. The act of accomplishing those goals resulted in a people encouraged, renewed, and excited about their future.

Nehemiah shows us the kind of impact one individual exercising convictional leadership can have on a nation. Consistency and commitment to a clear purpose coupled with clear and consistent communication of purpose serve as powerful unifiers. Every person in an organization is capable of influencing those around them by demonstrating their commitment to organizational conviction through words and actions.

Nehemiah didn't lay every brick that went into rebuilding the walls of Jerusalem, but he acted as though he did. Every bricklayer felt he was there in spirit, if not in body. His leadership enabled those around him to do their jobs more effectively because they could see how their daily actions, no matter how mundane they seemed in isolation, were necessary to the ultimate outcome.

Under constant attack from the Samaritans, it would have been easy for those in the trenches to lose sight of their ultimate goal and retreat to a defensive posture. But Nehemiah showed everyone under his command how their individual efforts were allowing the city walls to be rebuilt. He reminded them how completing the wall was key to restoring the Jews to their homeland. Retreating and defending would have afforded the Jews a greater immediate sense of security, but it would not have allowed them to achieve their ultimate aim.

The last time we saw a similar unification of purpose was during World War II. Every riveter knew American lives depended on his or her attention to detail. Every janitor understood how maintaining the factories where armaments were made was relevant to his or her co-workers' ability to sustain the highest quality of manufacturing and assembly.

Your organization may not face the same kind of Herculean task that Nehemiah faced when rebuilding the walls of Jerusalem (or that the world faced in defeating the Axis powers). Nevertheless, if a business wants to lead in the marketplace, it requires similar leadership. As Nehemiah discovered through his strategic partnerships, leadership can be found and encouraged in many places. This notion is central to Scrumban.

Servant Leadership

Another common pattern among many high-performing organizations is the notion of servant leadership—a philosophy that traces its roots back thousands of years. The ancient Chinese philosopher Lao Tzu is said to have written:

> *The highest type of ruler is one of whose existence the people are barely aware. Next comes one whom they love and praise. Next comes one whom they fear. Next comes one whom they despise and defy.*
>
> *The Sage is self-effacing and scanty of words. When his task is accomplished and things have been completed, all the people say, "We ourselves have achieved it!"*

Servant leaders engender trust, which catalyzes higher levels of engagement among workers and evokes more discretionary effort and idea generation, resulting in accelerated change and innovation across an organization. In pure bottom-line terms, managers who empower and respect their staff get better performance in return.

The servant leader's primary objective is to enhance the growth of individuals in the organization and increase teamwork and personal involvement. Though servant leadership represents a long-term strategy, recent experiments in behavioral economics suggest that servant leaders produce better-coordinated teams that result in improved outcomes even over the short term.[1]

---

1. "Selfish or Servant Leadership? Evolutionary Predictions on Leadership Personalities in Coordination Games," http://tiny.cc/ScienceA.

Good Leaders Recognize Knowledge Work Is Different

As outlined in earlier chapters, knowledge work is highly variable and very different from other kinds of work. Scrumban provides many ways for organizations to manage this variability, but management has to educate itself about these capabilities to realize any benefit.

For example, a variety of mechanisms for improving planning and forecasting were introduced earlier in this book. While these methods can certainly be an aid to individual teams, fostering a greater awareness and adoption of these techniques and the principles behind them is necessary to improve the organization's collective understanding of knowledge work—and the development of effective approaches for managing through its differences.

Fighting Entropy

Entropy is the natural tendency of systems to move from order to disorder. To effectively sustain high performance in their teams, executives and managers must understand that every organization is a constantly changing environment.

Good video games share a common trait: They mimic entropy as players progress through the game. The path to successfully completing any given level will change each time the game is played, and the successful path is rarely repeated. To win, players have to constantly observe the game environment, think about how they're approaching play, and adjust their strategy and tactics as needed to reach their destination. Managers need to deal with entropy in their organizations in much the same way.

Any visible systems we put in place, whether they're tools we employ or frameworks like Scrum, continually degrade unless we're constantly observing our environment and adjusting our behavior. Fortunately, Scrumban provides a framework with tools to help organizations counteract entropy, but it requires managers to understand and use its capabilities for this toolset to be of any benefit.

Nurturing and Protecting Core Values

We can all cite examples of organizations outperforming competitors that are many times their size. Organizations that exhibit these levels of performance share common values, and senior managers or executives typically lead the charge in ensuring they take hold.

Although individual employees within an organization perform different tasks and often have different interests, the actual production of value is driven by an inherent reliance on one another to perform specified tasks. Leaders and top executives of high-performing organizations play a critical role in creating conditions that recognize this interdependence, and instill values that foster the sense of unity essential for mutual assistance.

Establishing the Proper Use of Metrics

Certain organization-wide conditions are necessary for high performance that can only be influenced by management. How an organization measures financial responsibility is one such example.

Goldratt's theory of constraints shows how adopting common metrics can help organizations overcome structural impediments to high performance. In *The Goal*,[2] these impediments were rooted in the use of cost accounting and efficiency metrics for management purposes, and shown to be sources of divergence of purpose and hidden agendas.

It's critical not only to identify metrics, but also to use them appropriately. Most importantly, metrics should be applied to motivate and set expectations, not to manipulate.

Unfortunately, most organizations employ metrics that effectively prevent key foundational patterns from emerging. The reason why these organizations find it so difficult to achieve a high-performing state is often a function of what gets measured rather than a lack of willingness or ability to improve.

Enhancing Leadership through Better Communication

Simon Sinek has proposed a simple but powerful thought model for inspirational leadership. In his model, he emphasizes thinking, acting, and communicating from the inside out.[3] What Sinek's model leverages is the recognition of real factors that drive certain human behaviors (a systems view, if you will, of the human element). At the heart of Sinek's model is the golden circle (Figure 8.1).

Sinek developed his model based on substantial research on the contrast between the world's most influential leaders and companies and those on the periphery. When asked why they thought customers chose to do business with their company, most in the periphery believed it was because of their great products, great prices, or great quality. The most successful and influential companies, however, believed it was because their products and services resonated with the "why" factor—people chose to do business with them because everything they did was focused on responding to why people choose to do what they do.

What Sinek emphasizes in the customer context is that people do not buy products and services because of what companies do or how they do it. In fact, rarely do competing companies differ substantially. Rather, customers buy particular products and services because their perception of why the selling organization does what it does convinces them they want its products and services more than its competitors' products and services.

---

2. *The Goal: A Process of Ongoing Improvement* by Eliyahu M. Goldratt.
3. We encourage readers to watch his TED talk on this subject at http://tiny.cc/TedTalkLeaders.

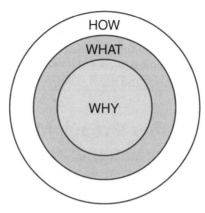

FIGURE 8.1   Adopting a systems view of human behaviors can improve communication and ultimately alignment of purpose among the employees of an organization.

The observations Sinek made in the context of consumer behavior are equally applicable to leadership. Employees who buy into their leaders' "why"—who share their leaders' convictions—are often more loyal, work harder, and show greater commitment. Scrumban frameworks afford leaders many opportunities to reinforce their "why" factor, but it's up to the individuals to recognize and leverage these capabilities if they want to reap the benefits.

Putting It All Together

As human beings, we have the ability to think about thinking. We can read books like this one and learn about ways of thinking that can have a positive impact on our work and in our lives. However, we can't function if we have to consciously think about every decision we make. Consequently, just as we develop habits of action (such as the act of getting dressed—we don't have to consciously think about how to put on our clothes in the morning), we must also develop habits of thinking. To properly function, we must work to ensure that our prior learning is ingrained into habit so that it becomes automatic.

Sound convictional leadership is a by-product of convictional intelligence, and our convictional intelligence is very much a function of our habits of mind. Just as we automatically know how to get dressed in the morning, so we develop habits of mind to which we no longer give actual thought. If we want to improve our ability to lead with conviction, then it is very likely that we need to become more conscious of changing certain habits of mind. It's one thing to learn about the concepts discussed in this section; it's quite another to "know" them and have them become a matter of reflex or intuition.

Steve Jobs was a master of intuition in matters of design. Apple employees have recounted stories of him holding the prototype of the iPhone, closing his eyes, running his hands around every part of the surface, and ordering modifications until it was "just right." It was Jobs's instincts, and not an antiseptic exercise of design principles (of which he undoubtedly had some conscious awareness), that led to the right decisions. Good convictional leaders nurture habits of thinking that allow them to "just know" the right ways to think and act.[4]

Reinforcing Leadership through Management

Not surprisingly, the management methods on which Scrumban is based identify a common set of values that should be fostered to create and sustain real Agility. The most important are summarized here:

1. *Adopting a systems/process focus*: Great leaders understand and encourage systems thinking. They seek to visualize the flow of work and information across the system as a whole, and are vigilant about identifying structural issues that encourage premature local optimizations, like the cost accounting methods in *The Goal* that were actually impeding value creation instead of optimizing it.

2. *Establishing a constancy of purpose*: The two top concerns for management should be the day-to-day operations of the business and the organization's future performance. High-performing teams have no doubts about what they're doing and why they're doing it. When the independent parts of a system understand they are working toward a common purpose, they can collaborate far more effectively than if they view themselves and their performance in isolation.

   It's essential for management to remind those in their system of their shared vision and help them articulate it. Management must also be vigilant against conveying any sense of a shifting vision or purpose. Constant shifting in these arenas can create distrust, which seriously erodes the factors that support high performance.

3. *Creating a community of trust*: High-performing teams can exist only within communities of trust. It's up to leaders to align incentives to produce a high level of trust among teams to support better performance and results.

   To this end, since trust is about perceived care, competence, and integrity (discussed further later in this chapter), these values need to be demonstrated through action and interaction. High-trust environments share many traits: In them, people feel safe acknowledging what they do not know, there is

---

4. For further reading on this subject, we recommend Albert Mohler's *The Conviction to Lead: 25 Principles for Leadership That Matters* (Baker Books, 2012). Though written for an audience of Christian religious leaders, its lessons can be applied in many other contexts.

genuine participation instead of hollow words, and there are clear strategies, direct talk, and fairness.

4. *Demonstrating a commitment to quality*: W. Edwards Deming was a statistician best known as a father of quality management. The "quality" label is really misleading, however, because Deming's work really demonstrates that quality is more of a means to an end. Deming provided us with management methods capable of creating sustained business success. His principles are best summed up as follows:

Management's failure to plan for the future leads to loss of market share, which in turn leads to the loss of jobs. Management must therefore be judged not only by current results, but also by whether it is executing against innovative plans to stay in business, protect investment, ensure future profitability, and provide more jobs through improved products and services.

A long-term commitment to new learning and new philosophy is required of any management that seeks any kind of transformation. The timid and the fainthearted, and the people who expect quick results, are doomed to disappointment.

Though most of Deming's work was done within the manufacturing context, it applies equally well to services. His work reflected that 94% of business problems are derived from the processes we put in place rather than the people working within those processes, and it demonstrated that lower costs and increased market shares are produced when management focuses on the ultimate responsibility for the quality of the organization's products and services. Scaling Agility to an enterprise-wide level requires a similar commitment.

A true systems thinker, Deming didn't believe any system was capable of understanding itself. Consequently, he devised an approach that individuals could use to begin to understand the systems within which they worked (believing the first step to a system understanding itself started with the individual). He specifically advocated that all managers needed to develop this system of profound knowledge to be effective. This system consists of four parts:

- Understanding the overall processes of the entire system (the interaction across all suppliers, producers, and recipients)
- Knowledge of the variation in the system (its range and causes)
- Concepts explaining knowledge and the limits of what can be known
- The psychology of human nature

Combining systems understanding and commitment to quality, senior management will be positioned to foster organizations that are truly Agile, maintain costs, increase value, and lead their markets over time. As a framework, Scrumban is naturally structured to help managers gain an understanding of an organization's IT processes at a systems level. Are you starting to see how all of the leadership principles and values detailed in this chapter interact as a complete system?

5. *Showing respect for people*: Software development is primarily a creative activity, and people are the creative elements that make it happen. Moreover, software development takes place within complex systems, and people serve as the agents that exchange information. Regardless of how well we design our processes, failure to respect the people within them ultimately leads to failure.

Ken Blanchard reminded the world that people who feel good about themselves produce good results. It only makes sense, then, for leaders and managers to nurture natural intrinsic motivators:

- *Curiosity*: Provide an environment with plenty of things to investigate and think about.
- *Honor*: High-performing employees take pride in having their personal values reflected within the work they perform.
- *Acceptance*: Create environments that approve of people for who they are.
- *Mastery*: Nurture mastery by stretching people to perform work at the edge of their abilities.
- *Power*: Provide people with the ability to influence their environments.
- *Freedom*: Allow people sufficient degrees of independence within their work and responsibilities.
- *Relatedness*: Foster environments where good social relationships thrive.
- *Order*: Create stable environments with the right balance of rules and policies.
- *Goals*: Nurture environments where personal purpose can be fulfilled through work.
- *Status*: Enhance status through recognition of accomplishments and responsibilities.

Leadership may also do well to question the use of traditional extrinsic motivators such as individual bonuses as a motivational tool, since management experts have suggested this practice actually reduces the intrinsic motivation employees get from work and undermines some of the interest in the job itself.

6. *Demonstrating integrity*: One of the many ways management ensures integrity in a system derives from how it elects to apply metrics across the organization. Do the chosen metrics reflect a direct connection between work performance and business value? Do the chosen metrics reflect a true understanding of the nature of work being evaluated? Are metrics used appropriately (to motivate and set expectations, rather than to manipulate or impose fear)?

With respect to the nature of work being evaluated, perhaps one of Deming's most important contributions to effective management methods lies in his work related to statistical process control (SPC). SPC allows us to manage variability in systems and work tasks based on a statistical evaluation of actual results. In other words, it enables us to eliminate all arbitrary numerical targets in favor of data that's truly meaningful.

With SPC, we seek to understand system capabilities in terms of probabilities. For example, over time we might be able to collect data that shows a team completes 80% of similarly sized user stories every 2.5 days. With that information in hand, we can move away from using prospective estimates to project how long it will take to complete work and instead rely on probabilistic forecasting.

Attention to establishing these kinds of measurements is a foundational element of the Toyota production system, and Scrumban relies on it in similar fashion. We can't ensure integrity in our systems if we never pay attention to the nature of our work and intelligently deal with things like variability.

7. *Creating a commitment to continuous improvement*: There are several ways managers can leverage a Scrumban framework to nurture mindsets committed to continuous improvement. Doing so starts with the notion of agreement—specifically, the Kanban Method's second principle of obtaining everyone's agreement to pursue incremental, evolutionary change. It continues with practices such as visualizing improvement efforts in conjunction with adopting katas and disciplined approaches to specific needs (such as problem solving or risk management).

8. *Establishing reliable processes for conflict resolution*: Delivering a difficult message is a lot like throwing a hand grenade: You can't diplomatically throw a hand grenade, nor can you necessarily outrun the consequences. Yet choosing not to deliver a difficult message is like hanging on to a hand grenade once you've pulled the pin.

Whether we're dealing with failed projects or seeking to manage underperforming employees, it's human nature to avoid difficult conversations. Recognizing this inherent difficulty and establishing consistent and reliable mechanisms to avoid and resolve the conflicts that inevitably arise is one of the more significant contributions managers and leaders can make toward fostering a culture that happily delivers results.

A common denominator to all of these values is the manner in which they support the creation of thinking systems—systems that continuously learn and adapt. Business organizations that learn fast are superior to those that don't—they're capable of identifying and responding to challenges and opportunities faster than those that don't. This ability to learn as a system is particularly important for software development teams, but true Agility comes when the entire organization is aligned in this manner.

Dan Mezick's book *The Culture Game* offers an interesting perspective on how incorporating game mechanics into the way we work represents a great mechanism for helping organizations accelerate team learning. Building on Jane McGonigal's definition of a "good game" as any activity with clear goals, clear rules, frequent feedback, and optional participation, he suggests that working in an organization is, in fact, a game. Most of the time, the game we call work isn't fun to play because the goals, rules, and feedback mechanics are poorly structured. Citing his experiences at Zappos, Mezick suggests how game mechanics can be leveraged to structure our cultures in ways that can quickly generate improved results.

Encouraging Thinking Systems and Push versus Pull

Strengthening the foundations that create thinking systems (adaptive capabilities) has the additional advantage of supporting an evolution from "push" to "pull" styles of management. Most IT organizations—even those that have adopted Scrum—follow deeply ingrained practices of assigning work. From a systems perspective, this is the equivalent of pushing demand onto a system for processing.

Push systems are speculative. They assume the system actually has the capacity to take on the work when it's pushed upon it. This mode focuses on maximizing the utilization of the workers within the system rather than the workflow itself. Put another way, we tend to focus on watching the runners rather than the baton.

In pull systems, the system is measured and managed in ways to make it more predictable. Through visualization and improved understanding of the system, pull systems place more initiative and responsibility on the workers to maintain and improve predictable workflow. As a consequence, there tend to be shorter and faster feedback loops and greater opportunities for immediate defect fixes.

Encouraging Servant Leadership

Servant leadership can be fostered by creating environments that support developing those characteristics central to the role of a servant leader. In the context of IT organizations, these include the following:

1. *Listening*: Emphasize listening effectively to others.
2. *Empathy*: Understand others' feelings and perspectives.
3. *Self-awareness*: Understand your own values, feelings, strengths and weaknesses.
4. *Responsibility*: Assume responsibility for outcomes, but also help others take on responsibility.
5. *Persuasion*: Influence others through persuasiveness.

6. *Conceptualization*: Integrate present realities with future possibilities.
7. *Foresight*: Demonstrate intuition about how the past, present, and future are connected.
8. *Coaching/mentoring*: Invest time and effort to foster leadership in others, because it is a natural trait that can be nurtured at every level.

    Good leaders get people to follow them; great leaders help develop other people worth following. Great leaders build leadership teams of outstanding individuals who share the same convictions and vision. They understand that mentoring others to be leaders is a process, culminating in freedom. Those persons whom we mentor to become leaders with us must also be enabled to lead in their own ways—but always toward the common vision and shared convictions.
9. *Systems thinking*: Understand systems as an interdependent whole, and not as a collection of independent parts.
10. *Empirical decision making*: Collect information through observation, experience, and experimentation. Make business decisions based on this data and an evaluation of cost, risk, and opportunity.

Adaptive Risk Management and Local Decision Making

Most organizations don't suffer from a lack of innovation. Rather, they're unable to achieve high performance because they can't choose which ideas represent the best course of action. This is why making good decisions—and making them happen quickly—is another hallmark of high-performing organizations.

Think about it: Every success, every misstep, and every opportunity seized or missed is the result of a decision that someone made or failed to make. If your organization can't make the right decisions quickly and effectively, and then execute those decisions consistently, your business will lose ground to its competitors.

Establishing mechanisms for making good decisions and placing the decision-making process as close to the "front lines" as possible immensely improve an organization's performance. IT leaders and managers can take advantage of Scrumban's ability to leverage risk management techniques and enable meaningful local decision-making capabilities. The prioritization of work is a familiar arena in which to make such efforts in IT work.

Facilitating Evolving Roles

We already know Scrumban emphasizes starting with what you do, and respecting current roles and responsibilities in the process. Because Scrumban is not a specific workflow methodology, however, it doesn't prescribe specific roles to be played as work is performed, nor does the insight it brings require new roles or practices.

That said, the process of discovery inherent in Scrumban may ultimately call for teams or organizations to consider changing, adding, or removing traditional roles and their associated practices. If changes are made to traditional Scrum roles, then clearly the teams involved are no longer practicing Scrum. I believe that's okay—provided the decision has been made with a sufficient understanding of why it makes sense for the current context.

It's more common, however, to find holdovers from non-Agile roles in many Scrum contexts. Though their traditional work may no longer be relevant to "new" processes, the individuals who held traditional roles may not immediately adapt and start delivering value to newly defined work processes. Following are some examples of transformations that individuals in common roles can make in a Scrumban context that can ease the path to fulfilling essential purposes envisioned within a more traditional Scrum framework.[5]

Product Manager

Product managers often represent a development organization's only connection to the ultimate customer, and frequently assume the role of product owner in Scrum. While deference should be given to the domain knowledge a product manager brings to the development process, the Scrumban framework reinforces the overall awareness that these individuals are merely proxies for actual customers. This opens up more opportunities to challenge conventional wisdom in ways that can lead to better outcomes.

Coaching Tip!

Check out the additional perspective I provide on the product owner/ product manager function in the Appendix.

For example, in Chapter 6, we considered how facilitating the right capabilities within the product owner function is critical to helping the organization realize shared understandings of value and prioritization. Good product management requires skills that allow individuals to understand the marketplace, elements of product engineering, and effective project management. Great products and services are the result of a continual focus on ensuring that their design, production, and marketing are united under a single, cohesive vision. It behooves all employees to recognize how the Scrumban framework can help ensure this essential focus is brought to bear.

---

5. Many of these examples of role-based guidance are derived from recent Kanban leadership retreats, and are summarized by Frank Vega at http://tiny.cc/RoleBasedGuidance.

In particular, we can help others understand how Scrumban expands opportunities for product managers to identify and improve workflow management associated with "upstream" interactions—that is, those taking place before work enters the development queue. Perhaps the most significant opportunity results from working within a framework that encourages the incorporation of more meaningful risk profiles for work items. Fostering the development and integration of scientific methods to prioritize work can ease many common challenges found in more traditional contexts.

Additionally, Scrumban's statistically based forecasting and planning capabilities enable managers to schedule releases at a sustainable pace—one that balances development, delivery, and quality with the needs of the business and its customers.

All of these opportunities represent significant shifts away from the approaches that typically dominate traditional versions of the product owner's role. More importantly, they can be realized within a framework that supports evolving these functions over time based on what works in the context of a given system.

Business Analyst

Like product managers, business analysts have opportunities to gradually evolve their traditional roles within the guidance offered by a Scrumban framework. For example, these professionals are perfectly positioned to reinforce system views by helping to "shape" new demands entering the workflow. Rather than being just a voice for customer demands (requests), business analysts can assess how variations among work items will influence workflow performance (measured in terms of quality, throughput, lead times, and others) and help teams proactively understand how these impacts play out.

In their communications with business stakeholders, business analysts also have an opportunity to ensure an improved understanding of target dates based on meaningful probabilities and associated risks, whether working in tandem with a product manager or filling this role directly.

Project Manager/Scrum Master

Even though Scrum has been around for many years, the role of Scrum master is still often misunderstood. The framework's key expectations from this role include the following:

- Being a facilitator
- Being a coach
- Helping the team remove impediments
- Being the framework custodian

Scrum masters are responsible for ensuring Scrum is understood and properly enacted. They perform this feat by ensuring the team adheres to Scrum's theories, practices, and rules. They're also charged with helping everyone involved with the team adjust their interactions to maximize value creation. These activities range from helping product owners identify and improve techniques for managing backlogs to coaching the development team on ways to work within environments where Scrum practices (or Agile practices in general) are not fully adopted and understood.

Despite the advanced "maturity" required to serve in this role effectively, there can be many reasons why an organization might prefer to transition existing employees into this role. Unfortunately, this practice often results in individuals never fully implementing the Scrum master role as intended. Even worse are scenarios where the organization elects to rotate the role among existing team members—a serious mistake.

Scrumban helps to ease new Scrum masters into their intended role by supporting many functions through its visualization and management framework. For example, a new Scrum master doesn't have to guide the product owner on managing prioritization if empirical techniques are adopted under the Scrumban framework. Visual workflow, additional metrics, and expanded management tools can be leaned on to improve their own and their team's recognition of key patterns because the framework enables team members to actually see and measure the influence of specific policies (such as limiting work in progress by value stream, helping to clarify how they choose to handle expedited requests, and elucidating the nature of activities and events needed to replenish the workflow's "ready" queue).

As understandings and practices mature, the Scrum master role is naturally suited to helping the team take advantage of new capabilities for developing probabilistic expectations and forecasts for delivery, required resources, and similar needs. These professionals are most likely to take a lead role in negotiating service level agreements or expectations with customers and partners, and can rely on elements of the framework to build trust around them.

Quality Assurance

Agile software development frameworks like Scrum radically transform more traditional quality assurance practices. Frameworks like Scrum emphasize the formation of cross-functional teams capable of working on all phases of work simultaneously. Unfortunately, there's often an imbalance between the number of testers and developers when organizations adopt Agile practices (plus minimal automation support), so development work quickly begins to outpace quality assurance as sprints are undertaken.

QA personnel can respond to such challenges by focusing their efforts on new approaches. First, they can identify ways to increase testing efficiency across the whole team. For example, which automation options can be employed to reduce manual regression efforts? Can developers write automation tests to further balance the workload? Can developers employ more unit testing to reduce the number of bugs and cycles requiring tester involvement?

The most significant evolution of all occurs when QA personnel adopt the mindset of being the champion of the product and the user. Rather than finding bugs or defects, the QA process should focus on identifying issues of performance, security, and related factors. QA personnel can further create balance and add value by engaging in risk-based testing (in which they identify where to focus quality efforts in a similar way to how risk profiles can enhance work item prioritization). In other words, the QA unit should take responsibility for ensuring the right product is being delivered over the product being delivered right, and pursue it in a manner that makes the most sense for their particular context.

The team and its QA members can explore different ways of executing against their new roles. One approach might be for QA members to serve as subject-matter experts (e.g., automation, architectural, testing) who float among engineers in the development process, supporting delivery where the need to focus is deemed greatest.

A final comment on evolving roles: Many organizations retain policies and approaches that perpetuate the Myth of the Appointed Leaders—that is, the notion that leadership, at any level, is responsible for levels of performance. To illustrate this myth in action, Gerald Weinberg recounted how he worked with one manager to experiment with introducing Agile approaches on a limited basis before making a decision on proceeding with a broader implementation.[6] After the first experiment ended very successfully, Weinberg was certain the manager was reaching out to accelerate the timetable for a broader implementation. Much to Weinberg's surprise, he was actually calling to cancel the entire program.

When he asked, "Which would you rather have: a team that never fails, but you don't know who's responsible for their success, or a team that fails regularly, but you know exactly whom to blame?" Weinberg received an unexpected response. "The regular failure, of course. I know how to manage when I can pick out the good guys and the bad guys, but how can I manage when I can't?"

Systems thinking clearly illustrates that while individuals might influence success or failure, one individual rarely (if ever) determines outcomes. Yet we tenaciously hold on to the belief that leaders make all the difference because of the comfort it provides. Scrumban can help raise awareness of policies and mechanisms that help to perpetuate this myth (e.g., financially rewarding managers for team successes). Unfortunately, there's no magic bullet for helping to make them disappear!

---

6. I encountered this story in Weinberg's collection of articles called *Agile Impressions*.

Tying It All Together

While teams and organizations will benefit from adopting the Scrumban framework for their operations, widespread and sustained success can be achieved only when leadership is invested in reinforcing the vision, values, and practices to make it happen. When the path is unclear, however, employees can leverage the Scrumban framework to discover clarity and catalyze necessary change.

Chapter 9

MATURING: LIKE A FINE WINE, SCRUMBAN CAN GET BETTER WITH AGE

IN THIS CHAPTER
- Prioritizing and Managing Change
- Common Opportunities for Improvement
- Amplifying Capabilities Beyond the Team (Organizational Agility)

It does not depend, then, merely upon what one sees, but what one sees depends upon how one sees; all observation is not just a receiving, a discovering, but also a bringing forth, and insofar as it is that, how the observer himself is constituted is indeed decisive.

—*Soren Kierkegaard*

Coaching Tip!

Enthusiasm is great, but don't be too quick to pursue change. Master what you're currently doing first.

As mentioned in previous chapters, visible practices, tools, and techniques—the things we can see and measure with relative ease—result from the action of invisible forces that ultimately dictate how effectively an organization can align its delivery of goods or services with perceived value in its markets. To operate at the highest levels of performance, we need to recognize and manage these invisible forces—a challenge with which Scrumban can help.

Heavily influenced by Lean principles, Scrumban is a long-term strategy. It is biased toward basing decisions on a long-term view, even if it means sacrificing short-term gains. From a process standpoint, its chosen path to high performance is to first maximize flow efficiency, then to pragmatically optimize the use of resources. While the need to manage resources is always present, taming flow is a necessary precondition for resource optimization.

Prioritizing and Managing Change

If you want to achieve high performance, then you need to instill a strong drive for learning and the pursuit of "perfection," although perfection can never be achieved. Scrumban supports these efforts through a pragmatic approach of emphasizing practical experiments that probe the unknown.

Because Scrumban easily integrates with other frameworks and models (such as A3 Thinking and Cynefin), we can use it to create disciplined approaches that scale across an entire organization and that validate (or invalidate) current understandings and generate new insights. With each experiment, the learnings form the basis for the next in a continuous cycle.

Scrumban is also a human strategy, with a central assumption being that if people are not performing to the best of their abilities, the fault lies with the system and not with the people. It is structured to maximize learning based on the belief that the best source for suggestions on how to improve a system is the people within it.

Business leaders and managers intent on maximizing performance in their organization should foster ways for people to effectively increase their understanding of their system of work and enable them to improve it. Scrumban provides the framework to make this happen. Like any other framework, it's not something you can simply implement and put on auto-pilot—practitioners still need to think and act.

Managing Maturity

Teams must possess a minimum level of capabilities before they can improve. Basically, they need to understand what is happening and what they should aim for. As they grow and mature, it's equally important (if not more so) to continually assess their capabilities in the following areas:

- Visualize evolutions and trends in their capabilities.
- Guide them on what and where to focus efforts for maximum impact.
- Measure the impact of their efforts.
- Motivate them to evolve and improve even more.

When starting off, some simple rules of thumb are obvious. Teams that need to gain control over their situation usually focus on visualization. Those that have worked without a formalized underlying process usually focus on defining policies. Teams having difficulties managing work in progress (WIP) usually focus on limiting that work.

As teams mature in their capabilities, however, it no longer helps to focus on just one or two principles while neglecting others. As with any endeavor, the cost of addressing "surface" principles is less than the cost of becoming more skilled. Teams need to balance their capabilities across all arenas if these arenas are to influence one another. In this way, Scrum and Scrumban are not very different, although Scrumban is less reliant on maintaining level degrees of capabilities to drive and sustain an enhanced delivery of business value.

Having a mechanism in place to evaluate progress and capabilities is a first step toward understanding how to best nurture the maturation of those capabilities. Let's review a few paradigms that teams can adopt in this regard.

Flight Levels

When introducing Scrumban as a concept, it's easy to think of its principles and practices as limited to the development team environment. I've tried to demonstrate throughout this book, however, that Scrumban's principles and practices can and should extend across many layers of the organization. Introducing these principles to the broader organization requires different approaches and skills.

I find the concept of Kanban Method flight levels developed by Klaus Leopold a helpful guide. He created this paradigm as a way to communicate why the Kanban Method framework is far more effective when used beyond individual team boundaries. The four "flight levels" he defined are equally germane to Scrumban frameworks:

- *Level 1: No input coordination*: Scrumban is applied within an organizational unit such as a team or department, and is often characterized by highly specialized persons working together, such as cross-functional teams working on a small product or subsystem. At this level, work is "thrown over the fence." There's no coordinated replenishment of incoming work. The units often serve numerous stakeholders, and trying to coordinate the prioritization efforts of a large volume of stakeholders on a single visual board is perceived as an impossible task. Another common characteristic of units practicing Scrumban at this level is their processing of a large amount of expedited work, especially as stakeholders' priorities change.

  Scrumban will improve efficiencies within the unit, but the lack of input coordination means there will still be a lot of working on the "wrong things," just more efficiently. Improvements have a negligible impact on the organization's overall service delivery.

  Theoretically, existing Scrum teams should not be operating at this level. The product owner role, product backlog, sprint planning sessions, and related Scrum elements should be providing a substantial amount of input coordination. But you can't judge a book by its cover, which is why it's important to look beyond the surface.

- *Level 2: Coordinated input*: Scrumban is still employed and focused on a unit level, but there's now some coordinated effort to limit the amount of work entering the system's input queue. Scrum's existing framework actually delivers many capabilities associated with this level, though they are likely to vary from unit to unit.

- *Level 3: Value streams*: This may be the first level of significant new capabilities for some existing Scrum teams. The target at this level is not individual teams or departments, but rather parts of a system-wide value stream that requires the coordination of multiple organizational units (e.g., teams, departments). Ideally, organizations functioning at this level will focus on the overall value stream and not just an isolated part.
- *Level 4: Scrumban at scale*: This "portfolio"- or "program"-level implementation involves the coordination of inputs and service deliveries across multiple teams, units, and divisions. Typically, the value streams for individual projects and products are different, and the work item type at this level is usually defined in terms of functionality (e.g., high-level descriptions are often referred to as "sagas"). These work items are broken down into smaller bits (epics, user stories, or requirements) at other levels (level 3, 2, or 1 systems).

  The major benefit of using Scrumban at this level is that it provides a framework for managing the relative importance of complex undertakings that are competing for time and resources. Scrumban's practices force the organization to make more conscious decisions about what to prioritize, and to focus on balancing demand with capabilities. This is also the level where organizations learn what it means to make risk-based decisions about what to finish next instead of working on everything at once (which often results in completing nothing at all).

Leopold also uses the wonderful analogy of a keyboard to illustrate why it's important to avoid thinking of Kanban/Scrumban as a framework that's limited to simply helping teams improve their performance:

> *Imagine your company is a keyboard, and each team within it is in charge of one single key. Your customers want you to write love letters for them. Your "A Team" can optimize for as long and as much as it wants until its ability to strike the "A" key is the best it can be. Your customer's love letter, however, will not be completed any faster as a result of their optimizations. Many of the other teams play an important role in creating the final system output. Apply this analogy to your own organization. The quality and speed at which value is delivered to your end customer will be influenced more by managing the interaction between your individual teams than it will by managing the performance of one or two teams in isolation.*

Whether it's just you and your team implementing Scrumban on your own, or a coordinated effort to adopt its practices across the organization, these flight levels will help communicate why achieving the highest levels of business performance ultimately requires the adoption of similar thinking and capabilities across the entire organization.

Measuring the Depth of Capabilities

In any organization, it's not uncommon for some teams to master improvements on their own while others struggle to cover the basics. Understanding the depth to which teams are practicing core principles and practices helps determine the following elements:

- The degree to which a team has implemented each core principle
- The impact Scrumban practices have made in terms of managing work and producing better business results
- The principles on which teams should focus their current efforts

Christophe Achouiantz and Johan Nordin developed a simple and effective approach for both evaluating and visualizing a unit's "depth of Kanban." They based their work on material produced by David Anderson, Håkan Forss, and Mike Burrows.

Achouiantz and Nordin's approach incorporated a series of "yes/no" questions related to each of Kanban's core practices (visualization, limiting WIP, managing flow, making policies explicit, implementing feedback loops, and engaging in continuous improvement). It also included an assessment component measuring the impact of these practices (Figure 9.1). The results are then plotted on a radar graph with axes corresponding to each practice (Figure 9.2).

Achouiantz first used this tool in an organization that was implementing Kanban for the primary purpose of engaging its IT teams in continuously improving in a sustainable way. To achieve this goal, these teams required a minimum level of capability to begin this journey—specifically, clarity of execution and clarity of purpose. Achouiantz ultimately quantified these capabilities in the context of the framework, and found referencing them was helpful in both communicating concepts and capturing trends over time.

The darkest area at the center of the radar graph reflects Achouiantz's estimate of the "critical mass" a team needs to reach to start improving *on its own*. If an evaluation shows a team was "in the red," it is considered a signal to step in. This approach ensured that the kickstart process Achouiantz and Nordin utilized (which is modeled in Chapter 5) resulted in teams operating within the "Improving Sustainably" area.

From the perspective of managing maturity, understanding the "depth" of core practices is less relevant than using the process as a framework for triggering

Visualize
1. Work (all, according to current policies)
2. Work Types
3. Workflow ("process", way-of-working, value stream)
4. 'Next' & 'Done'
5. Current Team Focus (avatars)
6. Blocks
7. Current Policies (DoD, DoR, capacity allocations, etc.)
8. Ready for Pull ("done" within the workflow/in columns)
9. Metrics (lead-times, local cycle times, SLA targets, etc.)
10. WIP limits
11. Inter-work dependencies (hierarchical, parent-child, etc.)
12. Inter-workflow dependencies
13. Risk dimensions (cost-of-delay, technical risk, market risk)

Make Policies Explicit—All Policies must be CURRENT (known and actually used)
1. Definition of Work Types and Work Item (template)
2. How to pull work (selection from 'Next'/prioritization of WIP)
3. Who and when manages the 'Next' and 'Done' queues
4. Staff allocation / work assignment (individual focus)
5. Definition of Ready for 'Next'
6. Who, when and how to estimate work size
7. Limit size of work items (work breakdown)
8. How to select & prepare work for the 'Next' queue
9. Definition of Done at all steps (seen as a Target Condition)
10. Knowledge spreading/sharing strategy
11. Class-of-Service
12. Capacity allocation

Effects (seeing Evidence of...)
1. Team members are seeing and understanding the Big Picture (team-level vs. local situations)
2. Better 'team spirit" (helping each-others to complete work, respect)
3. Focus on removing blocks
4. Focusing on finishing work rather than starting new work
5. Team is working on the "right" thing ("right" prioritization)
6. Limiting work to team's capacity (limited stress, optimal leadtimes)
7. Team has motivation to drive improvements
8. Local process evolution (visualization, workflow, policies, WIP limits)
9. Increase depth of Kanban implementation
10. Process evolution was model-driven
11. Process or management policy evolution as a result of mentormentee
12. Inter-workflow or management policy evolution due to operations review

Depth of Kanban Implementation

Team: Date:

Limit Work in Progress
1. No WIP limit, but commitment to finishing work over starting new (eventually reaching a WIP level that "feels OK" for the team)
2. Some explicit WIP limits, at lower level than workflow (a.k.a Proto-Kanban): personal Kanban, WIP limit per person, WIP limits for some columns or swim-lanes, workflow with infinite limits on "done" queues, etc.
3. Explicit WIP limit at workflow level - Single workflow full pull
4. Multiple interdependent workflows with pull system

Implement Feedback Loops
1. Daily Team standups
2. Key stakeholders (mngt, customers, other groups) are regularly updated on the current situation
3. Managers go and see (walk the 'gemba') regularly
4. Regular discussions with upstream and downstream partners
5. Regular presentations and discussions about Financial performance
6. Regular presentations and discussions about Quality KPI (defect rate, customer satisfaction, etc.)
7. "Regularly" means once per month or more often

Manage Flow
1. Daily planning meetings (as "daily" as agreed by policies)
2. Blocks out of team control are escalated for resolution
3. Next is re-prioritized continuously (no commitment in Next)-Deferred Pull decisions (dynamic prioritization)
4. CFDs (updated at least once a week)
5. Control Charts (updated at least once a week)
6. Size of ongoing work items is limited (large work is broken down)
7. Flexible staff allocation (swarming)
8. Cadence is established (planning, delivering, retrospective)
9. Flow metrics (number of days blocked, lead-time efficiency)
10. SLA expectations and forecasts (lead-time targets)
11. Capacity Allocations

Improve
1. The group knows why it exists and its criteria for success
2. Regular Retrospectives/Kaizen events
3. The team knows its current condition (may require metrics)
4. True North exists, is communicated and shared by the team
5. The team knows the current target condition (the challenge)
6. There is a validation criteria (test) for the current target condition to know when the target condition is reached
7. The team knows what obstacles are preventing them from reaching the target condition
8. The team knows what obstacle is being currently addressed
9. The team knows what is the next step in resolving the current obstacle (PDCA)
10. The team go and see what they have learned from taking that step

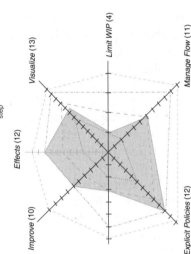

FIGURE 9.1   Simple yes/no questions assess a team's capabilities in six areas of critical practices.

Source: Christophe Achouiantz.

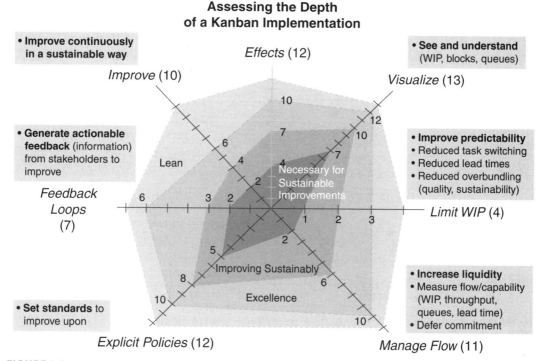

FIGURE 9.2   Field experience helped the creators of this radar graph define ranges of capabilities to identify when teams were operating at key levels of performance.

Source: Christophe Achouiantz.

discussions. For example, the simple act of going through the assessment process will catalyze discussions on how to improve the way a team works. Similarly, visualizing capabilities will help teams that were motivated to improve in one area recognize their need to balance out their efforts across others (Figure 9.3).

It takes only a cursory glance at the chart in Figure 9.3 to appreciate that this team is exhibiting highly evolved practices across most of Kanban's core principles. The team shows a borderline ability to limit WIP, however.

Ultimately, each team should decide whether it makes sense to concentrate on some principles over others. Team members need to remember that the cost of going "deeper" is likely to be much greater than the cost of achieving earlier degrees of capability. They also need to account for the fact these principles influence one another, providing the greatest return on effort when improvement efforts are directed toward proportionate versus linear development.

Some Caveats

Assessment frameworks such as Achouiantz and Nordin's model will produce useless or confusing results if used as a basis for comparison or across multiple

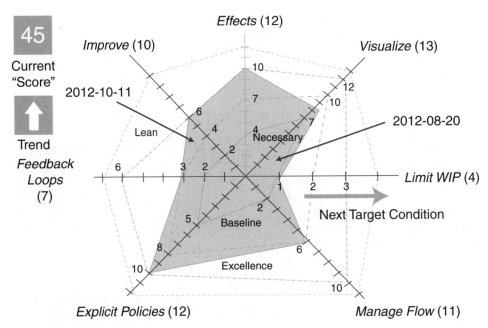

FIGURE 9.3 Plotting a team's capabilities on the radar chart helps it (and its coaches) prioritize areas ripe for improvement.

Source: Christophe Achouiantz.

teams—especially if you attempt to apply the model "as is" in an environment other than the one for which it was designed. Instead, the framework should be used only to gain a clearer perspective of a team's evolution over time. It helps answer questions like "Did the team get better?" and "Why or why not?"

In this way, Achouiantz and Nordin's framework shares characteristics with story points and team velocity; velocity is relative to each team, and most relevant to identifying patterns over time. The most appropriate use of a "depth of practices" evaluation is to trigger team-level discussions related to different aspects of Scrumban and the ways in which they can help the team improve its capabilities.

Another Approach

Mike Burrows has evolved the Kanban depth assessment tool further, focusing on using the Kanban Method's values, rather than core principles and practices, as a barometer. His tool measures depth on a four-point scale applied to evaluation-related questions associated with core values (Figure 9.4).

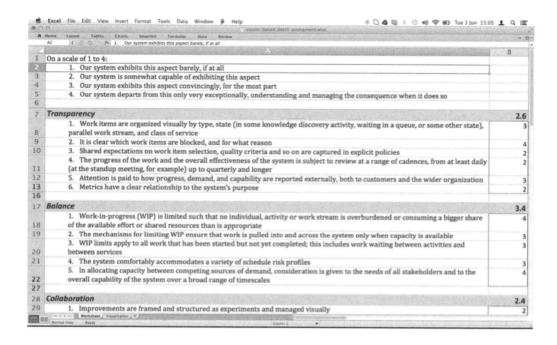

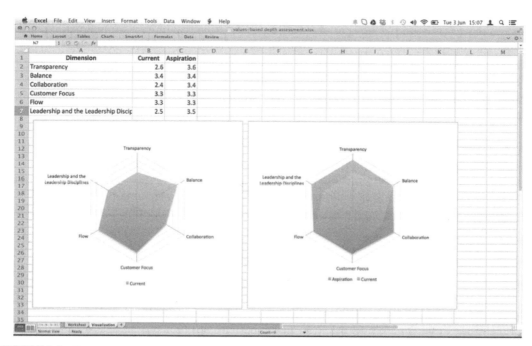

FIGURE 9.4   This team assessment tool focuses on evaluating how well a team is practicing core values versus practices.

Source: Mike Burrows (© David J. Anderson & Associates. All rights reserved. Used with permission.)

This approach does seem to represent an improvement over assessing a simple checklist of practices. Just as thought leaders in the Kanban community will continue to build on this work, so Scrumban practitioners can use these models to construct and refine the approaches that work best for them.[1]

Evolving Your Core Capabilities

Throughout this book, I've identified various approaches that teams and organizations can experiment with to continuously improve their practices. The Scrum master can play an instrumental role in providing suggestions and guidance on how teams might experiment—albeit while remembering that Scrum masters are guides and need to become managers of work rather than managers of people.

With this point in mind, let's return to some of the core mechanics that teams can address as their understanding of Scrumban matures. We'll start with managing flow, as this represents an overarching, long-term priority.

Manage Flow

Teams are most efficient, and typically have greatest control over their work, when they reach a state of laminar (or smooth) flow. Laminar flow is desirable because it makes systems more predictable.

Scrum seeks to optimize flow by emphasizing the creation of true, cross-functional teams. Not all organizations are prepared to embrace this outcome, however. Scrumban lets us evolve more resilient capabilities that better absorb variety when cross-functional capabilities aren't present (though it won't magically eliminate the tension with resource optimization—more on that in a moment). Some straightforward approaches include the following techniques:

- Recognizing different kinds of work (for better management of variety)
- Making the mix of work very visible—including the different kinds of risk associated with it (better prioritization)
- Designing systems so they allow work to be pulled in a way that maintains predictability across each kind of work (allows us to identify and resolve bottlenecks)
- Capturing this design in policies (prioritization rules, limits, time buffers, and other constraints—hidden policies interfere with managing flow!)

Regardless of how proficient a team becomes in basic Scrum practices, the Scrumban framework allows the members to explore a variety of options to pursue more laminar flows. These professionals may start with kanban system basics and

---

1. For further exploration of this tool, visit http://tiny.cc/Rebooted and Chapter 23 in Mike's book *Kanban from the Inside* (Michael Burrows, Blue Hole Press, 2014).

ultimately move on to managing broader options and characteristics, such as the adoption of specific engineering practices, or expanding team skill sets.

To this end, kanban systems that manage a variety of work item types, manage work through several classes of service, incorporate frequent system replenishment (sprint backlog/ready queue), and achieve frequent delivery will naturally exhibit high flow efficiency. Consequently, teams and organizations should seek to acquire and improve these characteristics over time.

A major complicating factor when optimizing flow efficiency is the natural business tension to want it all—that is, to seek resource optimization in parallel with flow efficiency. This tension comes down to business strategy, and the underlying principles on which Scrumban is based can help inform this debate. In this context, it's important to emphasize that although we ultimately want to optimize both, Scrumban prioritizes flow efficiency first, over resource optimization. Thus the business should be encouraged to support this prioritization as a means of achieving its desired end state.

One reason it's difficult to simultaneously achieve high flow efficiency and high resource efficiency is the need to contend with the natural variations in knowledge work (e.g., variations in arrival time, size, and complexity of the work). Depending on the context of your environment, some of this variation can be managed without losing the ability to be innovative and responsive to the market. You can do this by implementing the following tactics:

- Reducing batch sizes
- Reducing hand-offs
- Using a mixed-feature portfolio that includes work items with different priorities and sizes
- Reducing iteration length or eliminating iterations altogether
- Avoiding the temptation to encompass work within specific projects (projects are the equivalent of morning and evening rush-hour traffic jams in our regular work processes)
- Avoiding the use of mechanisms and processes that support load balancing, swarming, or the creation of ad hoc processes (so it becomes easier to find the natural bottlenecks or other problems and address them)

Another way for Agile teams to improve flow efficiency is to merge their teams into bigger departments, where members all work within a single workflow of services with multiple sources of demand, across multiple work item types, and a variety of risks are processed using different classes of services and without batch transfers (time-boxed iterations). The Japanese call this concept *heijunka*.

Practice Tip

Warning Heijunka may not be a viable option for many Scrum environments. When practicing heijunka, teams and organizations should ensure they're increasing flow efficiency between the points of customer commitment and actual delivery versus artificially increasing it by measuring flow only inside their sprints.

The purpose of a heijunka system is to force an appropriate mix of products into the backlog. This outcome is desirable because a single work item type of flow can't deliver our end product instantaneously to the customer (and some degree of push will always be required). Being prepared to do the difficult things, such as mixing work item types within a single system, enables us to learn to do them smoothly. Heijunka systems make it obvious how the tension between flow efficiency and resource optimization renders the process of achieving laminar flow particularly challenging.

Limit WIP

Limiting WIP is not easy. Even with efforts to visualize work, much can remain invisible—we're simply blind to it until it appears. One commonly neglected mechanism for limiting WIP is making hidden WIP visible. But how do we find hidden WIP?

The answer is actually quite obvious: Always assume it's there, and then look for it lurking in the "shadows." Here are three common places to find hidden WIP:

- *Large-size work items*: If your user stories are too big, there's a good chance hidden WIP is lurking inside them. This hidden work manifests itself as dark matter (the natural expansion of work as our understanding improves) or rework (defects resulting from poor understanding of work). User stories may get bogged down because one or more hidden tasks is hard to complete.
- *Too much focus on the team over the individual*: Limiting team WIP is one of the first evolutions a team achieves when adopting Kanban/Scrumban practices. Unfortunately, this often results in a failure to consider the impact of individual WIP on the overall flow. For example, a team might be "successfully" working within a WIP limit of five or six items even though one or two people are involved in every story. While people may complete the work, overloading their individual capacities defeats the very purpose of limiting WIP. Pay attention to the realities of the board!
- *Incomplete inventories*: We all rationalize why certain work items don't belong on the board. One common example is development teams omitting multiple support tasks from their boards because they aren't considered "real work." Similarly, teams with a variety of administrative tasks don't visualize them because they aren't "real work." All work is real. Reflect it on your board.

We can't manage all our work if we don't recognize it. As teams gain a better understanding of Scrumban principles, addressing hidden WIP usually represents "low-hanging fruit" teams can identify and address without much difficulty.

Manage Bottlenecks and Improve Flow

As teams begin using Scrumban to visualize and manage flow, we emphasize the importance of better understanding our systems. Our initial goal should always be to ensure they're stable, because attempting to improve a system in flux is counterproductive.

Workflow visualizations create physical evidence of bottlenecks in the form of backups (an accumulation of work to be done) and starvation (an absence of work for downstream processes). Establishing WIP limits tends to resolve backups (at least to the point of making them less visible). Starvation is easy to see regardless of whether WIP limits are in place.

It's important to understand the clear distinction between a "bottleneck" and a "constraint" in this context. A bottleneck is a resource subjected to more demand than it can satisfy. A system can have many bottlenecks.

A constraint, by comparison, is the bottleneck *with the least capacity in the entire system*. This bottleneck doesn't become the "constraint" until we decide to recognize and manage it. For this, we can apply the five focusing steps from Goldratt's theory of constraints:

1. *Identify the constraint*: Strengthening anything except the weakest link in a chain is a waste of time, so identifying these points is critical.
2. *Exploit the constraint*: The output of the constraint dictates the output of the entire system. Maximizing the output of your constraint is often the key to improving overall output, but consideration must be given to other factors when people represent the constraint (as is usually the case in knowledge work like software development).
3. *Subordinate everything else to the constraint*: The very nature of a constraint means everything else in the system is capable of producing more. Allowing other processes to produce to their capacity creates large inventories of backed-up work to be processed, longer lead times, and frequent expediting of tasks. It's equally important to ensure the constraint is never starved for work.
4. *Elevate the constraint*: Only after you've maximized the capacity of the existing system should you consider expanding it by adding more resources, such as additional developers. In most contexts, it's possible to achieve significant gains through appropriate management methods. Investing in more resources earlier than you need them unnecessarily increases risk.
5. *Prevent inertia*: Once you improve or elevate a constraint, it may no longer be the weakest link in your system. Continuously monitoring and managing your system is critical to achieving sustained performance.

As indicated previously, one drawback of applying the theory of constraints in a knowledge work setting lies in its objective of eliminating all waste. This represents a problem for two reasons.

First, many of the "non-value-adding" steps that this theory seeks to eliminate are performed by humans, not machines. With humans come human dynamics—people have emotional attachments to their work. Sometimes that relationship arises because certain practices are central to their professional identity; at other times, social status is the issue at hand. Consequently, efforts to eliminate "waste" often meet with emotional resistance in a form that can be very difficult to detect.

This is where Scrumban's system of visualizations, metrics, feedback mechanisms, and katas ultimately provides the motivation for necessary change as sources of delay are reduced and eliminated. Although the professional identities of the people involved will still be affected, the changes implemented will become lasting and sustainable because they are ultimately self-motivated and not imposed by outside forces.

Second, Goldratt's theory of constraints is great for optimizing workflow, but is less useful in regard to optimizing the work process itself. Let's assume we have a system where every 4 to 8 hours one analyst is able to break down a user story into discrete tasks necessary to complete development. Let's further assume this system has four developers who work on those tasks, and each developer is able to complete all of the tasks necessary to complete development within 12 to 16 hours. The constraint in this system lies with the analyst, as the developers can complete more work than the analyst can provide.

Now consider a scenario where that original constraint is elevated. Enough analysts are added to produce a sufficient amount of new work to keep the developers working to capacity. Such a system may no longer have an identifiable constraint from a workflow perspective. From an individual user story/work item perspective, however, the elevation of the analyst constraint has had no impact. It still takes the same amount of time for a user story/work item to pass through both stages: 4 to 8 hours for analysis and 12 to 16 hours for development.

If it is relevant to reduce the amount of time a work item spends in process, then it's even more relevant to focus on ways to improve the work process itself. In the example presented here, the process constraint is based on the amount of time a work item must spend in process in each phase.

Avoid Patterns of Unsafe Change

In writing about the Kanban Method's sustainability agenda, Mike Burrows has identified three troubling attitudes demonstrated by many managers and their organizations in regard to change. These patterns are not specifically addressed in most Scrum contexts:

- *Bravado*: A tendency to overreach, initiating change with little understanding or attention to its implementation, and putting the integrity of the organization and the well-being of its people at risk. This kind of change is often "too fast," and almost certainly fails to take into account any consideration of capabilities for managing change or whether it will lead to sustainable improvements.

- *Complacency*: The situation in which management inaction becomes a major cause of organizational failure. This pattern is typically labeled "too slow" when viewed in the context of addressing what's needed.
- *Tampering*: A concept mentioned before, which draws on the work of W. Edwards Deming. It relates to the propensity of managers to correct normal variations and interfere with an existing process. This pattern of change can be labeled "too random."

The Kanban Method's principle of respecting current roles and processes is what makes it an evolutionary change method, and an acknowledgment of the need to take change seriously. For this reason, it is recommended that Kanban be introduced with two simple perspectives designed to avoid the patterns of unsafe change described by Burrows:

- Acknowledging that what the organization currently does both serves and frustrates the customer
- Acknowledging that how the organization currently works both succeeds and fails to work for those inside the system

When these realities and their potential root causes are exposed in kanban systems, they become the subject of feedback loops and changes will start to happen. Each change—regardless of its success—is informative and improves shared understandings. The resulting learnings foster yet more opportunities for change and make it far more likely that successful change will ultimately be implemented safely and sustainably.

Create a Disciplined Approach to Improvement

No matter the frameworks involved, creating sustainable Lean and Agile practices across an organization usually requires a substantial degree of "cultural" change. Fail here and you will ultimately trap yourself in a never-ending cycle of poor performance.

In the context of this topic, culture is embedded in statements such as "This is how we do it here." A new process or change plan won't influence the existing culture. Cultural change starts with the change process itself, which in turn is where Scrumban can play an important role.

One approach for aiding the change process involves creating a "change team" that includes diverse members from across the organization. Such an approach places responsibility for change on a group of people, and forces everyone to come together for a single purpose while bringing their differing views and perspectives to the process.

Diversity of the team in terms of both function and hierarchy is critical, as the contrasts between functions and hierarchies typically yield far superior joint decision making than a single department—even a project management office (PMO)—can achieve on its own. The length of time the team will serve is also critical. These efforts have a way of becoming institutionalized, which is generally counterproductive to true Agility (Agile teams should be motivated to continuously improve through self-direction and collaboration).

Should you go this route, however, the first goal for any "change team" should be to improve how the organization makes improvements. The team members should be charged with improving the way changes are made to how work is performed. Some ideal frameworks for use when pursuing such changes are existing retrospectives (something Scrum teams are already familiar with) and evangelizing disciplines like A3 Thinking.

Retrospectives answer some very important questions:

- What went well last time?
- What didn't go well last time?
- What should we seek to improve this time? (A prioritization scheme)

A discipline like A3 creates an environment of collaboration and keeps everyone interested and engaged in the outcome as well as the process.

Katas and the Importance of Habit

Aristotle said, "We are what we repeatedly do. Excellence, then, is not an act, but a habit." The power of habits is critical to sustained success.

The concept of a kata (a Japanese word describing detailed patterns of movement) was introduced in Chapter 4, where we considered how organizations like Toyota have adopted A3 Thinking as a disciplined approach to problem solving. A kata is something that Toyota's employees repeatedly practice. Katas create the equivalent of "muscle memory" within the organization—a rapid and intuitive response for taking action without having to resort to a slower, more consciously logical process. Ultimately, a kata represents a synthesis of thought and behavior in skillful action.

Scrumban calls for us to improve the way we work through collaboration and scientific experimentation. Improvements represent nothing more than a series of experiments. Though it comes from a manufacturing context, the framework of the Toyota kata is an experimentation framework that we can easily adapt to software development.

- First we plan:
    - Understand the direction in which we want to go (our vision or ultimate objective)
    - Understand the current condition (where we're at)
    - Set a challenge (a target condition—something to achieve that lies between our current condition and our vision)

- Then we execute:
  - Take action
  - Measure results
  - Evaluate and learn

In the context of your kata, your vision should be process focused and not necessarily something that can actually be achieved. For example, any of the following would be a perfectly valid vision for a software development organization:

- Zero defects in production
- Satisfy 99% of customer demands
- Deliver on demand the highest-value needs first

Scrumban's visualization practices make it easier for teams and organizations to identify appropriate visions for their katas. Similarly, Scrumban's bias toward scientific measurements of both process (cycle time, WIP, queue size, takt time/iteration length) and outcomes (lead time, throughput) feed us the right kind of data—data that informs us about current conditions. Scrum alone may ultimately expose problems, but it is more limited in providing data and explicit techniques that aid in defining those problems in a scientific way.

A good kata will require you to set a target condition for experiments that is beyond your current knowledge—ideally, this target will be achievable, but not so obvious that it doesn't stretch you in any fashion (you want to learn from the actions you undertake). Here are some examples of meaningful target conditions in the context of a software development environment:

- Reducing lead time from 45 days to 30 days
- Reducing average WIP from 20 stories to 15 stories
- Deploying to production on a fixed release date schedule every 3 weeks

At this point, you should be able to appreciate how Scrumban provides Scrum teams with a robust framework to experiment with changes in the work process, and to visualize and measure the impact of those changes in a way that Scrum alone doesn't provide for.

One final thought: You should embed a "coaching kata" within your improvement kata—a framework for helping the team master the process of learning. Many aspects of a "coaching kata" are already evident within a disciplined process like A3 Thinking; others may require more reflection.

Further Evolving the Understanding and Management of Risk

Most process experts and business managers have a tendency to overemphasize factors that expand system capabilities (Figure 9.5). This is probably because we tend

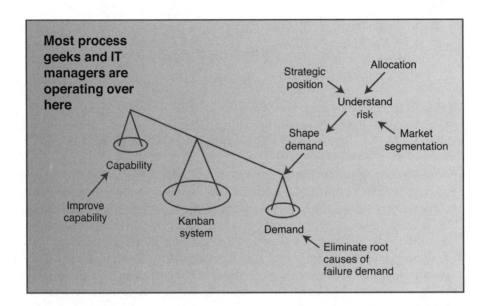

FIGURE 9.5   While the Scrumban framework can help teams and organizations improve their capacity to deliver work, it is equally well positioned to help them influence incoming work demands.

to see capacity as the only side of the demand–capacity equation over which we have any control. The reality, however, is that risk management enables us to shape the demands placed upon our system. Specifically, Scrumban provides supportive data and encourages collaborative conversations with stakeholders that create options giving us more control over the demand side of the equation.

More robust approaches to managing risk start with the understanding that most uncertainties arise from incomplete knowledge. These uncertainties can stem from a variety of sources related to three aspects of the programs we manage (including our own biases in attempting to understand and manage them):

- The activities of the project or program
- Our knowledge of the planned and actual behaviors of the project or program
- Our perception of the project or program based on data and information we receive about its behaviors

Risk-Handling Strategies

As we seek to improve our understanding and management of risk, it's useful to recognize that the risk management strategies we develop determine how we manage risk. These strategies usually encompass the following elements:

- *Assumption*: Assuming the consequences of risk (understanding the potential impacts and ensuring resources are available to deal with them)
- *Avoidance*: Changing the situation that creates the risk so as to avoid it altogether
- *Mitigation*: Proactively planning to reduce the risk
- *Transfer*: Shifting consequences of the risk to another party (or recovering from another party shifting the consequences to us)

Examples of Maturing Practices

Here's a brief sampling of methods that maturing systems can explore to create balanced systems by focusing on the "other" side of the equation.

Shaping Demand

The ability to identify the risk profiles of different work types is empowering, because it opens up the possibility of establishing policies and expectations around the delivery of work, the items that may need to be grouped together, the implications of failing to deliver on time, and the stakeholders who should most appropriately bear that risk. The development of classes of service, for example, is a tremendous tool. Less mature Scrumban implementations inform us about overall performance, but this may not be sufficient to overcome the psychological barriers associated with risk.

Consider a scenario where your team has developed lead time metrics across all work types. This set of tools has put you in a position to guarantee delivery of 85% of your items within a specific time frame (Figure 9.6).

Now, if you categorized work items based on different risk classifications, you could develop more granularized metrics across these classes. As Figure 9.7 indicates, the probable delivery dates for different types of work are actually quite diverse. The lead time data relating to each class of service reflects different distributions, and provides "ammunition" for negotiating reasonable delivery expectations based on the nature of the work at issue.

Lead Time Distribution

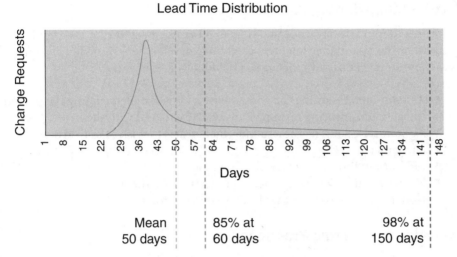

Mean	85% at	98% at
50 days	60 days	150 days

FIGURE 9.6   Measuring the lead time of all work types provides a coarse understanding of probable delivery time.

	Engineering Ready ②	Development		Testing		Deployment Ready ∞	Done
		Ongoing ③	Done	Verification ③	Acceptance		
Expedite ①				▨			
Fixed Date ②		▨		▨			
Standard ③	▨			▨			
Intangible ①			▨				

FIGURE 9.7   With work types broken out, it's easy to measure and visualize their diverse lead time distributions.

Improving Subjective Risk Assessment Capabilities

We should always be wary of rationalized effectiveness—a major pitfall of risk management. Most efforts dealing with risk management are subjective, and we tend to rationalize their effectiveness rather than rely upon more objective measurements as mentioned in Chapter 8. So what should we look for?

First, test for a placebo effect. Absent independent, objective measures of risk management, perceptions of success may merely reflect stakeholders "feeling" better about a situation simply because something has been "addressed." Indicators of false success can include the following:

- Claims of effectiveness because an approach is "structured." There are lots of structured methods that don't work. (Astrology, for example, is structured.)
- Claims of a "change in culture." "Culture" changes may be beneficial, but they don't necessarily correlate with improved risk management.
- Claims of reliance upon proven scientific or mathematical models. Can the people employing them demonstrate that those models have been appropriately applied? The mere existence of "proven" models is meaningless.
- Claims of "consensus building." Consensus is not the goal; better analysis and management of risks is the goal. Efforts that simply build consensus to go down a disastrous path simply ensure that you'll travel that wrong path faster.
- Claims that any efforts are better than no efforts. That may not be true; uninformed or misinformed efforts are just as likely to cause harm as benefit.

Second, improve subjective risk assessments through better calibration of both their initial generation (training and techniques that improve accuracy) and ultimate evaluation.

Consider some subjective risk assessments we might be called upon to make in a work context (such as an IT security specialist saying there is a 90% probability that no hacking attempt will be made in the current year). Studies have identified a substantial difference in accuracy between people trained on calibration techniques and untrained people. Untrained individuals claiming a 90% confidence level in their assessments are actually correct between 52% and 78% of the time. Individuals trained in risk assessment who make the same level of confidence claims are correct between 85% and 95% of the time.

One approach to help individuals become more calibrated in their subjective risk assessments is to provide better understanding of scoring methods (such as point estimations in Scrum). We tend to view scoring methods as ordinal scales without considering differences in magnitude. Consider a five-point scale. Eating four meals from a one-star restaurant will not produce the same satisfaction as eating one meal from a four-star restaurant. If we don't consider this type of difference as we apply scaled scoring systems, the quality of our subjective risk assessments will remain poor.

It's also important to help individuals recognize that past performance can cause us to artificially elevate our confidence levels when predicting risks. Sometimes this inflation occurs because we underestimate what we've learned from past experiences (convincing ourselves we saw something coming in hindsight). Sometimes it happens because we treat near misses and successes as similar outcomes. Finally, sometimes it reflects that we have a successful track record.

For example, does an IT security manager with a history of presiding over a completely virus-free, hacker-free environment for five years longer than his or her peers necessarily bring better capabilities to the table? Surprisingly, the answer is "no." Recent statistical analyses have shown that performance outliers may not reflect anything other than sheer luck. For the person involved, however, the experience is more likely to create a false sense of confidence with regard to future assessments.

Expanding Your Risk Management Horizons

In the introduction to risk management in Chapter 6, we identified three essential areas where it resides: market based, environmental, and work based. Chapter 6 also provided some typical risk profiles associated with work items, demonstrating how the demarcation of different classes of service often represents a particularly effective mechanism for managing them.

As their understanding of risk concepts matures, teams and organizations can begin to engage in broader and more sophisticated degrees of risk identification and management. As always, this effort should be driven by context. The degree to which an organization engages in risk management, however, is not necessarily correlated with its "maturity." "Mature" teams and organizations recognize what's appropriate for their particular needs and act accordingly.

With this caveat in mind, let's examine some additional risk areas that intersect with information technology functions. First, however, it may be helpful to think about risk as falling within one of two broad categories—internal or external. External risks can be market based (economic, regulatory/compliance), environmental, and even work based (vendor/supplier). Internal risks tend to fall within either the environmental (hiring practices/policies) or work-based (engineering practices/technical debt) arenas.

Your People

People working together effectively enable organizations to achieve their goals. An organization's first opportunity for managing risk, therefore, lies in its hiring practices.

A substantial cost is associated with every candidate search; likewise, a substantial cost is associated with the natural "learning curve" of new employees. Learning to hire for your specific culture is one of the most effective ways to control the risks linked to a poor hire, and striking the right balance between current and anticipated responsibilities is equal parts science and art.

Consider the role of Scrum master. I've previously discussed the differences in responsibilities between traditional project managers and Scrum masters. In a maturing system where Scrumban is employed, it may be relevant to ensure new candidates are capable of coaching or participating in some of the more sophisticated forecasting and modeling techniques, especially if your organization is moving in these directions.

For example, teams that are new to Agile methodologies quickly realize that being "Agile" in the real world is never as easy as it appears in theory. Hiring individuals with experience in similar environments, however, can accelerate the maturing of your teams. These hires can also address the flip side of this scenario, when mature Agile teams become frustrated that new team members don't "get" Agility.

Unfortunately, in many larger organizations IT managers rely too heavily on human resources professionals to drive the candidate sourcing and screening process. We've touched upon the dampening influences that traditional approaches in finance and legal functions can have when they aren't structured with a systems perspective. Would you expect the human resources function to be any different?

Roles are traditionally defined in terms of technologies, skill sets, and responsibilities. If your teams are maturing under Scrumban, your understanding of the key factors that influence success across your systems is far more important to defining the skills and characteristics needed for success.

In her book *Hiring Geeks That Fit*,[2] Johanna Rothman brings considerable insight and perspective to the hiring process, describing how organizations can begin actively managing risk before team members are hired, and detailing opportunities to minimize potential issues once they begin working. Ultimately, paying attention to the nature and quality of your system, and nurturing relationships with the people in them, is critical to hiring and retaining those individuals best suited to contributing to your organization's success.

A final thought on the hiring process: Far too often, candidates are screened and interviewed using a less than illuminating question-and-answer format. Behavioral interview techniques give you an opportunity to expose a great deal about how a person is likely to respond to situations common to your environment. Incorporating an "audition" element into your hiring practices can be similarly illuminating. For example, asking candidates to review and comment on another engineer's code (or asking candidates to bring in some of their own code for review by other engineers) can provide tremendous insight as to how those individuals might fit into an Agile environment (where code reviews should be ongoing).

Policies and Practices

A management model that conveys mistrust and controls against unwanted behavior is unlikely to achieve performance goals. That said, it's important to underscore the

---

2. Johanna Rothman, *Hiring Geeks That Fit* (Leanpub, 2013).

notion that governance frameworks, oversight, and controls are not inherently bad. What matters is their implementation.

Perhaps you've noticed a common theme here: Traditional management approaches across business functions often prevent organizations from achieving their objectives. Addressing these areas falls under what Jez Humble calls "adaptive risk management." Humble has highlighted several ways in which traditional approaches can impede the adoption of sustainable high performance specifically within IT (Table 9.1).

TABLE 9.1   Risk Management Compared

Traditional Risk Management "Theater"	Adaptive Risk Management
Rule based and static: New rules need to be created when new technologies are encountered.	*Principle-based and dynamic*: Can be applied to new situations not contemplated when the rules were first written.
Use controls to prevent accidents and bad behavior: Can unintentionally create new risks, such as over-reliance on emergency change processes because standard process is too slow.	*Use transparency to avoid accidents and bad behavior*: When it's easy to see what everyone else is doing, people are more careful.
Assumes humans are the problem: Operates on theory that if humans follow the system, nothing bad will happen. Ignores the reality that process specifications always require interpretation and adaptation.	*Assumes systems drift toward failure*: Systems and environments are constantly changing. Humans solve problems and must be relied on to make judgment calls.
Mandatory code reviews: Often enforced by check-in gates where approval is needed to merge code. This can be inefficient and delays feedback on nontrivial regressions.	*Continuous code reviews*: Colleagues review each other's code before check-ins, technical leads review all check-ins made by their team, and code review tools allow people to comment on each other's work once it is in the trunk.
Manual testing: Often made a precondition for integration. As with mandatory code reviews, this delays feedback on the systemic effect of code changes.	*Automated unit and acceptance testing*: These rapidly inform engineers whether they have introduced a known regression into the trunk. Can be run on workstations before a commit.
Comprehensive documentation: Used in the event of a failure to discover the human error that is the root cause.	*Deployment pipelines*: Provide complete traceability of changes from check-in to release and detect risky changes automatically.
Segregation of duties: Act as barriers to knowledge sharing, feedback, and collaboration. Reduce the kind of situational awareness that is essential to an effective response in the event of an incident.	*Situational awareness*: Created through tools that make it easy to monitor, analyze, and correlate relevant data (like much of the Scrumban framework!)

Consciously moving your organization toward adaptive risk management principles enhances the likelihood it will realize sustained benefits from practices like test-driven development (TDD), acceptance test-driven development (ATDD), and more. Similarly, recognizing your organizational culture is not yet in a position to support and sustain such practices can save you time and heartache that would otherwise result from attempting to adopt potentially positive practices too early.

Scaling beyond IT

Especially For:
Managers & Executives

Trying to familiarize yourself with all the ways you can integrate Scrumban with other frameworks can be like trying to drink from a firehose: The information can come so quickly and in such a large volume that it's impossible to understand it all in one pass. As teams and organizations increase their understanding of Scrumban, however, they gain the ability to drink more and more from that firehose. This chapter on "maturing" was written in recognition of this reality.

To this end, this section addresses additional concepts that become more relevant as teams and organizations reach later stages of their journey. This is by no means an exhaustive list; it simply represents some additional frameworks I've used in various contexts.

Beyond Budgeting (Agile Budgeting)

Many organizations struggle with taking Agile beyond IT because most Agile frameworks don't provide any guidance regarding governance structures. This leads to the false assumption that Agile approaches are sustainable under existing practices. In reality, many practices directly conflict with the values and principles that create Agility, and ultimately stifle the organization's capabilities.

Beyond Budgeting is a framework that arose from the world of corporate finance and represents a set of specific leadership and governance principles based on the same Lean, Agile, and systems thinking foundation as Scrumban. Because Scrumban is naturally structured to integrate management models, the two frameworks are particularly complementary. Beyond Budgeting represents an excellent source of the organizational guidance needed to sustain an environment where Lean and Agile principles can thrive.

Scrumban has its roots in IT (knowledge work). Though it can be applied across many different contexts, its origins make it particularly rich in mechanisms that improve our understanding and management of processes like software development. In other words, its framework is oriented toward integrating IT/knowledge work processes within the holistic system represented by the business organizations of which we are a part.

The Beyond Budgeting framework is similarly oriented toward its roots (finance and executive management). Budgeting and other financial mechanisms represent components of traditional command-and-control structures that interfere with Agile methodologies. The Beyond Budgeting framework recognizes this fact and provides the same kind of understanding and enabling mechanisms for management that Scrumban delivers to development teams.

Interestingly, just as Scrumban has evolved concepts of Lean thinking to better manage the inherent variability of knowledge work, so Beyond Budgeting has adopted a similar approach with regard to organizational governance:

> *The more complex the environment, and the "tighter" the targets, the more flexibility the control system must have: "only variety can absorb variety." Failure to provide "requisite variety" will result in instability (boom and bust) and ultimately system failure.*

The Beyond Budgeting Institute's assessment of why a contrasting governance model is needed to support adaptive Agile environments is also illuminating (Table 9.2).

When mid-size and larger organizations seek to become "Agile," a lot of effort is devoted to figuring out how to constrain new practices so they fit within existing management policies and structures. Beyond Budgeting takes a different tack. It advocates changing traditional management practices so the organization can realize the full benefits of the new practices. Because its origins are in finance, its persuasive authority may resonate more with executive management than a framework whose roots are in IT.

One of the most stubborn myths in traditional management is that detailed cost budgets combined with strict oversight are the only way to

- Effectively forecast and manage expenses
- Prioritize efforts
- Allocate resources

The fear of the consequences associated with eliminating budgeting inevitably becomes an impediment to approaches that support greater Agility.

Rather than attacking policies that require detailed cost budgets and tight controls, it can be more effective to initiate discussions about deficiencies in our traditional approaches, and to shift the debate toward a more relevant need—how to distinguish between "good" and "bad" costs (and more effectively manage each). Let's first consider the deficiencies. Traditional cost budgeting fails because the work to which they're related has the following characteristics:

TABLE 9.2   A Summary of Contrasting Models between Traditional Organizations and Organizations That Operate as Adaptive Systems

	Traditional	Adaptive
Organizational model	▪ Organization is viewed as a collection of replaceable parts (and the parts determine the performance of the whole). ▪ Organization is seen as having clear and predictable "cause and effect" relationships.	▪ Organization is viewed holistically, and it's recognized the interaction of the parts throughout the entire system determines performance. ▪ Organization is seen as a web of relationships that are unpredictable.
Management model	▪ Goal is to maximize shareholder value. ▪ Goal is on the "ends" (targets), and the means are fixed to meet the ends. ▪ Leadership believes central planning, coordination, and control are necessary to manage and achieve desired outcomes. ▪ Economies of scale drive cost management. ▪ Change is reactive and project driven.	▪ Goal is to adapt and endure over a long period of time. ▪ Focus is on the "means" (processes and people), and it's understood the ends will take care of themselves. ▪ Leadership focuses on setting direction; the organization is self-organizing and self-regulating. ▪ Economies of flow drive cost management. ▪ Change is integrative, continuous, and adaptive.

- Volatile
- Uncertain
- Complex
- Ambiguous

Do these characteristics sound familiar? They should, because they are the same challenges Scrumban helps us better manage through its framework.

Now consider the mechanisms Scrumban relies on to help us manage these challenges. We seek to visualize how we work and what we're working on. We measure our work scientifically and respond dynamically. We seek to defer decisions until the last possible moment, by localizing and optimizing our decision making with good processes and good information.

With Scrumban in place, the organization actually has a framework for addressing the financial and managerial deficiencies associated with traditional cost budgeting. It simply needs to evolve its traditional processes in the same way IT evolves its work processes to begin realizing these benefits.

This implies shifting the focus to what's more relevant. Managing the organization through traditional financial mechanisms like cost budgeting, however, imposes financial blinders on the organization. We end up with a narrow focus on the costs of a process without considering what we receive in return. In other words, we neglect to consider whether the expenditure at issue is "good" (in the sense that the business will ultimately receive more in benefits than it spends) or "bad" (in the sense that the business will receive less in benefits than it spends).

Good costs violate the rules of accounting. Yes, they legitimately represent a cost or expense from an accounting standpoint, but they are actually investments. Because traditional thinking effectively disguises this reality from us, organizations have come to focus their management efforts on making all costs as low as possible. What we should really be addressing, however, is how to identify and optimize our "good" costs.

With this understanding as a backdrop, let's consider an additional weakness of cost budgeting—the fact that budget-approving managers will always have less information about the organization's real needs than the business units engaged in the actual performance of work. So why not give the people at the front line more control?

Beyond Budgeting principles incorporate a variety of approaches to address these needs. Some of the more relevant include these tactics:

- Activity accounting
- Trend reporting
- Moving from absolute to relative performance target setting and evaluations
- Rolling forecasts

It's beyond the scope of this book to speak about these activities in great detail, but one does merit closer attention because of its particular relevance to Scrumban teams—target setting and evaluation.

For an evaluation of performance to be meaningful, it must refer to high-quality targets. A common problem with the way organizations evaluate performance derives from their propensity to blindly follow the numbers and fail to apply any kind of common sense in evaluating the context in which those numbers were generated. Put simply, it's easier to just compare one number against the other.

Because target setting and evaluation is prospective in nature, no target can ever hope to be perfect. Unforeseen things may happen; assumptions will likely change. Consequently, organizations need to establish more meaningful performance assessments than simply evaluating whether something is delivered "within budget" or whether a key performance indicator (KPI) is "healthy."

Consider a cost budget as a target. It's a predefined, absolute number that's established before work begins. Does this mean that business units or projects that operate "within budget" are always "good"? What if the unit failed to pursue value-creating opportunities because operating within budget was its top priority? Is a release or project that finishes on time and within budget successful if low quality was delivered? Has a business performed well when it achieves its target for market share because its main competitor unexpectedly went out of business?

The same considerations hold true for individual performance bonuses. Should we reward chance factors that allowed one person to make his or her target easily while another had to struggle immensely? Or should we acknowledge that other business objectives suffered because making a target became somebody's sole focus?

Now let's think about performance in general. We've said high performance is about making continuous improvements and delivering on promises. The only way we can truly assess whether we're performing at a "high" level is by measuring whether we're performing above "average"—being better than our peers against whom we can (and should) compare ourselves. In other words, high performance is relative.

Sports leagues represent the ultimate environment for relative performance measures. We can easily recognize how ineffective it would be for a baseball team to set a goal of scoring 650 runs per season. What matters is winning more games than your opponents, and the number of total runs it will take to achieve that end is relative. Many first-place teams score fewer total runs than their opponents. We would find it unthinkable to reward a losing team for making its targeted run production if the team failed to win its division—yet more often than not the business realm operates under a functional equivalent of this paradigm.

Just as we test the quality of our software code against functional requirements to determine whether it's ready for delivery to the customer, so we should test our measured performance to understand what the outcomes actually represent (especially with regard to relative targets). Performing this type of assessment is more difficult than simply evaluating the numbers—it requires leadership and a change in thinking.

Agile Contracting

As an alternative path to Agility, Scrumban amplifies Scrum's existing bias toward principles based on collaboration, transparency, and trust. Just as traditional management methods can interfere with these values (and thus the successful adoption and sustainability of Agility), business contracts can become similar impediments. Agile contracting is the equivalent of the Beyond Budgeting framework for legal affairs, and is relevant regardless of whether your IT operations are purchasing or delivering services dependent upon Agile methodologies.

As we know from systems thinking, actors within complex systems tend to do what seems best based on the limited scope of their roles and responsibilities without a clear understanding of the larger impact of their actions on the whole system.

Lawyers are especially prone to this habit, because they know that when something goes wrong in a business relationship, one of the first places where everyone looks is the contract they were responsible for negotiating and drafting. As a consequence, most lawyers tend to "locally optimize" contracts, in the same way that development teams without a systems understanding locally optimize their performance. Thus, if you are developing customized software for others or outsourcing development services from contractors, traditional contract approaches conspire against the Agile objectives that your development processes are built upon.

Because American jurisprudence is based on the precedent established by previous cases, most contract structures have their roots in pre-technology arenas like construction. Construction is related to knowledge work in the same way as manufacturing. There are many similarities, but there are also substantial differences, especially when Agile methodologies are involved. Consider these factors:

- Like manufacturing processes, construction work is often defined in great detail before the building process ever begins. The process of performing the work is fairly predictable. Software development is far more variable and inherently less well defined.
- In traditional construction projects, there's typically a long delay before something of value is delivered. Agile development work, in contrast, emphasizes frequent, incremental delivery of value.
- In traditional construction projects, feedback on the work performed is weak and usually delivered late in the process. Agile software development emphasizes frequent feedback loops.
- In traditional construction projects, customers usually face substantial problems if contracts are terminated early. In Agile development work, early termination is rarely problematic, as work is being delivered incrementally for the duration of the relationship.

Fortunately, the structural and legal aspects of Agile contracting are not substantially different from traditional approaches. They simply require adopting a fresh perspective that focuses on different things. Thus, whereas traditional contracts focus on problems (what happens when things go wrong), Agile contracts focus on operational process and delivery.

Common contract provisions requiring this changed perspective often relate to risk points (contracts are a form of risk management), and include such terms as the definition of scope and deliverables, change management provisions, penalties and incentives, payment schemes, warranty provisions, limitation of liability provisions, delivery and acceptance, and contract termination. Let's consider scope of work as an example. Parties drafting a traditional contract would likely spend a great deal of time and effort trying to define the scope of work with great specificity. In contrast, parties drafting an Agile contract would focus on defining a high-level backlog of work, placing greater emphasis on establishing the process through which user stories/work items are broken down and pulled into the development queue.

The Long Tail of Profitability

Chris Anderson's theory of the long tail outlines how market niches represent potential high-profit opportunities (see http://tiny.cc/long-tail). One approach that organizations can use to begin identifying and capitalizing on these opportunities involves transferring product innovation to the user community.

Maturing organizations can apply this concept to the prioritization of feature options. Features options are typically generated through a strategy lens, a market lens, and a risk lens. Why not use the long-tail framework as a new lens—a lens that can identify niche features for which certain users will pay a premium. Armed with this additional perspective, the business can select a combination of features that combine the minimum functionality needed to compete in the marketplace (what David Anderson calls "table stakes") with highly profitable add-ons. This "killer" combination will maximize both viability and profitability for the organization at very early stages. (For further reading on this application of "Long Tail" thinking, visit http://codegenesys.com/scrumban/long-tail.)

Tying It All Together

Teams and organizations can follow an infinite number of paths as they increase their understandings and capabilities using Scrumban. While the majority of techniques and practices outlined in this chapter represent more robust modes of operating, many rely on extension of the Scrumban framework to areas of the business beyond the software development and IT workflows where it is first introduced.

If there's a theme to underscore here, it's the continued emphasis on improving our understanding and management of risk. While Scrumban shares this focus with Kanban, it is uniquely positioned to enhance capabilities at both the team and larger system levels.

Chapter 10

MODELING: TO BOLDLY GO WHERE FEW HAVE GONE BEFORE

IN THIS CHAPTER

- Better Predictability through Probabilistic versus Deterministic Forecasting
- Evolutions in Modeling
- Examples of Modeling

The material covered in this chapter represents advanced topics for teams and organizations that have mastered the fundamentals and are interested in further refining their forecasting and planning techniques. If you're new to Scrumban/Kanban principles, I recommend treating your first time through this chapter as merely an orientation to advanced practices toward which your team or organization can mature.

As you might imagine, it would be possible to write an entire book on modeling principles and techniques. For this reason, I focus on the more pragmatic aspects by providing a basic background on modeling and showing how the planning techniques described in earlier chapters can evolve into more sophisticated practices.

Why Model?

Software development is inevitably filled with risk and variability. Elevated levels of uncertainty and risk make it challenging to develop accurate forecasts, and poor forecasting reduces predictability and erodes stakeholder trust.

Software development will never be without risk. Modeling represents a safe way to run experiments that enable us to assess the impact of risks before they occur and to proactively make better-informed decisions (not only are we able to minimize the likelihood of an event, but we are also able to better manage its consequences). Moreover, the nature and quality of discussions surrounding time forecasts and resource requirements take on an entirely different tenor when buttressed by information gleaned from a good model. All these factors contribute substantially toward building trust among stakeholders.

Here's the bottom line: Even a modest amount of time and effort in modeling can produce significant returns—financial and otherwise.

Starting with Metrics and Distribution Patterns

It bears repeating that one of the most significant ways Scrumban helps teams improve their performance and work conditions is through the collection and analysis of new data. Plotting this data over time allows us to gain insights regarding the frequency with which different results are distributed.

For planning and forecasting purposes, it's extremely useful to know that future results generated by a given process are likely to follow some sort of pattern. To this end, readers with a background in statistics will recognize Erlang, gamma, Poisson, and Weibull as distribution patterns against which results and events can be mapped.

Analyzing data across a variety of contexts illuminates how many of the metrics generated from kanban systems tend to follow one or more of these distribution patterns. When we can apply a known pattern to a given data set, in essence we can benefit from a summary characterization of that data within a concise set of parameters (shape and scale, typically). We can then manipulate the data against these patterns to perform more sophisticated planning and forecasting.

When we assume a data set follows a particular distribution pattern, we're essentially claiming that the underlying process also conforms to that particular distribution. If we're correct in making this claim, the additional information will sharpen our ultimate analysis; if we're incorrect, it will weaken it. As Sam Savage suggests, "In the valley of single numbers, the man with a bad distribution is king." The point is that any tool that can help reduce uncertainty is good. Knowing the range of the distribution and the shape of a random variable greatly reduces uncertainty.

Why Patterns Are Relevant

Why is it relevant to know that certain kanban system metrics tend to follow specific patterns?

First, applying "known" distribution patterns is particularly helpful when we don't have a lot of actual data to work with (such as when we start gathering data or when a particular team or system is relatively new). We can make reasonable forecasts at this stage simply by extrapolating against a predictable pattern as opposed to waiting for more data to be generated. That said, as more data is gathered, we can begin to produce even more accurate assumptions and forecasts by resampling the specific pattern of our actual results. In both stages, the existence of recognized patterns improves the usefulness and precision of our forecasting.

Second, we can examine the shape of our data, then refer to the science of "shapes," and finally start to draw conclusions about the behavior of our system compared to others that generate the same shape. If we want our system to behave like another system, then we likely need to make its shape resemble that of our target. In other words, evaluating the differences between the two shapes is likely to expose the practical areas we can address to make the outcomes more alike.

The particular shape of a pattern can also provide insights about making a system more predictable. Generally speaking, the wider the shape of our distribution, the wider our forecast ranges between the values associated with the results percentile within which they fall. As a consequence, our probabilistic predictions will be less reliable. Consider cycle times, for example (which Troy Magennis and others have confirmed follow a Weibull pattern). If your lead time distribution has a wide shape, taking steps that narrow the distribution will make your system more predictable. Options to explore in this case include the following:

- Minimizing lead times to reduce the likelihood of work items being impacted by an environmental blocker (aggressively limiting WIP as one approach).
- Improving focus. Ensure your teams never start a new work item unless existing items are blocked.
- Attacking the root causes of blocked work items (reducing their likelihood). This may call for adopting more disciplined approaches to problem solving, such as A3 Thinking.

Any efforts that reduce a kanban system's risk of delay will ultimately narrow the Weibull shape of its lead time distribution and improve predictability. A suggested value for the "shape" parameter of your distribution curve is 1 (which equates to an exponential distribution). Most projects will have values around 1.5. A value less than 1 wouldn't be realistic because it suggests a "reducing mortality" (a characteristic where the longer work is in progress, the lower the risk of delay). This outcome doesn't correlate with most known realities.

We can also look at patterns to better inform our Scrum practices. For example, analyzing distribution frequencies can help us determine the most appropriate length (duration) for our sprints or iterations, and the optimal number of user stories or work items by class of service, risk profile, or something else to incorporate within those sprints.

What Is Modeling?

A model is nothing more than a small-scale, mathematical framework designed to mimic a real-world system or process. We can use models to simulate actual work conditions and outcomes produced by our systems. More importantly, models enable us to run low-cost experiments of simulated changes, allowing us to determine the best approaches to obtain specific outcomes under given scenarios (like how to manage completing project x in y weeks for z dollars).

Modeling reality through repetitive simulations lets us produce the rough equivalent of actual performance data (assuming our models provide an accurate reflection of reality). Past performance may not be a guarantee of future results (there will always be outliers), but it does improve our understanding of the probability of various outcomes. (Figure 10.1 reflects a forecast project completion date based on repetitive simulations run through a modeling framework.)

More importantly, robust models enable us to identify which control variables are likely to have the most influence on our outcomes. They enable us to run "what if" experiments to inform our decision making—that is, experiments in which we isolate changes to a single variable and then compare the outcomes against the original benchmarks. These "what if" experiments can be used to determine which management strategies will most likely lead to a successful outcome when we tackle our modeled approach in real life.

Nate Silver is a statistician who has gained some measure of fame in recent years for his success in forecasting the outcomes of political elections. He recently published

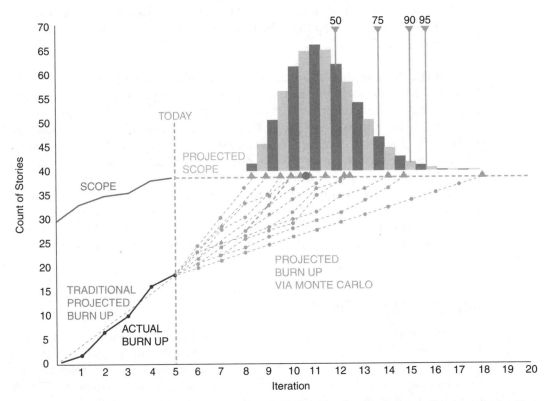

FIGURE 10.1   This chart plots a team's actual delivery of user stories over five iterations, then projects a probability distribution upon the remaining stories to forecast the number iterations needed to complete the projected backlog. This model shows us that simply continuing the slope of the actual burn-up will result in completing the remaining backlog of user stories less than 50% of the time.

Source: Rally Software.

an excellent article that outlines the characteristics of a good model in terms laymen can understand.[1] In summary, models should have the following characteristics:

- Be probabilistic and not deterministic
- Be empirical
- Respond sensibly to changes in input
- Avoid changing their rules midstream

In modeling Scrumban systems, we're interested in using better data, not more data. Consequently, it's important to incorporate parameters that directly influence lead time (I identify several examples later in this chapter when discussing what goes into building a robust model). Individual contexts will dictate whether less direct factors are also relevant to incorporate (vacations might represent one such example).

Reminder about the "Flaw of Averages"

I've previously alluded to how our natural inclination to apply average values in forecasting represents a "flaw of averages" to avoid. After all, you don't want to suffer the same plight of the statistician who drowned in a river whose "average depth" was 3 feet. For this reason, I recommend forecasting to values that represent at least the 80th to 85th percentile of modeled results (i.e., 80% to 85% of all items occur within the defined distribution).

In most software development environments, certain metrics tend to reflect distribution patterns that are skewed to the left with a very long tail of "outlier" results to the right (i.e., rather than reflecting a bell curve distribution, most results show up earlier on the *x*-axis). In such patterns, it's important to understand that the median result is typically a substantially lower value than the mean[2]—a reality few recognize early on. This reality is critical to realizing why applying average values to our planning and forecasting activities still represents imprecise estimates, at best.

Initial Considerations

It is moronic to predict without first establishing an error rate for the prediction and keeping track of one's past record of accuracy.

—Nassim Nicholas Taleb [Fooled by Randomness]

When Monte Carlo simulations are used to model schedules, it's important to ensure we do not attempt to treat all uncertainties in the same way. As outlined in Chapter 6,

---

1. http://tiny.cc/538Senate.
2. This means 50% of all samples will be less than the median, and hence *more than* 50% of the results will be less than the average.

there are two types of uncertainty—aleatory and epistemic. It can be helpful to recognize we have the option of applying distinct branches of probability theory to these different types of uncertainty.

Warning! Deep Geek Ahead!

These next few paragraphs are for those interested in some of the statistical underpinnings to good modeling.

The most common choices in probability theory are Bayesian and frequentist. The essential difference between the two approaches is that Bayesian theory optimizes for average-case performance rather than worst-case performance (and is the superior method when a good prior distribution over possible world states can be obtained, and good "average-case" performance is sufficient for your needs). Frequentist approaches generally don't account for good prior results.

When Bayesian updating can be efficiently computed (and its assumptions upheld), it is the optimal approach. In fact, even if some assumptions fail, Bayesian approaches can still be useful. But be wary: Bayesian methods make stronger assumptions than may be warranted.

Frequentist methods don't provide much of a coherent framework for constructing models and ask for worst-case guarantees. When dealing with weaker or adversarial assumptions, however, even simple models under frequentist approaches perform well. They can do so in very complicated domains (because there are fewer initial assumptions, less work is required to meet them). If you have no way of obtaining good prior results, or if you need guaranteed performance, the frequentist approach is superior.[3]

Monte Carlo simulations often apply a frequentist approach to modeling aleatory uncertainty, though either approach can be used. It's worth noting, however, that Bayesian inference from data modeled by a mixture distribution can also be performed via Monte Carlo simulation.[4]

Now that we have this "geek speak" out of the way, let's address some more pragmatic considerations for constructing our models. Ideal models have the following characteristics:

- They represent all work.
- They do not incorporate padding to accommodate uncertainty.
- They specifically account for different categories of risk through the appropriate branch of probability theory.

---

3. Conclusions summarized from Jacob Steinhardt's *Beyond Bayesians and Frequentists* (Stanford University, 2012).
4. Radford M. Neal. *Bayesian Mixture Modeling by Monte Carlo Simulation* (University of Toronto, 1991).

Suppose we want to assess the impact of adding or reducing resources to ongoing work. In a Scrumban system, this typically correlates to modifying WIP limits across different points in our software development flow. Scrumban enables the creation of a model to simulate the impact of a given change. The results provide an informed sense of the optimal skill balance for our team, moving us away from subjective decision making based on instinct and intuition, and toward scientifically based analysis.

In any statistical forecasting exercise, we must always be mindful of the model's underlying assumptions. The most common assumption is that our underlying process is stable and stationary.[5] This is why we should always ensure the system is stable before we attempt any kind of planning or forecasting based on empirical methods.

Another key modeling assumption is that our random variables are independent and logically distributed. In a Scrumban system, this translates to the following criteria:

- The workflow (as reflected by the visual board) is relatively static and will remain unchanged.
- The characteristic backlog upon which the forecast is based is representative of both the larger base from which data was collected and the work being projected (in other words, the distribution of different types of work, the effort involved, the business and technical domains, and so on are substantially the same).
- The team that will perform the forecasted work is the same as the team that produced the completed work upon which the variable value is based.

As differences between the reference process and the forecasted process increase, the quality of the model and its forecasts decrease. As some differences are always evident with the baseline models, it's important to understand that some differences will have a greater negative impact on the quality of your forecasts than others. For example, team make-up is probably the single most sensitive factor. "Substitute" team members will rarely possess exactly the same technical aptitude, domain knowledge, process knowledge, and communication skills as their predecessors.

Monte Carlo Simulations

Monte Carlo simulations involve performing a simulation against a model a number of times. For each step in the simulation, we manipulate a set of given input variables by selecting randomly generated values for each (within a predefined range). We

---

5. For example, suppose that you have an urn with six balls labeled "1" and four balls labeled "0." You mix the balls and draw one out, recording the value on the ball. You then replace it in the urn by adding two more balls of the same value. You then repeat the whole process again. This is an example of a nonstationary process.

record the frequency of measured outcomes to identify patterns in our results. Monte Carlo simulations are useful when a range of input conditions can significantly affect the final outcome produced by a process or system.

Monte Carlo simulations are commonly used to manage risk across a variety of industries and functions, but their application to software development activities is a relatively new phenomenon. They are, however, a suggested quantitative risk management technique in the project management body of knowledge. Troy Magennis is one of the leading contributors to the development of these techniques in the Lean software development arena, and much of this chapter is based on material he developed. Other significant contributors include Alexei Zheglov and Dimitar Bakardzhiev.

Models incorporate key control variables (system inputs) to simulate work undertaken against a representative backlog of work items. The selection of control variables is determined by choice, though at least one or two controls are necessary (more on this topic shortly). The potential values for each variable fall within a statistically calculated range (ideally calculated from historical data for each). As the simulation is run, random values from within the defined ranges across all variables are generated, producing different results for each full simulation.

Hundreds or even thousands of simulations may be run against the model to produce a large set of data results. Patterns are likely to emerge with regard to the frequency of measured results, highlighting the most likely outcomes (our system benchmark). In a Scrum or Scrumban context, for example, we might develop models around variables such as lead time and perhaps even risk profiles.

As with planning techniques that apply Little's law, Monte Carlo simulations depend on some key assumptions. One of the most important considerations is that the activity being simulated cannot be influenced by factors outside of your selected control variables.

Building on What You Already Do

Scrumban system models simulate work passing through your visualized workflow. The minimum elements that a model should account for include the work items in the proposed initial backlog, the value stream columns that those work items will flow through, and prior performance data for calculating the queue's historical takt time (or historical cycle time for each work column for a more granular model). The more granular the model, the better you will be able to measure the compounding effect of events that occur during development (such as defects, blockers, and dark matter). You will also be able to more accurately reproduce the impact of individual control variables.

It's easy enough to model outcomes manually. A good way to begin familiarizing yourself with simulations and modeling is to start by building upon the methods introduced in Chapter 6 (planning with Little's law). Here, we'll walk through one possible pathway a team or organization could pursue to improve upon its use of Little's law in release/project planning. To quickly recap, I applied the formula in Figure 10.2 to forecast the amount of time and resources it would take to complete a given project or release based on a given set of known values.

We know that project workflow typically follows a Z-curve pattern, and that we can apply Little's law only to the middle leg of this curve. To account for variability associated with the first and third legs, plus variability created by dark matter and failure demand, we calculate a project buffer based on the following formula:

Project buffer = Z-curve coefficient × [(1 + average failure demand + average dark matter) × (number of stories / average throughput)]

When this approach was introduced in Chapter 6, the potential traps and pitfalls associated with using "average" values were highlighted. These pitfalls are amplified when using variables for factors whose ranges of potential values aren't evenly distributed (or are outside the "normal" pattern). Uneven or highly variable distributions of possible outcomes can substantially skew forecasts that rely on "average" values.

Dimitar Bakardzhiev demonstrated how to improve the reliability of that approach by replacing calculated averages with probabilistically determined values (generated by running a Monte Carlo simulation to create a stochastic information packet [SIP] as the substitute).[6] What this essentially entails is generating an array of

$$\text{\# of User Stories} \left[\frac{\text{Average Lead Time}}{\text{Average WIP}} \right]$$

$$- OR -$$

$$\begin{matrix}\text{(Project/Release)} \\ \text{Lead Time}\end{matrix} = \left[\frac{\text{\# of User Stories}}{\text{Average Throughput}} \right]$$

$$- OR -$$

$$\text{\# of User Stories x Average Takt Time}$$

FIGURE 10.2   Mathematical representations for Little's law.

6. SIPs have become a standard method of communicating uncertainties through an array of possible values. They advance the modeling of uncertainty by being actionable (they can be used directly in calculations), additive (they can be aggregated across multiple platforms), and auditable (the data they contain is unambiguous).

possible values for some uncertain parameter based on historical data resampled via a Monte Carlo technique.

In the original example, I used averages for throughput, WIP, and lead times. Another improvement is to use takt time (the average time between two successive deliveries) rather than lead time in these calculations:

Lead time (projected duration) = number of user stories × average takt time

Average takt time = period of time / total number of items delivered

Takt time is preferable to lead time for a number of reasons, but primarily because most software development is done in parallel (i.e., team members work on a number of things simultaneously). This behavior is one of the major reasons why using average lead time for forecasting purposes can lead to inconsistent results.

To illustrate why this is so, let's assume three user stories are pulled into the work queue on the same day. The first user story is delivered on the third day, then the two remaining items are delivered on the sixth day. The first and second items would have measured takt times of 3 days. The first item's takt time is measured from the date on which work began (because there's no prior delivery to measure against). The second item's takt time is measured from the date the first item was delivered. The third item, however, has a measured takt time of 0 days, because it was delivered on the same day as the second item. Because takt time accounts for both lead time and WIP, it maintains the necessary relationships for Little's law while also accounting for parallel deliveries.

In this new model, we use Monte Carlo simulation techniques to create and apply both the SIP[7] for takt time (for each leg of the Z-curve) and to forecast project duration. From there, we evaluate the distribution pattern for the array of results generated (projects tends to follow a normal, "bell curve" type of pattern[8]), and select a distribution percentile against which to plan with greater confidence. Here's a recap of this changed process:

Lead time (projected duration) =
(number of user stories × SIP of takt time) [Z-curve first leg]
+ (number of user stories × SIP of takt time) [Z-curve second leg]
+ (number of user stories × SIP of takt time) [Z-curve third leg]

---

7. SIP Math comes from Harry Markowitz, the father of modern portfolio theory and a Nobel Prize winner (http://tiny.cc/sipmath).
8. From ScrumDo data analysis of more than 1000 projects.

Collect Your System's Historical Takt Time Data

Naturally, historical data is most relevant when applied to identical situations (e.g., the same team members, the same business domain, the same technologies). You should account for any variation in these factors.[9]

If you've been using Scrumban for some time (or tracking delivery dates of work items), collecting the historical data you need shouldn't be too difficult. Dimitar Bakardzhiev has produced a presentation[10] on this approach, and the examples in Figure 10.3 are taken from his material.

In this example, Dimitar developed his baseline data from a project that consisted of 27 work items. Comparing the delivered work against the project's cumulative flow diagram (CFD), he was able to determine that only 20 of those 27 items related to the second leg of the Z-curve (see Date Done column in left-hand set of data in Figure 10.3). The data from these 20 items will be used to generate a takt time SIP for the second leg of the curve. The same process was repeated for the items relating to the first and final legs of the curve, respectively.

Generate a Takt Time SIP with Monte Carlo Resampling

Using Microsoft Excel (most spreadsheet programs will suffice), Dimitar constructed a model that resampled the historical takt time 1000 times (essentially, recreating a

Project start	14.11.2011		
Date Done	Count of Done	Takt Time	Parallels
18.11.2011 r.	1	4	0
25.11.2011 r.	1	7	0
28.11.2011 r.	4	3	3
30.11.2011 r.	1	2	0
01.12.2011 r.	3	1	2
02.12.2011 r.	2	1	1
07.12.2011 r.	1	5	0
09.12.2011 r.	2	2	1
13.12.2011 r.	3	4	2
15.12.2011 r.	2	2	1
16.12.2011 r.	2	1	1
19.12.2011 r.	1	3	0
22.12.2011 r.	1	3	0
23.12.2011 r.	2	1	1
27.12.2011 r.	1	4	0
Grand Total	27		12

Takt Time	Work Items	Project Length
0	12	0
1	4	4
2	3	6
3	3	9
4	3	12
5	1	5
7	1	7
22	27	43

Project length	43
Avg TH	0,627906977
Avg 1/TH	1,592592593
Avg TT	1,592592593

FIGURE 10.3   Starting the process of building your SIP from historical data.

Source: Dimitar Bakardzhiev.

---

9. Each system will inform which adjustments, if any, should be made (with some variations being more significant than others). More importantly, rarely should you have to abandon modeling altogether simply because the systems and anticipated work you're seeking to forecast will be "significantly different." There is still substantial value to be derived from historical data.
10. http://tiny.cc/noestimatesmc.

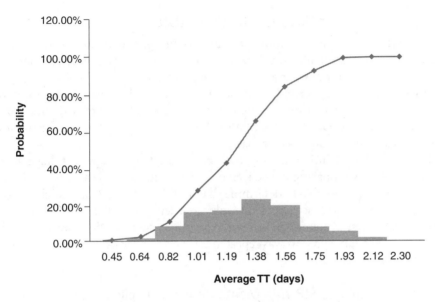

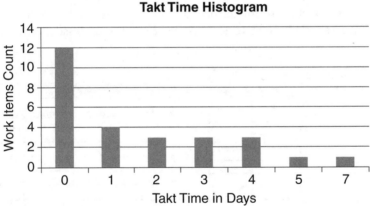

FIGURE 10.4   The resulting array of values is plotted and demonstrates a Weibull distribution pattern.

new 20-work-item project 1000 separate times, and assigning takt time values to each "new" work item based on a random selection from the original 20).

This modeling generated an array of project length and average takt time values, which could then be evaluated. In the example in Figure 10.4, we see Weibull (long tail) distributions for both takt time and delivery time.

Generate Project Delivery Time Probability with Monte Carlo Resampling

With a baseline SIP developed, we can use it to model the distribution outcomes for other projects of any size. As an example, let's assume you need to forecast a delivery date for a project using the same team (Figure 10.5).

#	T	Average TT
1	26	1.3
2	16	0.8
3	24	1.2
4	26	1.3
5	19	0.95
6	31	1.55

#	T	Average TT
989	25	1.25
990	29	1.45
991	17	0.85
992	22	1.1
993	26	1.3
994	20	1
995	24	1.2
996	24	1.2
997	34	1.7
998	16	0.8
999	22	1.1
1000	28	1.4

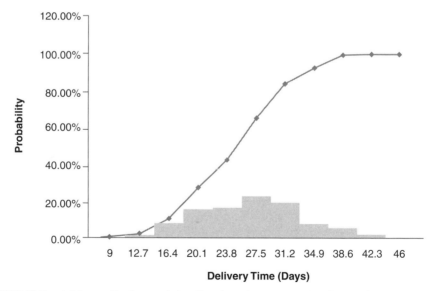

FIGURE 10.5   A Monte Carlo model reflecting the range of delivery time for a proposed project.

Your team would break down the requirements, adding work items for dark matter and failure demand (ideally based on historical data). Let's assume this process results in the team projecting a total of 100 user stories for this new project—12 to be delivered during the first leg of the Z-curve, 70 during the second leg, and 18 during the final leg (Figure 10.6).

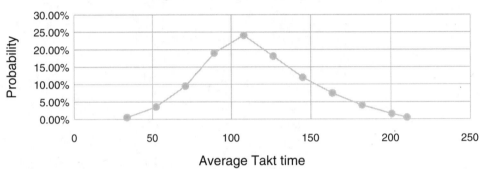

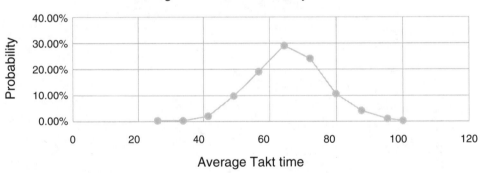

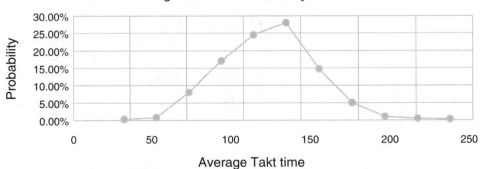

FIGURE 10.6   We still account for the Z-curve, but now substitute modeled outcomes for educated guesses.

Using the baseline SIP to model project outcomes will generate a probability distribution similar to the one reflected in the chart on the top in Figure 10.6. Selecting the delivery time value associated with the 85th percentile represents a very solid forecast (in the case of this example, sometime around 43 days).

Repeat the Simulation for Each Leg of the Z-Curve and Sum the Results

Once you've completed your simulations for each leg of the project Z-curve, all that's left is to sum the results.

It's Still Not Perfect

Several pitfalls are still possible with our revised forecasting approach. First, performance during the first leg of a project is driven by many factors, some of which relate to familiarity with the business domain, the technologies, and general housekeeping. Consequently, even when team members and technologies remain the same, a wide variation across individual projects is possible. The larger the sample size for these legs, the better.

Second, while historical performance should inform us about the number of stories to associate with each leg of the Z-curve, the final allocation should be made based on a collaborative review of the work.

Consideration of Major Risk Factors

The forecasting model highlighted in the preceding section is predicated upon data that relates to each leg of the Z-curve. Truly robust models, however, account for other major risk events that are not fully accommodated in this model. This consideration represents an important evolution in modeling, as major risks have the effect of shifting our results further out in time and/or changing the shape of the distribution pattern (Figure 10.7).

A Different Approach

It's feasible to adopt a different (outside-in) perspective to forecasting, without completely abandoning the application of Little's law. This approach simulates each step of work flowing through the system as cards are pulled and "held" in each column for a given time interval (based on the historical cycle time for that column). This highly granular method opens the door to many "what if" experiments. The passage of simulated time would be tracked as activity is undertaken (being careful to recognize and discount parallel workflows created by having multiple people engaged in work simultaneously).

These kinds of robust models can introduce commonly occurring events into the process as work is simulated. For example, if your team has an historical 20% defect rate, you would introduce a new work card (representing a defect) for every fifth user story processed in the simulation. Another example might be to have one out of every four cards become blocked at some point, thereby simulating a blocker experience

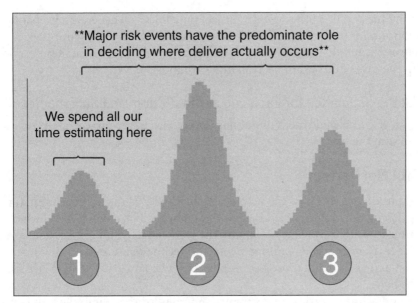

FIGURE 10.7   Risk factors not accounted for in the takt time model can still significantly influence project outcomes.

ratio of 25%. All of these granular variables were encompassed within the project buffer calculation utilized in our previous approach.

Under this more robust model, one full simulation cycle involves mimicking the movement of cards through the system and recording the passage of time until all the cards in the representative backlog are completed (including new cards representing bugs and defects, if they're modeled). One cycle produces a "completed" backlog along with a measurement of the time it took to achieve it and represents one potential outcome.

To transform a single manual simulation into a full-blown Monte Carlo simulation, you would have to repeat the same steps many times, using different random number selections (ideally SIPs generated from historical data) for each control variable (column cycle time, defect rate, blocker rate) at every decision point. The more times the simulation was completed, the more accurate the final estimate would be.

Such a model allows you to create reliable forecasts, but it still isn't sophisticated enough to provide a clear understanding of system influences that typically occur during development (a nod to a system's amplifying and dampening characteristics, which "hide" any direct cause and effect relationship between inputs and outputs). Manually running a number of simulations under even a simple model is very time consuming, however (and becomes an even more lengthy process as additional control variables are introduced). This is why developing computer-aided tools is necessary. A spreadsheet program like Microsoft Excel is not ideal, but it can suffice as a starting point.

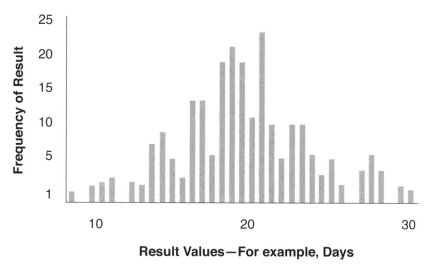

FIGURE 10.8   A distribution pattern emerges from plotting the outcome of the simulations.

As we've previously seen, visualizing the results of multiple simulations on a histogram allows us to see how results are distributed. The chart in Figure 10.8 plots how often a particular result was achieved across approximately 250 runs from one model. In this example, a peak distribution forms around 20 days. According to Troy Magennis and others, a normal distribution or bell curve pattern is typical for software development simulations unless highly skewed random number distributions are associated with the input variables.

Input Parameters: Weibull's Wobble But They Don't Fall Down

As previously noted, each input parameter in the model requires a range of possible values. Ideally, your model will randomly generate these values based on a function of the distribution pattern (generating SIPs is one such method).

For those who gravitate toward less complicated math, there's no question that the easiest option is to create and manipulate mathematical models that base random input parameter values on a uniform distribution pattern. Such simulations typically produce longer forecasts because a greater number of high values are associated with uniform patterns. Thus, if you apply a normal distribution to your number generation task and your model's projected delivery date is acceptable to the business, then you're in good shape. But what if you're on the edge?

This is where your mathematical recognition of a better representation of reality becomes very useful. As previously noted, many of the input variables we're likely to incorporate in a mathematical model for a Scrumban process reflect a non-uniform frequency distribution. These variables reflect "left-weighted" patterns, with a long right tail representing "outlier" results. Some of the common distribution patterns for these variables include the following:

- *Log normal*: This pattern tends to accentuate lower values, and is often too narrow in its distribution. Using this type of a distribution pattern for parameter generation may be appropriate for some input parameters, but is likely to skew forecasts toward more optimistic outcomes when applied to something like cycle time. External studies suggest defects and bugs follow this type of a pattern.
- *Gamma*: This is a good candidate for many variables, as it represents distributions that have low probabilities for intervals close to zero, with increasing probability evident up to a point, followed by a decreasing probability over time.

The probability distributions of many common parameters tend to follow a Weibull pattern. This is good news for a number of reasons.

First, Weibull has multiple shapes, which range from exponential to Rayleigh distributions, and all the properties needed from the distribution are proportional to the mean (proportionality depends solely on the shape parameter applied to the distribution). This is very useful because even though shape may vary, the median is always smaller than the mean.

More significantly, the Weibull distribution for key metrics is consistent across data generated from a variety of sources (from development work to operations) and styles (from waterfall to Scrum). Having one distribution pattern that fits a broad range of your work process makes for a more useful model.

Remember, you simply need a pattern that is wide enough to give a balanced forecast (and narrow enough to be reasonably predictable) until there's enough actual data to bootstrap from real samples (more on bootstrapping in a moment).

How to Create a Robust Model

Because some or all of the control variables (inputs) selected for any model are subject to varying degrees of uncertainty (including measurement of historical data, a lack of data, and an incomplete understanding of the system), there are limits on how much we can trust the accuracy of a model's output. For this reason, good modeling practice requires evaluating the level of confidence in the model. A good approach is to build a model incrementally, performing a sensitivity analysis at each stage to assess how much each control variable is contributing to output uncertainty (providing an order of importance for each input):

- Start with a simple model (no more than one or two control variables).
- Visually test the model by running one or two limited simulations.
- Run a Monte Carlo simulation of several hundred scenarios.

- Conduct a sensitivity analysis. Scatter plots are a simple but useful visual tool for this purpose. You can also base quantitative measures on the correlation between values or results of a regression analysis.
- Adjust the model if necessary, adding just one additional variable at a time and repeating the preceding steps.

Control variables you might want to build into a model for Scrum teams include the following examples:

- Average WIP (per column in your kanban system)
- Work items (user stories)
- Defect rates
- Blocking rates
- Ad hoc work/scope creep
- Team maturity (mature teams tend to work more efficiently and have quicker ramp-up times)
- Skill levels
- Familiarity with underlying work and technologies

Notice that these factors relate to many of the considerations we endeavored to account for in a more general way when planning under Little's law through recognition of the Z-curve.

A Sample "What If" Experiment

Troy Magennis has illustrated many ways kanban systems lend themselves to useful modeling. In this section, we'll consider one example within the context of the mobile app project at Mammoth Bank (our Chapter 6 planning scenario).

In Chapter 6, we applied Little's law to increase the reliability of our forecasting. In this example, we'll explore how modeling can help us address more granular decisions, such as the impact associated with increasing the number of developers or QA personnel on delivery time. Because Mammoth's virtualized workflow incorporates value stream mappings that relate closely with work skill sets (i.e., analysis/design, develop, test), it's relatively easy to construct a model to probabilistically forecast likely outcomes associated with different configurations.

When a project like Mammoth Bank's mobile app is running late, many managers are tempted to simply start adding programmers or other workers into the mix as a means of speeding up delivery. These knee-jerk reactions often have little to no impact on the delivery date. Here's an overview of the steps to model our way to a better decision:

1. We create a representative backlog of work items of the project at issue (number and type of work cards).
2. We perform a Monte Carlo simulation of the system (our Scrumban team) as currently configured to obtain a baseline result for this backlog.

3. We run separate experiments after making changes to control variables. In this scenario, our control variables are distinct skill sets that relate to each column within our kanban system. Specifically, we take the following steps:

   a. Increase the WIP limit of a single column in our model.

   b. Run a Monte Carlo simulation, recording the new result distributions.

   c. Compare these results to the baseline.

The project manager in our scenario, Julie, simulated a variety of options for one of the RAD teams on the project—a Scrum team with seven members (two analysts, three developers, and two QA engineers). Table 10.1 shows the data her modeling generated.

Julie's initial modeling experiment showed that increased testing capabilities would likely have the greatest effect in reducing delivery time. Converting this insight into actual hiring or assignment decisions requires independent judgment and perhaps a closer look at some other aspects.

For example, it would be useful to run a variety of experiments to test the cumulative impact of changes across multiple columns (such as adding one developer *and* one tester). Good models will produce results that indicate which combination of WIP increases (or decreases) produce the greatest overall improvement in system delivery time (the outcome Julie is looking to shorten).

Having run such experiments, Julie determined that adding one developer and two testers to the team would produce the best outcome (the shortest time to delivery). This configuration was forecast to reduce the overall project length to 52 days. Having satisfied herself that she had determined the best option for accelerating the project delivery date, Julie now needed to decide whether this option made sense from a financial standpoint.

Fortunately, this assessment was made easy by the fact that Mammoth Bank had determined it was losing $75,000 for every day the features in the entire product backlog were not available to end users. For ease of illustration, we'll assume that Julie was easily able to identify the financial loss associated with the features in her simulated backlog—$15,000 per day. Consequently, shaving 10-plus days off her team's delivery time meant the bank would produce a favorable financial impact in excess of $150,000 ($15,000 per day × 10 days)

TABLE 10.1   Data from Modeling Simulation

Column (Represented Skill)	Original WIP limit	New WIP Limit	Baseline Lead Time	New Lead Time	Change
Test/QA	2	3	62.75	58.25	−4.5
Developers	3	4	62.75	59.9	−2.85
Design/analysis	2	3	62.75	62.5	−0.25

BASELINE

Skill Set/Other	Number	Daily Cost	Time to Delivery[11]	Total Cost
Analysts	2	800	62.75	100,400
Developers	3	1,250	62.75	235,313
QA engineers	2	800	62.75	100,400
Total staff cost				436,113

PROPOSED

Skill Set/Other	Number	Daily Cost	Time to Delivery[11]	Total Cost
Analysts	2	800	52	83,200
Developers	4 (+1)	1,250	52	260,000
QA engineers	4 (+2)	800	52	166,400
Total staff cost				509,600

Scenario	Time to Delivery[11]	Staff Cost	Revenue Loss	Total Cost
Baseline	62.75	436,113	941,250	1,377,363
Proposed	52	509,600	780,000	1,289,600
Net impact	−10.75	73,487	−161,250	−87,763

FIGURE 10.9   Combining information from sophisticated modeling techniques with financial information.

The only thing left for Julie to determine is the additional cost that would be incurred from adding more team members into the mix. On average, each of Mammoth Bank's analysts and QA engineers is paid approximately $800 per day in salary and benefits. The cost for each developer is $1250 per day. With this data in hand, Julie can now assess the full overall impact of her proposed course of action (Figure 10.9).

The bottom line: By almost doubling the team size, Julie can reasonably ensure her team will deliver the project 11.75 days earlier (measured at the 90th percentile

---

11. These values are taken from the distribution of probable results generated by your modeling. To minimize risk, we recommend using a number that is taken from the 90th percentile or better.

of distributed result frequencies). Although the total staff cost is significantly greater under this scenario, after factoring business losses into the decision, Julie's modeling provides a high level of confidence that her proposed course of action represents a sound business decision.

Bootstrapping

Bootstrapping[12] is a statistical tool based on the premise that inferences about a general population from a set of sample data can be modeled by resampling that data and evaluating the relationship between the two. Because the actual data from the general population is unknown (we're accessing only a set of sample data), there's no way to truly calculate the error in a sample statistic against its population. In bootstrap resamples, however, the "population" is the original data sample. Because that data sample is a known quality, the quality of inference between the resample data and the original data set can be measured. This lets us extrapolate the result to the relationship between the sample set and the general population.

By way of example, assume we're interested in determining the average age of people around the world. It's neither realistic nor possible to measure the ages of all the people in the world, so we sample a portion of the population and measure their ages. From this single sample, however, we can obtain only one estimate of the mean. To extend this line of reasoning to the total population, we need some idea of the variability of this calculated mean.

One of the simplest bootstrap approaches involves taking the original data set of N ages and resampling it to form a new bootstrap sample of the same size (the new data set is generated from the original by using sampling with replacement so it won't be identical). By repeating this process several thousand times (typically between 1000 and 10,000 times), and computing the mean for each simulation, it becomes possible to create a histogram showing the distribution of the bootstrap means. This provides an estimate of the shape of the distribution, which we can use to answer questions about the extent to which the mean varies from the original sample (and then extrapolate that back to the general population).

Some Final Words

Scrumban is an incredibly robust framework that teams and organizations can employ to take more control over how they work and achieve sustainable levels of high performance over time. Perhaps its greatest strength derives from the fact that each team using it is empowered to determine the level of sophistication and mastery that best works for its context. I hope this book allows you and your teams to forge a comfortable path to better ways of working for yourselves and the organizations for which you work.

---

12. Bootstrapping was proposed in 1979 by the statistician Bradley Efron and is a special case of Monte Carlo simulations.

Appendix

MORE: FOR THE STOUT OF HEART

This appendix provides readers with resources that fall into the following categories:

- High-level summaries of core fundamentals
- Additional background on some of the many models, frameworks, disciplines, and approaches particularly susceptible to being "plugged in" to the Scrumban framework
- Complete case studies referenced in the main text
- Other resources and references to help with using Scrumban in your environment

Scrum in a Nutshell

Scrum is typically introduced by contrasting it with more traditional methods of software development such as waterfall. Those traditional methodologies tend to follow a sequential life cycle:

- The process begins with a detailed planning phase that analyzes, designs, and documents the end product in fine detail.
- The next phase involves identifying the specific tasks to be completed and the time needed to complete them (both estimated to varying degrees of detail).
- This work is then handed off to the customer or primary stakeholder for review. Only after the customer's or stakeholder's approval is obtained does work actually begin.
- Teams or individual developers start completing specialized work in assembly-line style.
- The developers' work is tested before being released to the customer.

Most significantly, various control mechanisms are used to ensure there are no deviations from what was originally planned and approved.

These traditional approaches have both strengths and weaknesses. On the plus side, they're very logical, they require thinking before acting, and they require documenting everything in great detail. Our fast-paced world, however, tends to amplify the weaknesses of these approaches.

First, innovation is often stifled under traditional methods. Great ideas don't always show up at the beginning of the development process, and great ideas that appear late in the release cycle end up being viewed as threats to delivery instead of opportunities for success.

Second, rigid processes don't allow us to respond to changes in the marketplace during the development cycle.

Third, the detailed documentation produced from hours and hours of effort usually receives little attention. As a consequence, a lot of time and effort is put into something that delivers very little end value to the customer. More significantly, when this documentation is referenced, it often exacerbates miscommunication rather than bringing clarification!

In the end, all these weaknesses conspire to ensure that traditional development processes produce products that are only as good as the initial idea. In contrast, Agile ways of working (of which Scrum is the most popular) focus on empowering cross-functional teams to make decisions so they can engage in rapid iteration and adapt to continuous customer input. They're fundamentally about getting things done, and helping to ensure what's being done is relevant to the needs of the customer.

The Scrum Work Process

Unlike those traditional approaches, Scrum structures product development in cycles called sprints. Sprints typically last no more than one month and are scheduled sequentially without intervening delays. Sprints are also time-boxed—they end on a specific date whether "scheduled" work is completed or not. They are never extended.

At the beginning of each sprint, cross-functional teams select "stories" (customer requirements expressed in a functional manner) from a prioritized list. The team commits to completing its chosen stories by the end of the sprint. Chosen items do not change during the sprint, and the team gathers for no more than 15 minutes each day to check on progress and adjust the steps needed to complete the remaining work.

At the end of each sprint, the team reviews completed work with business stakeholders to demonstrate its functionality. Feedback from this event (and the customer's continued use) is incorporated into subsequent sprints.

Scrum emphasizes that the working product delivered at the end of each sprint should be really "done," meaning code is integrated, tested, and potentially shippable. This is also radically different from the traditional approaches described earlier.

The scope of sprint retrospectives is not limited to a review of the product, however. Scrum emphasizes short development phases where teams are constantly inspecting both the product and the process used to create the product. It further emphasizes the importance of adapting product goals and process practices in a continuous mode.

Scrum Roles

There are three essential roles in Scrum: product owner, Scrum master, and team member.

The product owner represents the business side of the house and is responsible for maximizing return on investment (ROI). Product owners identify product features and constantly refine and reprioritize them based on their importance to the business. In actual day-to-day practice, business "value" remains a fuzzy term. Consequently, prioritization ends up being influenced by a variety of dynamic factors.

In some organizations, the product owner and the customer are the same person (this is very common for internal business applications). In other organizations, a vast marketplace might represent the customer, with a product manager or product marketing manager representing customers' interests. Either way, Scrum's product owner is different from a traditional product manager because the person filling the Scrum role is called upon to actively and frequently interact with the development team as sprints progress. Product owners are the ultimate authority as to which work gets done and when, as they are solely responsible for the business value of that work.

Team members are those individuals responsible for actually building the product defined by the product owner. A team typically consists of five to nine people and is cross-functional in nature, meaning all of the expertise required to build and deliver the potentially shippable product exists on each team. For a software product, the team might include individuals with skills in analysis, development, testing, user interface design, database design, and so on. Teams are intended to be "self-organizing" (self-managing), carrying a high degree of autonomy and accountability.

The team decides which stories it will commit to delivering each sprint, and how best to accomplish that commitment. Teams tend to be most productive when all members work exclusively on one product during the sprint and don't multitask across multiple items. Also, teams with infrequent membership changes are associated with higher productivity. Large application groups are often organized into multiple teams focused on different product features (with a close coordination of effort).

Scrum masters have limited but essential roles in the Scrum process. They are not team or project managers. Unlike a project manager, the Scrum master does not tell individual team members what to do or assign tasks. Rather, his or her role is to simply facilitate the process, supporting the team as it organizes and manages itself.

Scrum masters also educate and guide product owners, team members, and others within the business on how to use the Scrum process effectively. One of the Scrum master's most important roles is to protect the team from outside interference.

As Scrum exposes many risks and impediments to a successful sprint, an effective Scrum master will help resolve those issues. Although it's ideal to have a full-time

Scrum master, smaller teams will often have one of their members serve in this role (and carry a lighter work load to balance it out).

It's important that the Scrum master not be the product owner. The Scrum master is sometimes called upon to push back on the product owner (for example, if the product owner asks the team to work on a new deliverable in the middle of a sprint). The product owner also may not have a sufficient connection to the business issues to prioritize and refine work definitions effectively.

If a Scrum master was previously in a management position, he or she will need to significantly change the management mindset and style of interaction to be successful. An (ex-) project manager can sometimes step into the role, although this approach has met with mixed success.

Planning Poker

The team is responsible for providing estimates of the effort required for each item on the product backlog. Over time, a team should be able to track how much work it can do each sprint. This information can then be used to project a release date to complete all features, or to estimate how many features can be completed by a certain date (assuming no changed circumstances). In Scrum, we call this the "velocity" of the team. Velocity is typically expressed in the units utilized to create backlog item size estimates.

A variety of estimating techniques have been devised over the years to help teams estimate their work. Planning Poker is one of the most popular methods. With this approach, team members offer estimates by placing numbered cards face-down on the table (rather than speaking them aloud). Once everyone has "played," the cards are revealed and the different estimates discussed. This technique helps a group avoid the cognitive bias associated with anchoring, where the first suggestion sets a precedent for subsequent estimates.

Scrum and Scrumban: Some Quick Comparisons

Tables A.1 through A.8 summarize how Scrumban offers a path for overcoming some of the common challenges that Scrum teams face in fulfilling the essential purposes Scrum expects from its roles, events, and artifacts.

TABLE A.1   Scrum Roles

Description/Purpose	Common Challenges	How Scrumban Helps
Cross-functional and self-organizing teams. Designed to optimize flexibility, creativity, and productivity. Maximize feedback and accelerate ROI by efficiently delivering iterative product increments. Team is empowered to organize and manage work. Collective responsibility is fostered by discouraging subteams and specialization.	Psychological barriers to change. Operating on their own versus having specific individuals direct people and processes (adapting to the Scrum master role can be particularly challenging). Building effective cross-functional skill sets within a development team takes time and effort.	Emphasize system understanding and stability ahead of change. Respect and retain current roles while developing a shared understanding of the current work process and policies. Work more effectively while evolving at a comfortable pace. Aid the transition to a prescribed Scrum destination, or adapt roles, ceremonies, and processes to a state that works best for a given system at a given time.

TABLE A.2   Scrum Ceremonies

Description/Purpose	Common Challenges	How Scrumban Helps
Four formal events for inspection and adaption: Sprint Planning, Daily Scrum, Sprint Review, and Sprint Retrospective. Each ceremony serves a specific purpose and is essential to Scrum. Typically involve degrees of collaboration designed to promote: ■ Mutual understanding (transparency) ■ Individual buy-in ■ Shared commitment toward a commonly understood outcome ■ A culture of continuous improvement	Many organizations modify or omit ceremonies as a solution to exposed problems and dysfunctions (benefits Scrum would otherwise deliver are never realized). Less mature teams tend to focus on the wrong issues and unnecessarily lengthen the time investment. Seasoned Scrum masters can help teams learn to manage ceremonies more effectively, but individual capabilities can vary significantly and the end result is often hit or miss.	Can replace the intended functions of modified or omitted ceremonies. Teams can work more effectively in "broken" systems as they're enabled to evolve. Scrum-like frameworks aren't condemned to underperform. Reduce or eliminate the time required to complete many ceremonies by effectively incorporating their functions within daily work or other mechanisms.

TABLE A.3   Product Backlog

Description/Purpose	Common Challenges	How Scrumban Helps
A dynamic, ordered list of everything that might be needed in the product.	Organizations often frustrate the purpose and function of the product owner role by assigning it to multiple individuals.	Work demands from all sources are visualized; can be managed with greater transparency.
The product owner is responsible for the content, availability, and prioritization.	Subjective prioritization and risk management techniques.	Scientifically based mechanisms to identify and measure risk are emphasized.
Maximizes transparency of key information to promote a shared understanding of work and business objectives.	Effectiveness depends on individual capabilities.	Visualized classes of service support just-in-time localized prioritization (more informed handling of work with different value and risk).
Team is collectively responsible for refining the backlog.	Inordinate focus on templating language and similar aids over delivering value and minimizing risk.	Visualization and measurement of work flow through the value stream helps overcome an inordinate focus on mechanics (such as templating language).
	Grouping mechanisms such as theming and slotting are invented with little business awareness.	

TABLE A.4   Release Planning

Description/Purpose	Common Challenges	How Scrumban Helps
Planning in an Agile context should be iterative, be consistent with self-organizing teams, and support empirical process control (meaning plans emphasize insight over direction or commitment).	Planning and estimating largely depend on a single metric—velocity.	Enhanced recognition and management of risk factors, additional metrics, and techniques allowing for probabilistic forecasting (based on Little's law) enhance the reliability of forecasting and improve its scalability across larger enterprises.
Agile release plans should be dynamic, and increase in accuracy as the results of each sprint are incorporated.	Reliable forecasting is difficult to achieve because it is subjective and unique to each team. This fundamental nature of velocity makes estimating difficult to scale.	The integration of real options theory and similar models into a Scrumban framework affords more flexibility with release planning.
Agile release cycles should be kept as short as possible (definitely less than 1 year) to ensure "course corrections" can be made as early as possible.	Though it's possible to adjust deadline, scope, resources, and quality for any given project, only deadline and scope tend to be effectively controllable in most Scrum contexts.	

TABLE A.5   Sprint Time-Box

Description/Purpose	Common Challenges	How Scrumban Helps
Limited to one calendar month to ensure a routine "inspect and adapt" cadence. Has a short-enough duration that market needs won't change between the time a commitment to complete work is made and the time the completed work is delivered. Protects the team from scope creep. Eliminates ad hoc work requests that interfere with productivity. Team commits to completing only work that it estimates is realistic to achieve.	Duration is often established based on organizational desire for alignment, but actually the nature and complexity of work can vary from team to team. Some environments change more rapidly than others, meaning market needs can change during a sprint. Insulating the team from work requests is rarely pragmatic. Emergency work is a part of all businesses, and we need mechanics for managing it. Full scope of knowledge work is discoverable only as work is performed.	Discovery and understanding of the systems across which work is performed are used to set sprint duration (or transition out of time-boxed development altogether). Prioritization and commitment to specific work is not limited to the start of a time-box. Visualization and cost of delay metrics (CD3) reduce subjectivity and allow for just-in-time prioritization throughout the workflow. Visualization of different classes of service improves recognition and management of different business needs.

TABLE A.6   Daily Stand-ups

Description/Purpose	Common Challenges	How Scrumban Helps
Fifteen-minute time-boxed event to synchronize activities and plan the next 24 hours of work. Optimizes the probability of meeting the sprint goal. A key "inspect and adapt" meeting to help eliminate the need for other meetings, improve communications, promote quick decision making, and improve the team's overall knowledge.	Can turn into meaningless "status" meetings rather than true synchronization and planning efforts. Impediments managed after they manifest themselves. Probability of meeting the sprint goal is still subject to the inherent variability of work. Less likelihood of developing disciplined approaches for recognizing patterns in impediments because continuous improvement efforts are managed outside Scrum's core framework.	Kanban board as a "real-time" information radiator shifts the focus away from status and impediments and toward opportunities for inspection and adaption. Greater focus on the work, rather than the worker, reduces the need to manage psychological barriers. Visualization enables scaled stand-ups across larger or multiple teams (improving shared understandings). Bias toward integrating disciplined approaches (katas) improves scaling and mobility of team members.

TABLE A.7   Sprint Review

Description/Purpose	Common Challenges	How Scrumban Helps
Four-hour, time-boxed meeting (for 1-month sprints) to inspect product increments. Inspect and provide feedback on completed work; collaborate to identify ways to optimize value. A revised (reprioritized) product backlog is produced defining the probable work items for the next sprint. Opportunity for the entire team to improve their knowledge of business objectives and the suitability and quality of the incremental product delivery.	Often perceived as the measurement of performance and accountability to stakeholders. Ends up being misused to protect reputations in low-trust environments rather than to improve delivery. Work is frequently optimized prematurely to meet presentation demands from stakeholders.	Supplemental mechanisms for building trust are more effective than or equally as effective as the sprint review, making it less likely for the review to be misused. Having multiple definitions of done across each value-adding step improves overall work quality and reduces the likelihood of premature optimization aimed at preserving stakeholder trust.

TABLE A.8   Sprint Retrospective

Description/Purpose	Common Challenges	How Scrumban Helps
Three-hour, time-boxed meeting that occurs after the sprint review and before the next sprint planning meeting. A continuous improvement process to counteract the natural forces of entropy (moving from order to chaos) and to sustain higher levels of Agility and performance. Opportunity to inspect how the last sprint went in terms of people, relationships, process, and tools. Identify potential improvements to the way the team works; create a plan for implementing them.	Sprint mechanism does not naturally encourage or provide for capacity to be allocated toward ongoing improvement efforts. Recognized opportunities to improve tend to be subjective or based on anecdotal evidence rather than empirical analysis.	Visualization framework eases management of striking a balance between delivering work and executing against improvement efforts. Greater emphasis on the analysis of empirical data (and providing more such data to measure) makes the continuous improvement process more effective and more scalable. Disciplined, scientific approaches to problem solving, risk management, and continuous improvement (katas) create more adaptive "thinking systems."

Scrumban Roadmap: A Quick Reference for Getting Started

Chapter 5 provides a detailed overview of one approach for introducing Scrumban to an organization or group of teams. The purpose of this quick reference is to provide a high-level summary of the practical steps to getting started.

Step 1: Visualize Your System

Having teams create a visual model of the systems in which they work (and ultimately a model of their workflow) is the first and most important step. Initial visualizations aren't intended to be perfect. Rather, their primary objective is to help teams gain a common understanding of how they are currently working. The entire team should be involved in this process. The key elements to identify are as follows:

- *Inputs*: The kind of work coming in to the team and where it comes from
- *Process steps*: The stages of discovery or refinement work passes through from the time the team first accepts it to the time it delivers completed work to others
- *Work performed by others outside the immediate team*: Shared resources, required approvals from other departments or business units, and so on
- *Outputs*: The team's completed work and to whom it is delivered

A visual representation of these elements is presented in Figure A.1.

Exercise 1: One way to get started is to have each team member identify two or three items he or she currently has in progress. As a group, discuss how each person received that work, what the team member is expected to accomplish based on its current state, and what happens to it once the individual's part is done.

After walking through several existing work items in this fashion, you should begin to recognize patterns that can be translated into a visual mapping similar to the diagram in Figure A.1.

Remember, the objective here is simply to visualize the different kinds of work your team undertakes (e.g., user stories, bug fixes, work estimation requests, ad hoc customer requests). Resist any urges to redesign how you work. These decisions will be made by the team over time as your understanding of the system improves.

Exercise 2: Engage your team members in some form of interactive training or exercise that will orient them to the core Scrumban practices that will be introduced through your initial efforts. The two chief practices are workflow visualization and the evolutionary change process. You may elect to include additional concepts such as limiting work in progress (WIP) and pull versus push. Ideally, you want new

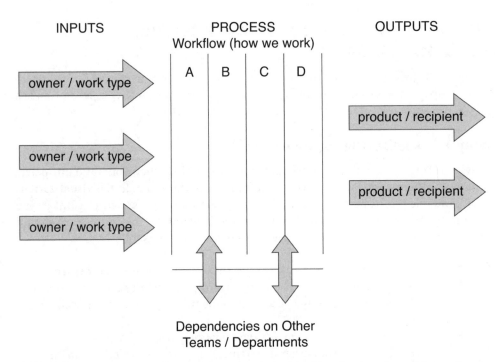

FIGURE A.1   A necessary first step to creating a working kanban board is to visualize the closed system to which it relates.

practitioners to recognize that these practices are minimally disruptive, and to experience the way they'll be carried out within the working context with which they're already familiar.

I specifically designed the GetScrumban game (Figure A.2) for this purpose, and certainly encourage its use as part of any kickstart process.

Exercise 3: With the initial understanding in place, have your teams expand upon their initial systems/workflow visualizations and create their first working kanban board (either a physical board, a virtual board, or both). At the end of Chapter 6 and also later in this appendix are several examples of board designs that teams can draw upon for inspiration. Don't neglect to consider "ticket" (work item) design at this point, assessing factors such as the following:

- Information necessary for a team member to make a good decision as to which of multiple work items should be worked on first
- Information needed to better understand how long it takes for work to move through the system or even each phase of the system

FIGURE A.2   The GetScrumban game (http://GetScrumban.com) simulates how a Scrum team can introduce Scrumban elements into its workflow to address common challenges.

Coaching Tip!

Encourage teams to keep initial designs simple!

Simplicity of design should be paramount—especially when teams are getting started. That said, the phases of work reflected in an initial board design should expand beyond just "To Do," "Doing," and "Done." Nevertheless, such a coarse workflow mapping may be the most appropriate starting point for some contexts.

When teams complete their initial designs, be sure to congratulate them on achieving their first concrete step toward not only becoming more effective, but also gaining more control over their own way of working! Each of the following "steps" to launching Scrumban in your environment primarily takes place in the context of day-to-day activities and interactions.

Step 2: Start Measuring Performance

Once teams populate their kanban boards with actual work items, they'll see how work "moves" from left to right across the board as progress occurs (Figure A.3). Revealing how work actually flows through your process is informative, but using new tools to measure and evaluate flow is even more valuable.

To facilitate shared understanding and collective responsibility, the board should always be treated as belonging to the entire team, and not just the manager or Scrum master. Similarly, conversations around information gleaned from the board should always be steered in directions that reinforce assessing the board as a reflection of the

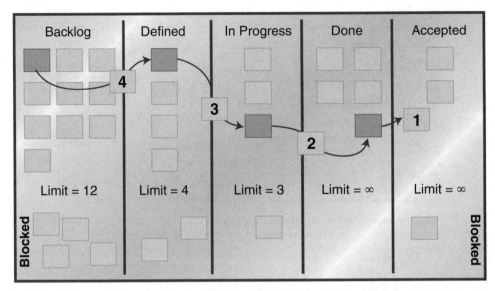

FIGURE A.3   Cards move across the board from left to right, with an emphasis on moving cards in the rightmost side (those closest to delivery) first.

entire system, and not as a collection of separate conversations focused on individual items or the work undertaken by individual members.

After allowing a day or two for teams to become accustomed to any new logistics associated with working with visual boards, coaches and Scrum masters should begin guiding teams on capturing and understanding some basic metrics. Among the most important to start with are these measures:

- *Amount of work in progress (WIP)*: Work that's been started but not yet finished.
- *Blockers*: Blocked items are just that, and can't move to the next stage of your process until the issue blocking them has been resolved.
- *Lead time*: The amount of time it takes for work to travel across the board.
- *Throughput*: The number of work items completed per a given time period.

Exercise 1: In daily stand-ups, coaches and Scrum masters can begin nurturing conversations in which these metrics can be used to help the team better understand its system:

- *Amount of work in progress*: Have the team divide its total WIP by the number of members on the team to get an average amount of WIP per person. Does the result show that each person is managing two things at a time? Five things at a time? Ten things at a time? Does the number seem like too much or too little?

- *Blockers*: Guide the team in asking pertinent questions about blockers. How often is work getting blocked? How long does it stay blocked? Do blockers tend to show up in just one or two parts of the process? The answers to these questions will help the team understand why work is being delayed (because of a lack of skill sets on the team, defects, or other reasons).
- *Lead time*: Does the team understand how long it's taking for work to move through the system? Capturing this information for each work item and plotting it in a histogram or other visual chart can lead to many insights. Encourage the team to explore such issues as whether some work types take longer than others and why. Evaluate which understandings can be developed from monitoring the relationship among these four basic metrics over time.
- *Throughput*: Marginally informative in isolation, tracking this number over time will help the team understand whether changes they make to their system affect the total amount of work completed.

Step 3: Stabilize Your System and Improve Focus with WIP Limits

At the end of Chapter 5, we discussed how Scrumban can be used to stabilize a system by establishing initial WIP limits within the system's workflow. Remember, it's necessary to stabilize a system before undertaking any effort to improve it, so attaining stability should be one of every team's first objectives.

Although we ultimately want to apply WIP limits based on the system's actual capacity, imposing totally random limits when working with a system for the first time allows the process of discovery to begin. Let's see how.

Exercise 1: Coaches and Scrum masters will need to guide team members toward understanding the true nature of their system, particularly how to tell whether it's stable or unstable. If it is an unstable system, which measures can be taken to stabilize it?

- Is any team member working on things that are not reflected on the board? Capturing all incoming and outgoing work is vital to assessing the system. If this goal isn't being achieved, determine which changes are needed to begin capturing this work.
- Are system lead times relatively stable or widely distributed?
- Does the cumulative flow diagram (CFD) reflect a balance between incoming requests and outgoing work?
- Encourage using WIP limits as an initial mechanic for stabilizing incoming and outgoing work. Measure and adapt as warranted.

Exercise 2: In parallel with their efforts on metrics, coaches and Scrum masters should further help team members seek out visual patterns exposed by their boards and metrics. The daily stand-ups should almost immediately move away from discussions of status. Team members no longer have to recite what they did yesterday, what they're planning to do today, and which potential impediments are obstructing them—all of this information appears on the board right in front of them! Instead, members are encouraged to explore issues relevant to flow and performance:

- Where is work backing up? Why is this happening? Which experiments can be conducted to expand our understanding?
- Are any parts of the system starved for work during the day? Why is this happening? Which mechanisms can we experiment with to avoid it?

Step 4: Improve Your Understanding and Management of Risk

Chapter 6 and later chapters explored how Scrumban can be used to improve our understanding and management of risk. Though ultimately one of the most important areas for a Scrumban team to attack, attempting to address risk too early can needlessly complicate your kickstart efforts. Consequently, we always encourage initiative leaders to proceed with caution here.

Don Reinertsen said, "If you quantify only one thing, quantify the cost of delay."[1] Thus, when the time is right for your team to begin thinking about risk, I recommend starting with concepts associated with cost of delay.

Exercise 1: In release planning and backlog grooming sessions with product owners, coaches and Scrum masters can begin helping product owners incorporate more consistent concepts of value into work descriptions. Have them attempt to quantify:

- The extent to which proposed work will increase revenue
- The extent to which proposed work will protect existing revenue (improvements or innovation that sustain market share)
- The extent to which proposed work will reduce costs
- The extent to which proposed work will avoid anticipated costs

With these preliminary valuations in place, guide product owners to new processes that will help them (and the team) make better business decisions as to which work should be prioritized based on anticipated impact to the business (Chapter 6 introduced a "weighted shortest job first" approach called CD3).

As familiarity with these approaches grows, guide the team in exploring how to integrate this new information into their visual management framework.

---

1. *Principles of Product Development Flow* (Celeritas Publishing, 2009).

Step 5: Continuously Improve

As reflected throughout the book, Scrumban is usually a journey of evolution, not revolution. Teams should continuously seek process improvements, and continuously improve their ability to identify and prioritize the efforts most relevant to the capabilities they want to improve.

Concepts alone don't change how we act and think. If we want to achieve meaningful and sustainable change, then we must make a deliberate and conscious choice to practice new behaviors—especially at the beginning. We want to identify and adopt routines that will help us take the concepts discussed in the book and turn them into new mental habits that will make their practice a reality.

Coaches and Scrum masters should use retrospectives as their vehicle of choice for introducing many of the habit-forming concepts we introduced in Chapter 9, such as the following:

- Fostering consistent and habitual thinking
    - Begin with something as basic as guiding the team on a process for conducting simple experiments (e.g., attacking average lead time by adopting a new team policy on blocked work items)
    - Extend by guiding the team to more disciplined regimens such as A3 problem solving
- Integrating and using team assessment tools to prioritize improvement efforts (i.e., understand which core capabilities are most deficient and take action to improve in those arenas first)
- Detecting and avoiding patterns of unsafe change

Using Scrumban to Introduce Scrum

Although Scrum (and Agile practices in general) are becoming more prevalent in software development, the act of exploring and adopting new ways of working can be quite overwhelming for many teams. There's a lot of new information to master and a host of emotional impacts to manage (don't underestimate the influence that emotions have on these efforts).

Some team members may be upset because they perceive the impending effort as an implicit indictment of their previous way of working—that is, a signal that it has been deemed a failure. Others will be concerned about changes in their roles or titles. The range of potential emotions is both wide and unpredictable. You need only consider the kaleidoscope of emotions that most of us feel on the first day of a new job (or a new school year) to gain some appreciation for what's at play—some anticipation, some anxiety, some doubt, and probably a handful of other feelings.

For these reasons, finding the right quantity of new information to introduce and the right pace at which to introduce it is critical to overall success. Introduce too much too quickly, and you run the risk of bogging teams down. Move too slowly, and the endeavor will be perceived as a waste of time and effort. Though seasoned coaches and Scrum masters will often gain an intuitive understanding of how to strike the right balance, I've found Scrumban to be an ideal framework for introducing Agile practices and Scrum to teams. Though every context is different, the general approach outlined in this section has proved successful across a wide range of environments. (Note that this approach assumes there is a seasoned coach working with the team who will come to play the role of Scrum master as Scrum events and artifacts are introduced.)

Step 1: Provide Context

Whether they choose to acknowledge it or not, teams and organizations interested in adopting Scrum (or Lean and Agile practices in general) are putting themselves on a journey of change. Typically, they are moving from a context that has traditionally assigned success and failure to a limited number of individuals (i.e., project managers and other leaders) to a context where success and failure are collectively owned and shared.

In preparing to embark on this journey, the coach/Scrum master needs to address two levels of context as a first step. The first contextual level is organizational: What are the organization's pain points driving the effort to change?

- Have there been issues with time to market?
- Is quality a growing concern?
- Has the organization encountered challenges in responding to changing conditions in the marketplace?

Being able to articulate the business reasons driving the need to improve is fundamental to establishing a shared business purpose around which everyone can rally.

The second context is local: Which pain points will the team have an opportunity to address as part of the effort?

- Is work seemingly thrust upon the team without regard to the team members' actual capacity to complete it within the desired time frame?
- Does the team feel isolated from the people who actually use and benefit from what they create?
- Does the team feel impotent about its ability to control or influence how they work?

Identifying conditions the team has a vested interest in improving is an important first step toward minimizing emotional barriers that would otherwise interfere with your efforts.

Even with these contexts defined, however, teams and organizations following a traditional approach to adopting Scrum—where Scrum represents both the vehicle for effectuating change and the change itself—consistently experience significant challenges. This occurs because although Scrum is a simple framework, teams are immediately burdened with learning new ways of working. Changes in habit take time and effort to implement, and it's fairly typical for new approaches to feel significantly more burdensome, yet less productive as learning curves are traversed. The psychological and emotional impact of this journey cannot be ignored. This is why I find Scrumban a superior framework for introducing Scrum to new teams.

Once organizational and team-level rallying points have been articulated, the coach/Scrum master needs to guide the team through a limited number of "new" objectives, concepts, and practices:

- First and foremost, it should be emphasized that the sole objective of this effort is to help the team members better understand how they currently work. The team will decide how to apply their new knowledge to address the organizational and team objectives that have been articulated.
- The team should be provided with a basic introduction to systems thinking, and encouraged to apply this perspective to improve their understanding of their work.
- The team should be introduced to basic mechanics for visualizing workflow (the concept of different work items and value streams). An initial kanban board should be developed from this exercise, and populated with existing work items.
- The team should be introduced to the concept of "pulling" work versus having it "pushed" upon them. This represents the most significant change they will be asked to undertake in performing their work.
- Another significant change to how the team works will likely be the notion of a daily stand-up. Rather than have these stand-ups follow a typical Scrum pattern, however, the team is simply called upon to spend 10–15 minutes each day examining the visual workflow and collectively addressing discoveries.

Note this approach doesn't require the team to learn new concepts (like a product backlog, time-boxed sprints, iterative and incremental delivery of a working product, and other concepts that are central to Scrum). Also, while it's possible (and preferable) to include nondevelopment functions at this stage (i.e., a product owner), doing so is not essential to getting started. Consequently, teams can be sufficiently oriented in less than a day to continue their present ways of working with minor adaptations that are neither complex nor burdensome.

Step 2: Introduce Scrum Elements in Response to Team Discoveries

The coach/Scrum master will use the daily stand-ups and his or her regular interactions with team members to identify opportunities for introducing additional Scrum or Scrumban concepts as appropriate. Although the exact order varies from context to context, I focus on these elements:

- *Physical space*: Guide the team in embracing changes that can improve collaboration. For example, take down cubicle walls, locate team members in the same physical area (if they have been dispersed throughout a building or campus), locate the information radiator of choice in a central area (e.g., whiteboard, large electronic screen), and incorporate technology to aid collaboration with remote workers.
- *Backlog*: Though we often think of backlogs in terms of defined products or projects, the reality for many development teams is that they need to address a variety of ad hoc requests outside of product development. I tend to diverge from the traditional Scrum framework here by allowing teams to recognize this work as part of their backlog.
- *Creating definitions of done*: This definition should ultimately include user acceptance testing (UAT), which will be a challenging change for teams used to having a UAT phase after long design and development phases.
- *User stories*: Though we start with work items, helping the team develop skills for writing good user stories will improve both flow and recognition of different work items. For application development teams, helping them begin to create work items as user stories that are feature related versus task oriented is a critical evolution to recognizing and delivering value over activity.
- *Iterations and related events*: Time-boxed sprints and the events around them provide a great structure for fostering a variety of activities that are essential to developing Lean and Agile mindsets. These include the notion of delivering working product on a regular cadence, improving the ways we break down work for execution, enhancing team communication and understanding of the actual work associated with producing any given item, and fostering disciplined approaches to continuous improvement.

Seasoned coaches recognize that events like sprint planning sessions and techniques like team estimation represent mechanisms that can help teams master practices that will improve Lean and Agile outcomes. In my mind, they are akin to the concrete steps to which all new Shu-level learners gravitate. Scrumban allows us to meter the pace at which teams are exposed to these concrete steps, facilitating the process of learning and mastering Scrum.

Neither Scrum nor Scrumban, however, will help teams realize their maximum effectiveness until the end user becomes part of the process. As alluded to earlier, coaches/Scrum masters can elect to involve non-IT functions at any point in the process.

Nevertheless, there are certain advantages to limiting initial efforts to only the development team. For example, many fundamental practices focus on helping the team better understand and manage workflow, and there's something to be said for keeping new learners singularly focused on a small number of things without distraction from other concepts.

Once iterations and related events are introduced, however, the product owner's involvement (and concepts relating to value, risk, and prioritization) becomes essential.

Step 3: Maturing

By introducing Scrum practices as solutions to perceived challenges, most teams will have incorporated all of the essential elements of the Scrum framework into their way of working within two to three months. Easing them into the framework in this fashion allows them to gain a deeper understanding of why and how each element fulfills certain functions. And team members will have achieved this maturity with minimal disruption to boot!

With this foundation in place, the team (and organization) has many paths that it can follow to attain further maturity. Naturally, I continue to emphasize maximizing the Scrumban framework to drive this maturity.

Scrumban and SAFe

Though it is well beyond the scope of this book to engage in a comparison of Scrumban and SAFe (the Scaled Agile Framework), this topic is important enough to warrant a few words.

SAFe is intended to provide a "recipe" that enterprises can theoretically follow to scale Agility across the organization. Like Scrumban, this framework is built upon Lean and Agile principles. Unlike Scrumban, it prescribes adopting specific practices at three distinct levels (the team, program, and portfolio areas).

Enterprises are naturally attracted to SAFe, especially because it provides the kind of concrete instructions that new Shu-level learners are eager to mimic. I question, however, whether it's effectively structured to help organizations achieve true adaptive capabilities as discussed within this book. Nonetheless, there are sound thinkers behind SAFe, and it continues to evolve as a framework. I remain steadfast in the view that good ideas can come from anywhere, and will continue to watch for improvements and new ideas that will no doubt result from its continued use.

Scrumban Stories: The Full Case Studies

There are a number of "Scrumban stories" referenced throughout this book. These stories are histories of how the Scrumban framework was used in a variety of contexts to ease or accelerate desired outcomes. This appendix includes four stories from a mix of industries (financial services, health care, information technology, and others). They relate to different-sized organizations (from startups to Fortune 50 corporations). They also describe how elements of the Scrumban framework were used both within and outside of a software development context.

Though the documenters of these studies are identified at the beginning of each story, I want to specifically call out and acknowledge Bennet Vallet, Ramon Tramontini, and Marcelo Walter for allowing us to include their previously documented studies in this publication.

Scrumban Story 1: Mammoth Bank (Part 1)

Industry: Financial services

Organization size: Enterprise

Documented by: Ajay Reddy

Background

It's 2013, and the IT organization at this Fortune 100 financial institution is eight years into an "Agile transformation." An outside firm was retained to lead the initial transition, a different company was hired three years later to assist with ongoing efforts, and now a third company is being engaged to help the institution realize the full extent of benefits originally targeted from this major undertaking.

This particular story is about the RAD Group and its Digital Data Team (the actual names have been changed to preserve confidentiality). RAD develops web and mobile applications for a mix of business units at the bank. As our story begins, RAD is under fire for slow and unreliable delivery. The bank is losing existing customers and prospective new business because its technology applications are lagging. Senior executives are up in arms, and RAD needs to find a solution to this situation fast.

Situation

Dissatisfaction on All Sides   RAD and its Data Team presented a challenging environment for any coach. The RAD Group was led by a well-respected engineer who had become extremely skeptical that any further value might be gained from additional training and coaching on Agile practices. His attitude reflected the group's overall "improvement fatigue." The business units were dissatisfied with the lengthy time to market associated with new applications coming out of RAD. The development teams were frustrated by constantly shifting priorities across and within the projects they worked on, forcing frequent context shifts as work was seemingly shifted from project to project with every sprint.

Further complicating the picture was the fact that most of RAD's work consisted of high-visibility projects serving a variety of high-profile business units (from residential mortgages to commercial lending). There was a constant shifting of priorities in RAD's work inventory, which exacerbated the long delivery cycles and missed deadlines, which in turn frustrated RAD's business customers. RAD had been assessed as a "highly Agile" group, and most of its members believed any perceived delays and reliability issues were directly attributable to the group's ability to quickly respond to the business units' changing priorities.

CodeGenesys was one of many resources employed by the bank's third consulting firm. Our coach was the fifth individual in a long line of consultants assigned to work with RAD. The first order of business was to extract data from existing tools and systems so as to objectively corroborate the expressed dissatisfactions of all stakeholders and see which additional information could be gleaned.

Understanding the Context   Most of the Data Team's work came in the form of "product enhancement requests." Data from the bank's Project Portfolio Management tool confirmed the business unit's anecdotal history: Customer lead time was extraordinarily long (the span of time between the date when an enhancement request was initiated until the date when it was actually delivered; see Table A.9).

TABLE A.9   Existing Data on Project Lead Times

Reported Project Size	Time Waiting in Project Queue	Actual Development Time	Total Customer Lead Time
Small	14	16	30
Small	24	9	33
Medium	16	14	30
Medium	15	27	42
Medium	23	17	40
Medium	24	36	60
Large	20	30	50
Large	25	42	67
Average	*20*	*24*	*44*
Median	*22*	*22*	*41*

Corroboration of the team's claimed sources of dissatisfaction, however, was slightly more challenging to produce from existing systems. A limited set of Scrumban practices were immediately introduced to gain better insight.

The Scrum Context

Commonly Encountered Challenges Though it had been several years since the bank had begun its transition to Agile practices, like most large transformations the process had started with a small number of teams. Scrum was the framework of choice for RAD's development teams, and the team members were still relatively new practitioners. These teams were contending with the following challenges, among others:

- *Limited cross-functionality*: The bank's complex technology systems required pockets of specialization, as did security and governance needs. These specialized resources were shared across teams, meaning they were not always available to address work items in progress.
- *External dependencies*: Sprint goals were often dependent upon receiving other work or approvals from outside groups (business and IT).
- *Unreliable estimates*: While the estimation process was beneficial in terms of enhancing a shared understanding of work, there was little correlation between team estimates and the actual time and effort required to complete stories. Forecasting the combined capabilities of multiple teams was also challenging.

Some Common Approaches A variety of techniques have been employed to help organizations address these challenges. Let's first consider the management of external dependencies.

Scrum emphasizes accountability as a mechanism for achieving Agility. If a team can't complete work by the end of the sprint, it dilutes accountability and gives the team an excuse not to deliver a product.

Teams often try to break dependencies by "empowering" a product owner to bypass or manage its reliance on external resources, but this rarely is effective (especially when the organization doesn't view the product owner as empowered). Another common response is for the team to define "done" in a way that affords team members full control over what's delivered. This doesn't necessarily equate to the work being truly "done" from the customer's perspective, however.

Another common response is for teams to attempt to manage their external dependencies by deferring their work until the dependent work is delivered. This isn't always an option, however, nor is it particularly Agile.

Some of the more effective ways teams have employed to overcome these challenges include the following steps:

- Assuming responsibility themselves (and securing the necessary capabilities to perform the work)
- Working against a test double (abstracting the dependency behind an interface)
- Negotiating an agreement (while understanding such agreements may affect feature prioritization of other teams)

Unfortunately, none of these "solutions" produces universal success, leaving teams to either employ a shotgun approach or rely upon the intuition of its Scrum masters and coaches to guide them toward an appropriate result.

Team estimating was one of several new practices Scrum brought to the table at Mammoth Bank. Estimating efforts was one way that teams were improving their knowledge about the work they were undertaking, and was still viewed as contributing to improved morale. These efforts were not proving beneficial in terms of helping the teams meet their sprint commitments, however, nor were they lending greater predictability to the delivery of completed work.

Analysis of the data from the seven prior sprints verified the high variance between estimates and actual performance, but failed to clarify a cause for this variance. Suspected culprits included the following candidates:

- No clear definition of done for many work items
- Too much work in progress per team member
- Too-short sprint duration (two weeks)
- Subject-matter experts not immediately addressing and completing work

Among the common approaches teams can pursue to address these issues are these methods:

- Enforcing clearer definitions of "done" across work items
- Limiting the number of open work items
- Negotiating increased sprint durations with stakeholders

The Scrumban Approach

Starting with an Improved Visual Workflow   Like many of the Scrum teams throughout RAD, the Data Team was using a basic Scrum board to visualize work progress during sprints (a physical board with three columns labeled "To Do," "Doing," and

"Done"). After a few days of observing the team in action, I introduced the concept of expanding the team's board to better capture the actual flow of work.

Because humans process visual presentations of data more effectively, improving workflow visualizations is a particularly powerful way to enhance shared understandings. I guided the team in expanding their board design so the "Doing" column was divided into multiple columns representing various phases of knowledge discovery (Figure A.4).

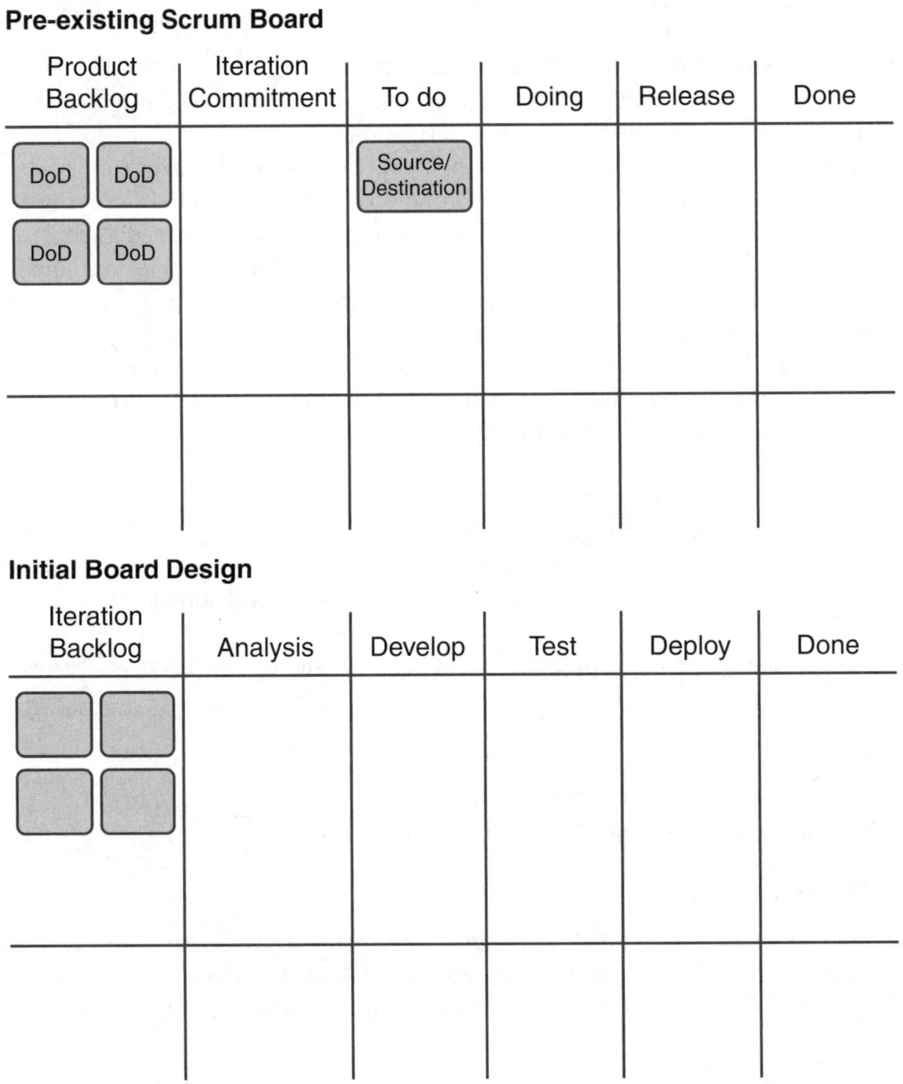

Pre-existing Scrum Board

Product Backlog	Iteration Commitment	To do	Doing	Release	Done
DoD DoD DoD DoD		Source/ Destination			

Initial Board Design

Iteration Backlog	Analysis	Develop	Test	Deploy	Done
▢▢ ▢▢					

FIGURE A.4   Initial visualization of workflow broken down into more granular phases.

Team members continued to update the board at least twice a day, or whenever they began work on a new item. Other than this slight modification to the visual design of their work board, the team didn't change anything about the way it worked (continuing a cadence of two-week sprints, and collectively estimating user story points as an integral component of their sprint planning process).

Learning and Evolving from New and Objective Data   Beyond providing an expanded visual presentation of workflow, the team's revised board designs led to the capture of new metrics.

Teams throughout the RAD Group relied on historical measures of story point velocity to drive story selection within individual sprints. This information was also used for longer-term forecasting of projects. Though teams had demonstrated improvements in their velocity over time, this data didn't correlate with the actual delivery of work. Once the team began actively measuring new things (specifically, lead times and the flow efficiency of each sprint), they expanded their understandings even further.

Visualizing these metrics enabled the team to recognize a number of things:

- *There was only a loose correlation between story points and actual lead time*: Though the Data Team had improved its story point estimating capabilities since its initial adoption of Scrum, a substantial degree of variation persisted in the amount of time it took to complete work on stories of the same size (Figure A.5).

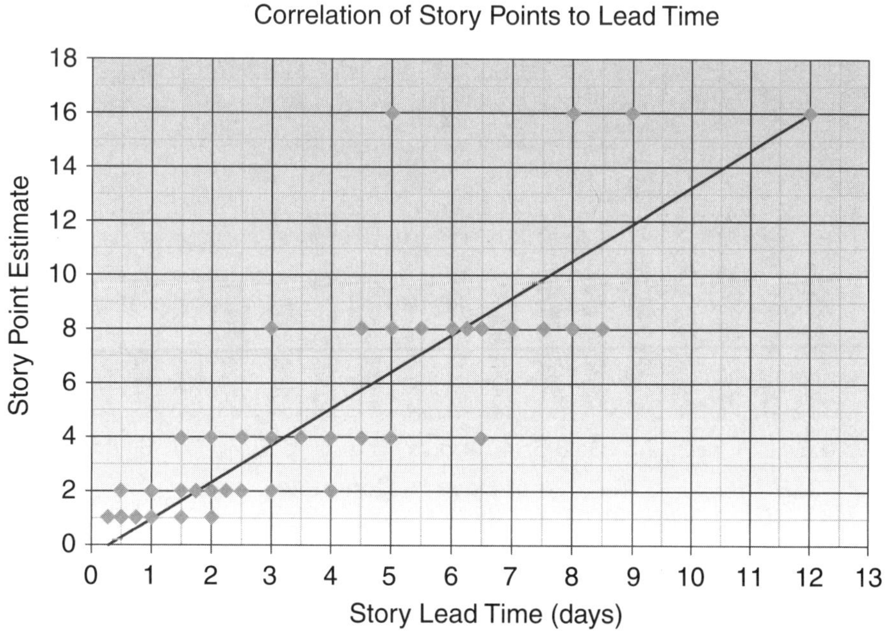

FIGURE A.5   The actual time required to deliver similarly sized work reflected great variability.

This data prompted the team to begin devising low-cost experiments that would help them better understand the root cause of this variation and improve their ability to better recognize and manage it.

■ *Different work types existed*: After several weeks of collecting data, I helped the team recognize patterns that seemed to be emerging within the team's lead time histogram (see Figure A.6).

First, and not unexpectedly, the distribution pattern corroborates what Scrumban practitioners intuitively understand—most user stories are completed within a relatively short time frame, but there's a long tail of outliers (reflecting the wide variability in work) that cause longer overall delivery rates.

Second, the data set was still relatively limited, but the pattern was *suggestive* of a bimodal distribution. Multimodal distribution patterns often signify the presence of different *types* of work—each with its own characteristics and patterns. Identifying different types of work is the first step to better understanding and managing them.

■ *Substantial waste was present in the system*: Once the team incorporated a "waiting area" for user stories awaiting approvals or contributions from external sources, it created the ability to better measure "waste" (a concept associated with Lean thinking).

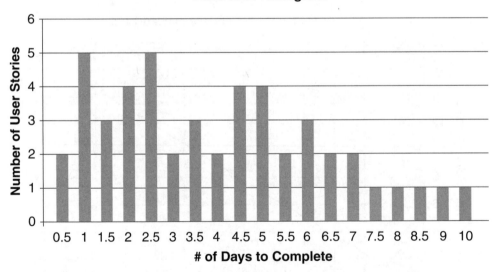

FIGURE A.6   (a) Patterns emerged when the lead time histogram was constructed. While the initial board design (b) did not take the changes into account, the revised board design (c) incorporated a "waiting area."

BEFORE:

Initial Board Design

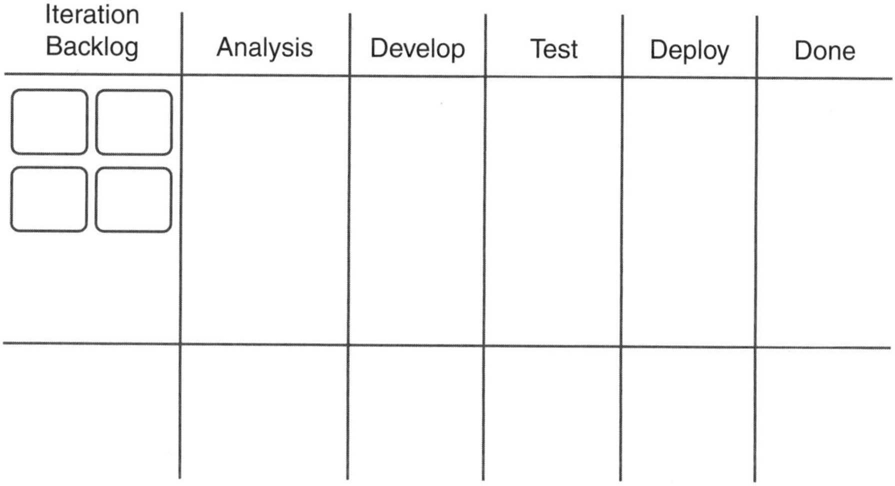

Iteration Backlog	Analysis	Develop	Test	Deploy	Done
☐☐ ☐☐					

AFTER:

Revised Board Design

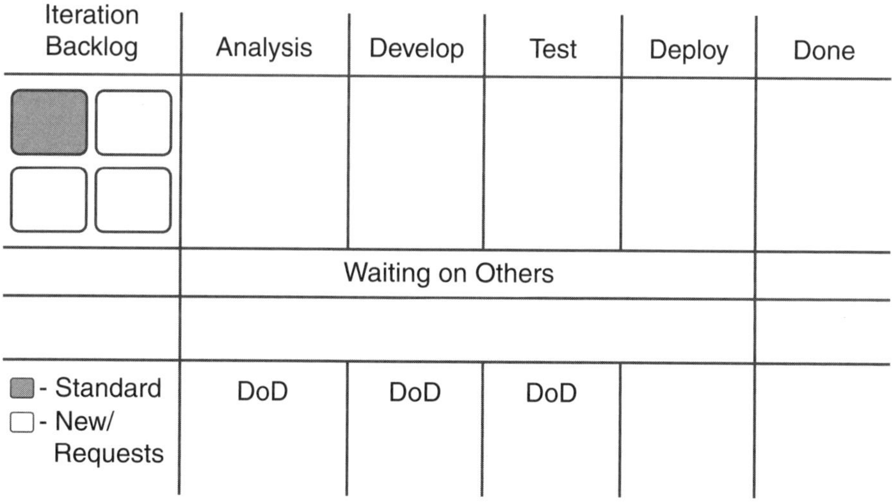

Iteration Backlog	Analysis	Develop	Test	Deploy	Done
▨☐ ☐☐					
	Waiting on Others				
▨- Standard ☐- New/ Requests	DoD	DoD	DoD		

FIGURE A.6   (continued)

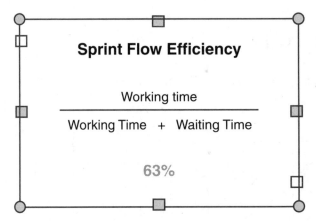

FIGURE A.7   By measuring time spent waiting for work from external dependencies, the team was able to recognize the full extent to which this time impacted its overall delivery time.

Flow efficiency is expressed as the ratio of actual touch time (working time) to total delivery time (measured from the date when the system commits to completing work to the time of that work's actual delivery). Figure A.7 shows this ratio.

Although the team's measurement evaluated flow efficiency only within the context of individual sprints, this was a great starting point for conversations and actions that would considerably improve time to market for applications produced by the entire RAD Group.

Results

Scrum wasn't failing RAD's Data Team as a development framework, but neither was the team positioned to capitalize on all of the framework's benefits.

The Scrum framework is purposefully simple, and relies on the collective capabilities of the entire team to deliver on its promised benefits. This necessarily includes the team's ability to properly identify and understand the problems and dysfunctions that Scrum exposes, and to effectively prioritize which of these issues to attack and determine how best to attack them. Consequently, team capabilities can plateau or stall owing to a variety of factors that have nothing to do with the framework itself. *Scrumban principles and practices help counteract these factors.*

In the case of RAD's Data Team, Scrumban helped team members develop a shared understanding of the way they were working. Its expanded visualizations and metrics exposed problems that were not obvious before its adoption and would have taken considerably more time to recognize and address during the team's regular retrospectives. More significantly, the Scrumban framework armed the team with new objective data—information that it used to negotiate service level expectations with

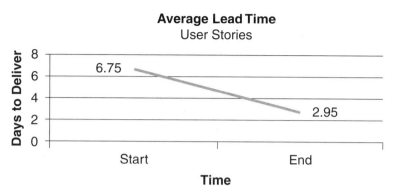

FIGURE A.8   The team realized a significant reduction in lead time simply from the initial process of discovery about their existing ways of working.

external sources, which in turn resulted in a substantially reduced waiting time (and associated variability) for their work.

Reduction in Delivery Time   Within 10 weeks of adopting their initial Scrumban practices, the Data Team reduced their average time to deliver completed work by 56%—more than halving the amount of time needed for work to move from the beginning to end of the work cycle (Figure A.8). This improvement was driven by several factors:

- *Taming of hidden influences*: The team's expanded visualizations of workflow across the value stream, of "dark matter" (i.e., work expansion discovered as part of the development process), and of waiting time based on external dependencies exposed significant factors influencing delivery time that were previously camouflaged.

    For example, the bank's PMO had mandated a two-week sprint duration for all Scrum teams in the IT organization (its chosen way of achieving organizational "alignment"). The kind of work undertaken by the Data Team, however, could not realistically deliver finished "value" in two-week cycles. Consequently, the team was breaking work into chunks that corresponded to different phases in the value stream, essentially replicating a waterfall process within a time-boxed cadence.

    This kind of dysfunction is exposed when everyone in a Scrum framework is doing his or her job. For example, the product owner or Scrum master should help the team recognize when user stories aren't delivering tangible value upon completion, or when a sprint goal is not really a sprint goal. Scrumban not only exposes these dysfunctions from a different perspective, but also offers a set of tools that teams can employ to overcome the behaviors that cause them.

- *Improved focus*: Although the team didn't explicitly adopt policies and practices around limiting work in progress until later on, visualizing workflow and then "dark matter" made it painfully obvious when attention and effort were divided among too many things. Consequently, there was a natural reaction to limit the amount of work in progress at any one time when the board became cluttered (impediments that often went unrecognized in the team's previous stand-ups).

   Even though Scrum implicitly limits work in progress through the sprint mechanic, the framework doesn't provide any explicit mechanisms for evaluating flow or managing the relationship between flow and WIP. This is an additional dimension Scrumban teams can utilize to their benefit.

- *Eliminating waste*: The nature of work performed by the Data Team required it to coordinate with a number of external units as work was undertaken, and the amount of time work was in a suspended state while the team waited for others to contribute or respond constituted waste. Figure A.9 reflects the extent to which the team's flow efficiency was improved simply through better management of these dependencies.

   The team intuitively recognized this cost of coordination and attempted to account for it in their story point estimations. Visualizing and measuring these interactions, however, armed the team with objective data it ultimately used to quickly negotiate improved turnaround times with some external units.

On a Path to Further Improvements   Empowered by their initial success and the sense of improved control over their own work, the Data Team's "improvement fatigue" evaporated, and they became highly motivated to continue their journey. They continued making further refinements to their visualizations, discovered new ways to minimize the shifting priorities that plagued them, and significantly improved their

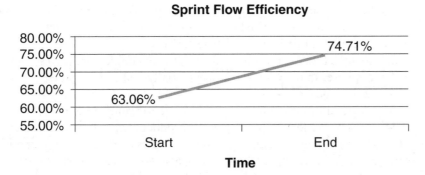

FIGURE A.9   The team was able to substantially improve its sprint flow efficiency simply by better managing its external dependencies.

ability to reliably forecast when work would be delivered. Read more about their path to those success stories in the next installment.

Scrumban Story 2: Mammoth Bank (Part 2)

Industry: Financial services

Organization size: Enterprise

Documented by: Ajay Reddy

Background

In this second story about the RAD Group at Mammoth Bank (developers of web and mobile applications), we learn about the group's continuing efforts to take control of issues plaguing their work.

In general, RAD had been under fire for slow and unreliable delivery. The bank was losing customers and opportunities because of lagging capabilities in its technology applications, and senior executives were up in arms. The group's recent success with decreasing delivery time had sparked renewed optimism among its members and a few folks in the business unit. Building on that success was critical to stemming customer losses due to lagging technologies.

Situation

Shifting Priorities   RAD was responsible for responding to the digital needs of several business units within the bank. Consequently, its backlog of pending work included multiple projects, each serving a different unit.

Upon the group's transition to Agile practices, a team of business analysts assumed the product owner role over this project portfolio. It was this team's job to work with the business units, understand their product needs, and define and prioritize those needs within the Scrum framework as they worked with individual teams.

A substantial effort had been made to create cross-functional Scrum teams as part of the transition. Though RAD's teams were fairly well balanced in their capabilities, as a practical matter they had to share a number of specialists across the group (database engineers, architects, IT operations, and others).

Under the bank's previous waterfall development approach, there was no real prioritization of work: The team simply began working on the next project in each business unit's queue on a rotating basis. Work was often interrupted by urgent needs escalated by a business unit. The queues were perpetually backed up, and the bank's move to Agile practices was intended to help improve response time to escalated needs, and to address the imbalance between demand and capacity.

The Scrum Context

Commonly Encountered Challenges   When the bank transitioned to Agile practices, the analyst/product owner team transitioned away from scheduling projects on a rotating basis and began prioritizing projects based on relative value. Despite this change, the group continued to contend with interruptions in the form of urgent requests and project escalations.

Scrum's time-boxed iterations had helped minimize work interruptions during sprints, but constantly moving teams between projects required adjustments to programming environment setups and familiarizing (or refamiliarizing) team members with the project particulars. It also made the coordination of shared resources extremely challenging. All of these factors negatively influenced overall performance.

On the upstream end of the workflow, the analyst/product owner team was constantly embroiled in negotiations with the business units around relative valuation—especially when a unit sought to escalate the priority of a given project. Although their initial valuations weren't inaccurate, changing circumstances over time caused actual value to fluctuate.

Within single project/product environments, the Scrum framework provides teams and organizations with a number of tools and capabilities to make better decisions and more quickly adapt to changing conditions. As Mammoth Bank's issues reflect, however, scaling Scrum across multiple teams, interdependencies, and projects can be quite challenging.

Some Common Approaches   Over the years, a variety of mechanisms have been developed to help organizations scale Scrum (or Agile approaches, in general) across large or multiple projects. These include adopting a Scrum-of-Scrums framework and creating specialized teams (such as feature teams, integration teams, coordination councils, and others). Mammoth Bank had adopted some of these approaches, but none was especially relevant to helping RAD's product owners gain better visibility and management over shifting priorities.

Adopting an "Enterprise Scrum" approach represented one potential solution to RAD's challenges. This approach, which was presented at the 2010 Hawaii International Conference on System Sciences, extends the Scrum framework to the program/portfolio management level. Time frames are expanded (quarterly "sprints"), backlogs are coarser, and roles are adapted to improve communication and coordination at a high level.[2]

While "Enterprise Scrum" and its subsequent evolutions represent a workable solution for some environments, undertaking such an endeavor at Mammoth was neither practical nor likely to produce immediate benefits. Implementing "Enterprise Scrum"—even a scaled-down version—would have required participation from

---

2. http://jeffsutherland.com/HICSS2010EnterpriseScrum.pdf.

senior executives within each of the business units plus broader participation from within the IT organization. With the organization already struggling on a number of fronts, it just wasn't feasible to pursue this path.

The Scaled Agile Framework (SAFe) represented another approach to solving RAD's challenges. Like "Enterprise Scrum" and its variants, however, SAFe requires a substantial degree of buy-in and participation across the organization. As Ken Schwaber and many other thought leaders have opined, it's questionable whether SAFe is truly Agile at all.[3]

RAD needed an approach that it could implement on a more limited scale and that would immediately improve its ability to better understand and manage the dynamic forces driving the challenges it was facing. Scrumban proved to be a viable alternative for the group.

The Scrumban Approach

Assessing and Visualizing Risk   Most development frameworks (including Scrum) have little to say about which projects to start, about when to stop and move on to something else, and about how to determine which work carries the greatest value. In these contexts, Scrum defers to whatever knowledge and schemes the product owner utilizes, though it certainly encourages product owners to develop appropriate mechanisms and skills in this regard.

Scrumban changes this landscape. It is biased toward establishing scientific approaches to risk and value assessments, and it enables teams and organizations to easily incorporate prioritization functions into its visualization framework. As a consequence, organizations and teams can visualize the impact of failing to complete work as time passes, giving them the opportunity to continually adjust local choices so as to complete work at every phase of the development cycle. More importantly, Scrumban reinforces the fact that delivering business value is the bottom-line objective of the team's work.

The frequency with which RAD's product owners had to contend with project escalation requests suggested they weren't recognizing common market risk profiles associated with pending projects. The Kanban Method promotes recognition and adaptive management of these risks in furtherance of its agenda to maximize service delivery to the business. To this end, it favors evaluating and visualizing the value/market risk relationship by using common "cost of delay" (or "impact of delay") profiles:

- *Urgent/emergency profile*: Represents the highest risk and most immediate impact to the business. Although the chart in Figure A.10 suggests the team's typical lead time will cause delivery to occur after an impact is experienced, this isn't necessarily the reality. Teams can effectively deal with these profiles

---

3. http://agile.dzone.com/articles/method-wars-scrum-vs-safe.

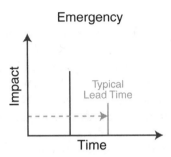

FIGURE A.10   Visualizing the cost of impact of an urgent/emergency risk profile.

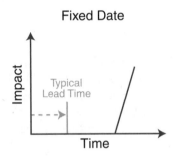

FIGURE A.11   Visualizing the cost of impact of a fixed date risk profile.

by establishing explicit work policies that call for everyone to immediately stop other work and swarm on these items to expedite their completion.

- *Fixed date profile*: Work with this profile represents medium to high risk, with an immediate impact on the business occurring if it is completed after the required delivery date (Figure A.11). Fixed-date costs of delay are often associated with legal commitments to customers or suppliers and regulatory requirements. Depending upon their due date, fixed-date items are best managed by selecting them for delivery over standard work (but not too early—it is often beneficial to complete other work first).

    If work is performed late, these projects and work items can be transformed into Emergency profiles (pragmatically, the only difference between emergency and fixed date profiles is that the latter affords the opportunity to plan). Conversely, if work is performed too early, you may be deferring other work, which can result in a greater overall cost of delay to the business.

- *Standard profile*: Represents medium risk to the business with a shallow and immediate impact (Figure A.12). The typical policy for such items is to process them on a first-in-first-out basis (using some prioritization scheme to select the order in which they're pulled into the system). Standard work items

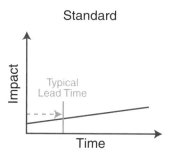

FIGURE A.12   Visualizing the cost of impact of a standard work item risk profile.

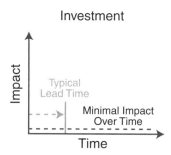

FIGURE A.13   Visualizing the cost of impact of an intangible risk profile.

can become more or less urgent over time, transforming into different risk profiles as warranted.

- *Intangible/investment profile*: Represents almost no risk and has a low to moderate impact on the organization. Intangible or investment work typically has no measurable cost of impact in the near future, and is performed as needed so the team may continue developing with high quality and speed (Figure A.13). Examples of such work include dealing with technical debt, emergent architectural issues, and general improvement efforts.

By developing information that allowed them to assign relevant risk profiles to pending projects (and ultimately to feature/user story prioritization), RAD's product owners were able to significantly reduce the number of incoming escalation requests.

Adopting a Common Language   RAD's improved understanding and management of risk was beneficial, but it was only one part of the equation. The product owner team soon discovered its valuation assessments for projects, and requested features and functionality within those projects, were increasingly being called into question.

The group had been employing a MoSCoW approach for its sprint backlog prioritization (categorizing work based on assessing which needs must, should, could, and would not be satisfied). While helpful, this scheme was product-centric, and didn't eliminate time-wasting debate for the product owner when it was necessary to evaluate the relative importance of different projects across business units. A different approach was needed.

One of RAD's team had begun experimenting with a prioritization scheme that was more quantifiable than MoSCoW—that is, they had begun evaluating story urgency in a cost of delay context. Because the mobile app they were developing served a diverse group of business stakeholders, the group had employed this approach to help it "negotiate" agreed-upon priorities for different features based on projected financial returns. The PMO opted to extend this implementation across the entire portfolio, and settled on using CD3 (cost of delay divided by duration) as an approach that could be easily applied at various levels. CD3 has gained traction among Agile teams, and in a typical Scrum context, is managed through the product owner role.

In assessing value, CD3 suggests quantifying value across several contexts:

- Projected increase in business revenue
- Projected decrease in business revenue (if not completed or until completed)
- Projected reduction in costs
- Projected avoidance of costs (such as fines or increased expenses)
- Knowledge acquisition (What's it worth to determine a path to success or failure? Can the knowledge to be discovered be obtained elsewhere and for what cost?)

CD3 is effectively a form of the "weighted shortest job first" queuing method. When applied at a user story level, it naturally encourages breaking work down into smaller batches—one of the easiest and most effective improvements a team can make in terms of improving flow, quality, and delivery of value.

Scrum Team Implications   Though RAD's development teams continued to employ time-boxed sprints as their primary mechanism for delivering the highest-value work first, the visualization of risk profiles and cost of delay within their work stream reinforced an important evolution—shifting the organizational focus away from measures of efficiency and cost and toward speed and delivery of value. Beyond alleviating the performance impediments caused by frequent context shifts in projects, this subtle change in focus ultimately helped to accelerate other evolutions at the team level.

More significantly, at least one of the teams began evaluating the potential advantages associated with prioritizing work at each phase of the value stream (the quantifiable measures associated with each story were amenable to updated calculations), with phase-specific factors (such as technology and skills risks) helping to inform the relative priority of a user story at each point in the workflow. As of this writing, the approach has yet to be implemented.

Results

Scrum wasn't failing RAD's Data Team as a development framework, but neither was it providing individual units with tools or mechanisms to help them assess and prioritize the value of projected work, to recognize how that value could change over time, or to evangelize these understandings across multiple business units. The Scrum framework is purposefully simple and relies on the collective capabilities of the entire team to fully deliver on its promised benefits. This necessarily includes the team's ability to properly identify and understand the problems and dysfunctions that Scrum exposes, to effectively prioritize which of these issues to attack, and to determine how best to attack them in the context of what the team controls. Consequently, capabilities can plateau or stall owing to a variety of factors that have nothing to do with the framework itself. *Scrumban principles and practices help counteract these factors.*

Percent Increase in ROI Within 10 months of implementing their first changes, RAD's product owner team had considerably improved the project's ROI—almost doubling the total return on investment to the company. This improvement was driven by several factors:

- *Minimizing project "interrupts" due to changing urgency*: No matter how perfectly RAD's teams were practicing Scrum, the core framework remained silent on helping the teams discover and manage changing urgencies in pending work. This program/portfolio-level perspective has definite implications at the team level. While Scrumban isn't the only approach that can address these challenges, it is often the most pragmatic option. It doesn't require broad organizational participation, and individual units can continuously adopt small changes over time that ultimately generate significant impact.
- *Minimizing the subjective nature of project valuations*: While Scrum and other Agile frameworks support and encourage similar outcomes, Scrumban includes a variety of mechanisms that help organizations move in this direction. More importantly, its practices reinforce and improve shared understandings in ways that are complementary to Scrum's roles, events, and artifacts.
- *Reinforcing evolutionary changes in thinking*: Perhaps the most important factor of all, changes in thinking are sustainable only when the people truly understand and appreciate their necessity. By reinforcing discovery and understandings through a variety of mechanisms, the Scrumban framework naturally encourages continual evolutions in thinking that will "stick" over time.

Scrumban Story 3: Siemens Health Care

Industry: Healthcare IT

Organization size: Enterprise

Documented by: Bennet Vallet, Director of Product Development

Background

Siemens Health Services is a global provider of IT solutions for the healthcare industry. In 2005, its development organization began adopting Scrum/XP practices in an effort to become more Agile. By 2011, the organization had achieved a mature state, and its 50 teams in the United States (along with sizable development operations in India and Europe) were producing new feature releases about once per year.

Shortly before Siemens's development organization undertook its transition to Agile practices, the company had embarked on an ambitious initiative to develop a new suite of software solutions that would compete against mature systems already in the market. This program's ability to leap past the competition would be driven by new technologies and the organization's ability to rapidly develop functionality. Unfortunately, continuing challenges around predictability, efficiency, and quality measures were putting this strategy in jeopardy.

Situation

Challenges at Every Level   Despite its success in adopting Agile practices, the organization was continuing to struggle with planning and coordinating development in its complex and highly regulated domain. Release deadlines had become intensely pressurized, with large amounts of overtime being expended to meet the challenge. Teams experienced difficulties planning and completing stories within their time-boxed sprints (one month), typically resulting in a mad rush during the last week to claim as many points as possible. This led to hasty and over-burdened testing, which was doubly challenging because a story's "doneness" required rigorous testing in a fully integrated environment.

On a program level, the organization struggled with establishing and meeting committed release dates. Team velocity metrics weren't providing sufficient insight for managing release development at scale, and overall efficiency and quality had plateaued. Corporate decision checkpoints and quality gates demanded greater capabilities. The company's strategy for success in the marketplace was being threatened by these organizational shortcomings.

The Scrum Context

Commonly Encountered Challenges   Unlike other scenarios where deficiencies in Scrum/XP practices are a significant contributing factor to larger challenges, the teams at Siemens were actually in very good shape. Scrum roles were followed, stable feature teams had been created, a mature product backlog process was in place, and their regular cadence of one-month sprints was engaged with proper sprint planning, reviews, and retrospectives. Agile practices such as CI, TDD, story-driven development, continuous customer interaction, pair programming, and relative point-based estimation were standard practices across all of the organization's teams.

Team metrics (e.g., velocity charts based on relative story points) assessed during sprint reviews usually reflected good results, but they weren't revealing the full picture. Too many features weren't reaching completion until the end of the release, and systemic bottlenecks were invisible. The available metrics weren't helping either the individual teams or the organization as a whole identify where problems lay or the actions needed to overcome them. Moreover, though these metrics had been in place for some time, they remained relatively unfamiliar to others in the general corporate culture.

Some Common Approaches   The managers at Siemens believed their teams' mastery of Agile practices, better planning, and harder work would lead to success. They had employed a variety of mechanisms to address their challenges (such as using feature teams and adopting Agile engineering practices), but were still coming up short.

Like others before them, executive management had chartered a small team of internal managers in the fall of 2011 to coordinate and drive efforts to improve the development organization's underlying processes. They began focusing their attention on principles of systems thinking, Lean thinking, and queuing through a variety of sources. Based on this, the group recognized a number of things:

- Their previous process improvement efforts were local optimizations of specific practices within functional domains (such as analysis, coding, and testing) that didn't necessarily improve the delivery system as a whole.
- Their failure to recognize and manage core Lean principles related to queues, "batch sizes," and resource utilization was unnecessarily elongating the release cycles.
- Many of their planning assumptions based on project management disciplines, rather than product development, needed to be reevaluated.

Early in their discussions, the group debated whether improvement efforts could be implemented solely at the enterprise level without having to change anything at the team level. Controlling and limiting the amount of work (specifically features) going to the teams was viewed as central to addressing these issues, and such an approach would ease adoption by not requiring any real change in team practices. It was decided that some changes needed to be made at the team level to achieve the desired results.

The Scrumban Approach

Siemens ultimately embraced an approach that called for layering the Kanban Method within the company's Scrum context. Having recognized that the problems didn't lie in the people or their skills, but rather in the organization's inability to effectively manage the flow of work in progress through its existing Scrum mechanisms, Siemens managers saw Kanban's visualization mechanics as an effective means to improve insight into systemic problems and patterns across the value stream. They also expected Kanban's additional metrics to provide greater transparency into actual progress (as well as to suggest specific interventions needed to improve the overall process performance). They had unknowingly decided upon Scrumban as their chosen approach to amplify the benefits that Scrum had begun to deliver.

Getting Started   Siemens approached its initiative as a holistic redesign. Borrowing from Russell Ackoff's principles of "idealized design," the organization's managers acted as if they were free to replace their existing system with whatever alternative they wanted. In short, they envisioned a new structure based on the results they wanted and worked backward.

The implementation team designed an approach that entailed establishing a common set of "explicit policies" to which all development teams would adhere, and provided a very high degree of consistency across work units, workflow, definitions of done, and metrics. It was determined that electronic boards should be used (large monitors displayed in each team room) that would be accessible in real time to all local and offshore developers. Electronic boards also enabled an enterprise management view across the program and provided a mechanism for real-time metric collection for each team and the program as a whole.

Siemens essentially maintained its existing feature, epic, and story hierarchy for the work units. New metrics, however, were introduced into the mix: "lead time" (defined as the amount of time required for a work item to move through defined phases of the value stream) and "throughput" (the number of work items that entered the "Done" step per unit of time, such as user stories per week).

Some of the key concepts Siemens was seeking to introduce into the Scrum teams' way of working would be counterintuitive and inconsistent with existing practices (practices such as limiting work in progress, adopting a pull versus push mindset, and avoiding full resource utilization). Formal education and training activities were used to introduce key concepts, but were not sufficient to ensure assimilation across the teams. Consequently, a limited number of external consultants were brought in to help, and internal employees were assigned to serve as Kanban coaches across existing

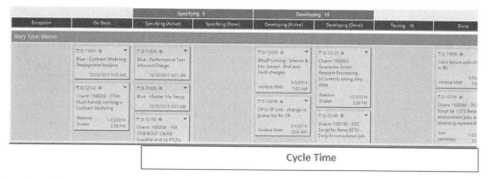

FIGURE A.14 Representation of how expanded workflow visualizations were among the first new capabilities introduced to Scrum teams at Siemens.

Scrum teams. In short order, teams were readied to begin working under newly defined policies and visualizing work on their new kanban boards (Figure A.14).

As previously noted, there was a particular focus on reinforcing and enhancing continuous improvement and quality management under this revised paradigm. Each column was assigned its own doneness criteria, and "doneness procedures" were incorporated into explicit policies. This ensured all quality steps were complete before a story was moved from one column (value phase) to the next to the next (e.g., moving a story from "specifying" to "developing"). Though most of these practices predated the adoption of kanban systems, the systems enabled improved visibility, focus, and rigor for test management practices. An additional policy was also implemented to enhance shared understandings of the quality picture—namely, displaying all defects on the board as separate work units.

Results

Scrum itself wasn't failing Siemens teams as a development framework, but neither was it enabling the organization to execute its business strategy as effectively as it needed to penetrate and aggressively compete in a mature marketplace.

Decreased Defects and Faster Defect Resolution   With its new framework in place, Siemens immediately reduced the number of defects created during release development by 60% and minimized the gap between defects created and defects resolved during the release (Figure A.15).

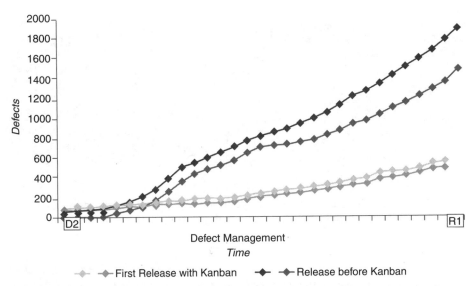

FIGURE A.15   Both the number of defects and the time needed to resolve them decreased substantially after introducing Scrumban mechanics.

Improved Ability to Identify Issues and Action Steps   It did not take long for the new metrics, and the reporting mechanisms used to visualize them (cumulative flow diagrams, scatter plots, and histograms—reporting visualizations not typically utilized in traditional Scrum contexts), to begin yielding benefits. At the team level, these new metrics helped the teams manage work in progress and clearly see real and potential variabilities in delivery. At the enterprise level, managers could now see capacity and other areas of systemic variability that could influence the release.

For example, during the first releases under this new framework, cumulative flow diagrams allowed management to recognize the potential for higher throughput in the developing phase by increasing test automation and rebalancing capacity. Similarly, scatter plots and histograms allowed teams to recognize lead time trends at different percentiles, to detect variability quickly, and, more importantly, to take action in addressing these issues on a proactive basis. A concrete example is the manner in which Siemens became able to track concrete and common measurements of throughput (i.e., the number of stories completed during a given unit of time). Systemic capacity imbalances became transparent, and the impact of work in progress on lead time and throughput was easily recognized and understood across all functional roles.

Decreased Lead Time   Under its pure Scrum framework, the Siemens development team's lead times varied considerably. As the scatter plot in Figure A.16 illustrates, there was a significant difference in the amount of time it took to complete stories at

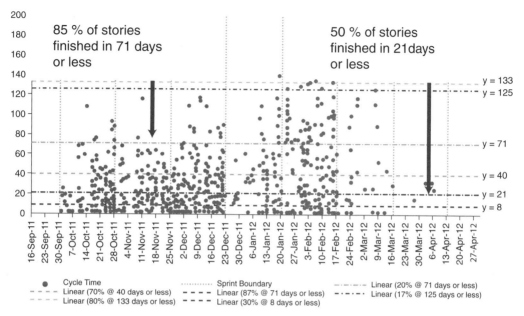

FIGURE A.16   A 50-day difference between lead time measurements for 50% of completed stories versus 85% of completed stories suggested a substantial amount of work in progress was being "ignored."

the 50th and 85th percentiles (lead times of 21 days or less and 71 days or less, respectively). This strongly suggested teams were not paying attention to work in progress.

The transition team members had initially decided to delay making WIP limits mandatory. They originally viewed WIP limits as more of an art than a science, and decided on trial and error as a means for each team to figure out its own WIP limits. The delay in implementing this practice was costly, as lead times under the new framework demonstrated the same upward pattern as seen in previous releases (Figure A.17).

Referencing cumulative flow diagrams, the Siemens teams soon recognized how managing WIP and aligning the story arrival rate with the departure rate affected both lead time and predictability. Figure A.18 shows how teams were bringing in more stories (arrivals) than they were completing (departures). The new metrics and reporting mechanisms provided a more complete picture at both individual team and program levels as to where capacity weaknesses existed. They also revealed where the group needed to make adjustments to improve throughput and efficiency. In addition, management was able to better forecast completion dates based on the number of stories remaining in the backlog.

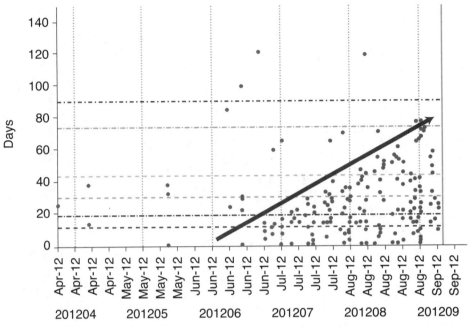

FIGURE A.17   Lead times reflected an upward trend over time with no WIP limits in place.

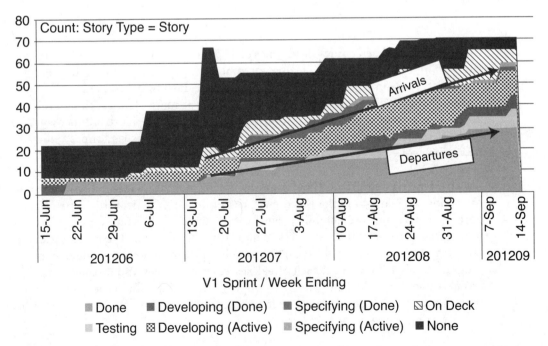

FIGURE A.18   This cumulative flow diagram shows how new work was being accepted into work queues faster than teams were able to finish it.

Once the teams adopted WIP limits, cycle time stabilized (Figure A.19). Lead time at the 85th percentile fell to 43 days or less, and overall lead time distributions trended in much more predictable ranges—an improvement of more than 40%.

In the team's second release under the new Scrumban framework, the metrics reflected it had achieved a high degree of lead time predictability (Figure A.20).

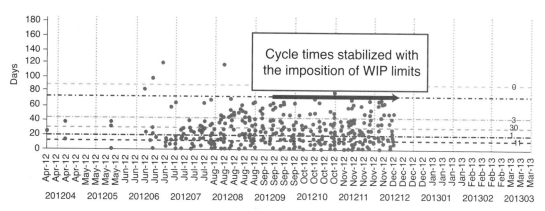

FIGURE A.19   Lead times quickly stabilized once explicit WIP limits were instituted across teams.

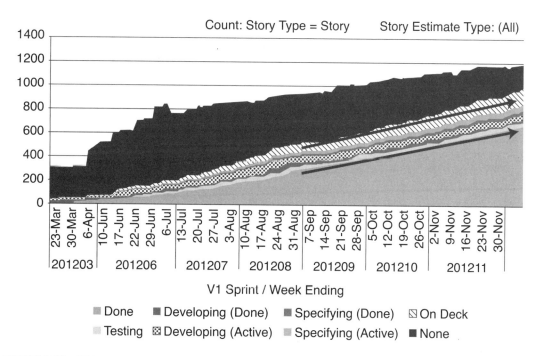

FIGURE A.20   This cumulative flow diagram reflects smooth flow and a balance between the rate at which new work is being accepted into work queues with the rate at which it is being delivered.

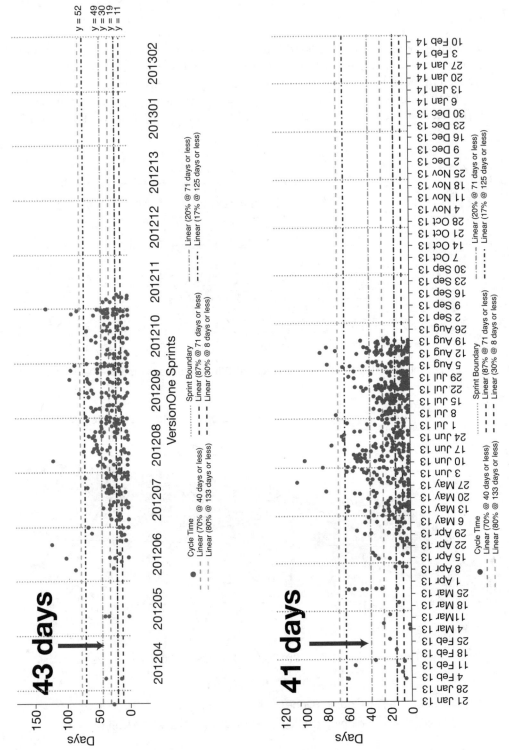

FIGURE A.21   Note the greater density of distribution in the lower chart.

Though lead times demonstrated similar distributions and ranges as with the first release, considerable improvements in the underlying numbers were realized. At the 85th percentile, stories were finishing within 41 days and variability was better controlled. Viewing the two scatter plots figures side by side bears this perception out (Figure A.21).

Increased Throughput   Improved lead time resulted in an increase in throughput (or story completion rate). As shown in Figure A.22, comparing the first release to the second, the Siemens team was able to reduce median lead time by 21.05% (resulting in a 33% increase in throughput). This occurred with no changes in story size or team composition.

Better Forecasting Using Lead Time   Siemens's analysis of lead time metrics indicated there was minimal correlation between estimated story points and actual lead time (Figure A.23).

Because Siemens had achieved predictable lead time, the company opted to experiment with a Monte Carlo simulation modeling tool. This tool was used to generate a distribution of likely feature and release completion dates.

By the time the team started planning for the second release, days of planning games and story point estimation were replaced by Scrum masters using the simulation tool fed by their team's own historical metrics. Throughout the release, the Scrum masters continued to update the tool's input periodically to provide updated metrics, which in turn further improved accuracy. These results proved that accuracy in making feature and release forecasts had been enhanced enormously.

Release	Median Cycle Time	Throughput per Day	Stories Completed
1st Kanban Release	19	3.52	525
2nd Kanban Release	15	5.28	787
Improvement	−21.05%	+33%	+33%

FIGURE A.22   The measurable results from instituting explicit WIP limits for the second release.

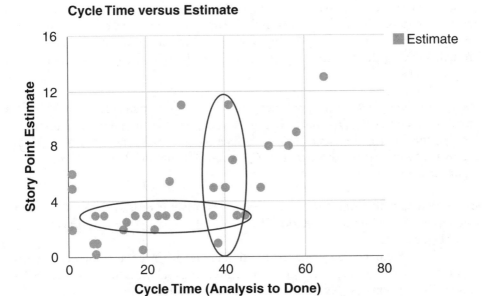

FIGURE A.23   There was little correlation between story point sizing and the actual time to deliver work.

Scrumban Story 4: Objective Solutions

Industry: Custom software development

Organization size: Enterprise

Documented by: Ramon Tramontini, Chief Operating Officer, and Marcelo Walter, Manager at Objective Solutions

Background

Objective Solutions develops software solutions that support the business operations of Brazil's major telecommunications companies. As an early leader of Agile practices in Brazil's software development community, it has developed its own tools and techniques over the years to support pragmatic implementations of Agile practices within its own operations and beyond.

This story chronicles the framework that Objective Solutions put in place to help it scale Agile practices as the size of its development organization grew from fewer than 20 members to more than 90 members in the span of five years. What's particularly interesting about this company's story is how it came to use a variety of techniques associated with the Kanban Method without prior awareness of that method, and how it used this framework to help its teams improve their mastery and adoption of Scrum/XP practices in a way that worked particularly well for their context.

Situation

The Starting Point   Like many development organizations, Objective Solutions began its journey toward Agility by adopting Scrum/XP practices. As of the end of 2009, its 17 team members had a good handle on essential Scrum practices and had adopted pair programming as a chosen Agile engineering practice.

The Scrum Context

Commonly Encountered Challenges   As Objective Solutions grew its operations, it faced a variety of challenges that teams and organizations commonly encounter along the journey to Agility. Some of these were related to difficulties in adapting to Scrum, others were associated with helping its teams master specific engineering practices, and still others related to general workflow. Although the organization didn't recognize it as such, Objective Solutions' application of the Scrumban framework across this variety of challenges is what makes its story so interesting. Among the specific applications we'll explore are the following:

- Coaching/training
    - Scaling pair programming
    - Coaching/training challenges
    - Pair member rotation
- Scrum framework
    - Sprint starvation
    - Parkinson's law
    - Unbalanced task board
    - Management influence versus self-organization
- General work process
    - Pull versus push
    - Bottlenecks

The Scrumban Approach

Scaling Pair Programming   One of the first and more obvious challenges Objective Solutions identified lay in scaling its pair programming efforts as the team grew. The organization was convinced of the basic tenet that two programmers can do a better job working collaboratively than they can do working individually, and this was initially borne out at a small scale. Mature pairs shift roles continuously, allowing the ideas to flow and avoiding dead ends in the development process. They get deeply immersed and engaged. The job gets done faster and better. The team learns and grows. In less mature teams, this outcome needs to be developed.

As the Objective Solutions team grew, the IT managers soon discovered that certain combinations of developers weren't flowing in the desired manner. Some combinations resulted in one developer dominating the process; others resulted in significantly decreased output and increased carelessness.

Looking for a state of flow across both collaboration and growth, Objective Solutions elected to incorporate a visual cue (a kanban) that signaled paired developers when to shift their respective responsibilities (where typically one programmer focuses on syntax, method logic, and related matters, while the other worries about design patterns, variable names, and development as a whole). It experimented with different time intervals to find an optimal pattern, but found this simple visual cue (and attendant policy) was all that was needed to ensure a continuous and consistent level of production and quality from the programming pairs.

Coaching/Training Challenges   As the development team grew, Objective Solutions transitioned senior members into team coaching roles. These individuals were no longer directly responsible for completing development tasks, but rather were charged with the responsibility to ensure their teams would deliver tasks within established time and quality standards. Pairs would call upon their coach as needed, with the three individuals working to resolve whatever challenge had impeded the pair's progress. This worked well at first, but once the group had grown to 11 pairs with only limited amounts of experience, the coach became trapped in an endless chain of reactive work. It was impossible to prevent problems before they happened.

Objective Solutions turned to another visual signal to resolve this problem. It developed a low-tech red flag signal that pairs could raise whenever they got stuck. These flags helped the organization see the reality of the group's limitations, but the company was still simply reacting to problems. When managers looked more closely at the problems, they identified three kinds of developer pairings:

- *Crybabies*: Typically inexperienced pairs who had a high dependency on the coach about what to do and how to do it. These pairs got "stuck" very easily.
- *Stubborn*: Pairs who spent too much time trying to solve problems on their own. Though the independent attitude is desirable, it has to be balanced against deadlines and rework caused by a technically insufficient solution.
- *Suicidals*: Pairs who think they're walking down the right path, but are actually upon a doomed trajectory.

Objective Solutions elected to modify its signaling system to include a yellow-colored flag. Though red flags were still raised whenever they got stuck on a task, every pair was now required to raise its yellow flag at the beginning of work. The coach was required to check in with these pairs at least once per day to monitor their work and proactively address any potential issues (with red flags taking priority). Not only did this basic kanban system help the team improve its understanding of current conditions, but it also allowed for implementation of a proactive management framework that made allowances for priority needs.

Pair Member Rotation   When Objective Solutions first introduced pair programming into its development process, it also adopted the recommended practice for "moving people around."[4] The initial policy allowed developers to select their own pairing combinations on a predefined day of the week. The organization selected this particular duration because it correlated to the average task size and because switches required the physical movement of workstations and personal belongings.

Soon, the same developers were always pairing together. While familiarity and chemistry are good things, "stability" in this context can lead to a lack of creativity, innovation, and evolution. In this context, self-organization was self-defeating.

Objective Solutions' first effort to address this situation was to assign pairs based on all the possible combinations. This worked for a while, but grew complex and cumbersome as the team grew. The organization ultimately created an algorithm that generated pair combinations based on a variety of parameters (e.g., skill levels, history of past pairings, seniority). The final call for pair combinations is up to the team, but a limited selection of choices based on these factors has helped the team break down prejudices and generate new ideas. A more consistent blending of the team's skills and ideas has proved able to drive better results over time.

Sprint Starvation   Objective Solutions' flagship product is both large and complex. At the time of this review, it consisted of more than 4000 Java classes, 1700 Oracle tables, and 26,000 automated tests. The organization was building on a daily basis and delivering a new version to its customers once per month.

Objective Solutions initially set its sprint size to fit the delivery schedule, but found it difficult to plan the backlog because of the immensity of the work undertaken (more than 1500 hours for each sprint). Because just keeping up with their day-to-day problems challenged team members, adequate planning for each sprint became a significant hurdle. The organization consistently underestimated its capacity (perhaps out of a healthy conservatism), resulting in work starvation at the end of each sprint.

Objective Solutions ultimately opted to adopt a continuous flow model, treating each task as its own sprint.

Parkinson's Law   Long before their adoption of Scrum and Agile practices, the development leaders at Objective Solutions recognized the reality of Parkinson's law—the natural tendency for work to fill the time available for its completion (or fit the given estimate). Over time, the organization saw the effect of Parkinson's law influencing

---

4. Rotating team members after fixed periods of working together.

its estimating capabilities. Because some work took longer to complete than was esti-mated (for reasons that often had more to do with external factors than imprecise efforts), the team expanded its estimates as they strived for greater predictability. As the team allowed more time for all work, however, it also began expanding its efforts.

Although Objective Solutions didn't really utilize Scrumban to address this per-ceived problem, its solution is worthy of mention because of the guiding mindset. The chosen mechanic was to eliminate team estimation altogether, placing the onus on a proxy product owner who worked closely with the team. In choosing this path, the primary consideration was the reality that the ultimate customer cared only about business value, with processes, controls, measurements, languages, and technologies all simply serving as the means to that end.

Could Objective Solutions have followed alternative paths? Absolutely. Would any of those have been better choices? Who's to say. The customers are satisfied, the organization's needs are being met, and the existing process is working well for the team. The mindset that drove this result will catalyze further changes when and if they become necessary—and that's a key characteristic of the Scrumban mindset.

Unbalanced Task Board, Bottlenecks, and Pull versus Push Systems   Shortly after adopting an expanded task board that more closely resembled the value stream mapping associated with a kanban system, the Objective Solutions team recognized the groups of work were grossly out of balance. As shown in Figure A.24, the four

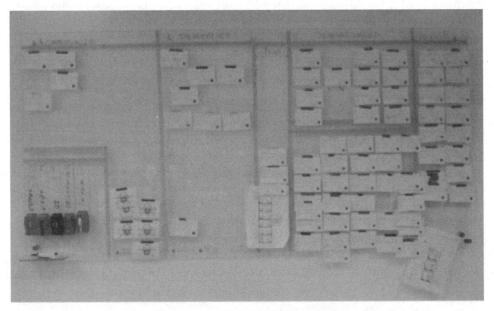

FIGURE A.24   Early visualizations soon reflected the number of unfinished tasks was far greater than the amount of actual work in progress.

primary columns associated with their board relate (from left to right) to the backlog, a contextualization phase (where the backlog items are broken down into tasks of 40 hours or less), an active development phase (split in two, with the top half representing work in progress and the bottom half representing items that are blocked for external reasons), and finally a review phase. As is apparent in Figure A.24, the quantity of unfinished tasks was significantly greater than the actual work in progress.

The Objective Solutions team recognized they couldn't solve their problem without first understanding it, so their first action was to simplify the visualization of their work. They merged the backlog and contextualization columns, and then created mini-task boards for each of the program pairs within the context of their development phase. These embedded pair task boards reflected the item each pair was currently working on, with a subcolumn for blocked tasks and another subcolumn for completed tasks awaiting review. This revised visualization greatly enhanced the visibility around each pair's work in progress (Figure A.25).

One of the first things the team members recognized from the revised visualization was that they were pushing work on the programming pairs. Code review had manifested itself as the team's greatest bottleneck, so new policies were put in place to require cross-pair reviewing. Before pulling a new task from the backlog, each team was required to pull a task on the review step of another team. This represented the first time the Objective Solutions team had consciously addressed a bottleneck.

What soon became apparent, however, was that the revised visualizations were not helping the team address a larger, more fundamental problem—not focusing on completing unfinished tasks. Though each pair's WIP was limited in the first scheme

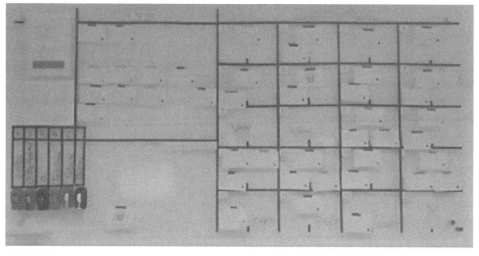

FIGURE A.25 Simplifying the kanban board made it easier for everyone to recognize the actual status of pending work.

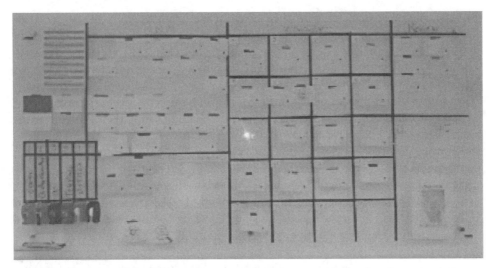

FIGURE A.26   Further enhancements to workflow visualization helped break down engrained habits of avoiding complex tasks.

(only one item could be actively coded at a time), this simply supported the developers' tendency to pull new work items rather than resolve more complicated, blocked tasks. This phenomenon, in turn, led to a mad dash toward the end of each sprint/delivery cycle. With a policy of having only one active item per pair, blocked tasks would remain behind an active item and automatically be elevated to current status once the active item was finished and ready for review. A common review column was returned to the board design to better visualize and manage that activity (Figure A.26).

Management Influence versus Self-Organization   One of the more interesting realizations the Objective Solutions team achieved through this journey was the recognition that management must often guide evolutions in the context of scaling, especially when teams are inexperienced. Sometimes teams will evolve in their own way; at other times a firmer hand is required. Managers need to find the balance between waiting and interfering, and there will always be trade-offs in those decisions. The Scrumban framework provides mechanisms to help inform decision makers, while influencing direction more effectively in a manner that still emphasizes a high degree of self-organization.

Results

Objective Solutions did not abandon Scrum or its Agile practices in employing Scrumban capabilities. Though its final way of working is not pure Scrum, it has defined a continually improving process that delivers the results the organization needs.

Faster Delivery and Better Quality   The Objective Solutions team's cumulative flow diagram reflects the tangible results of their efforts (Figure A.27). The amount of

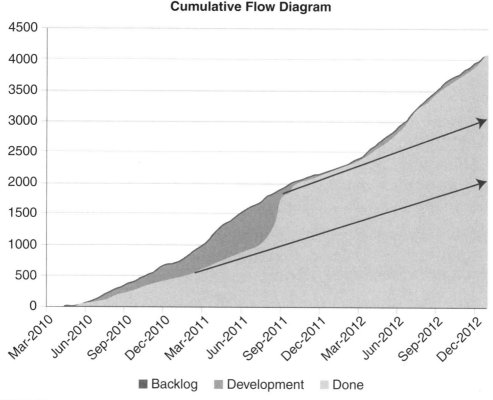

FIGURE A.27   The amount of work in progress was constantly growing (the widening dark band) until the team gained control over the situation.

work in progress was consistently large (and growing) before the team took steps to understand and address their workflow. Placing controls around allowable WIP substantially improved flow and rate of delivery.

In conjunction with these improvements, the group's average lead time decreased from a high of almost 25 days in May 2011 (as the team faced challenges with its growing numbers) to less than 5 days by March 2013. Though lead time spiked as high as 48 days in August 2013 (Figure A.28), this condition was short-lived (just one month in duration) and likely related to a variety of factors associated with the nature of work being undertaken at that point, in conjunction with the efforts being made to gain control over the workflow challenges.

Finally, the team saw a significant decrease in the amount of time it was spending on addressing quality issues that arose during development (Figure A.29). This decrease was a significant achievement when placed in the context of growing the team from 17 to 90 members during the same time frame.

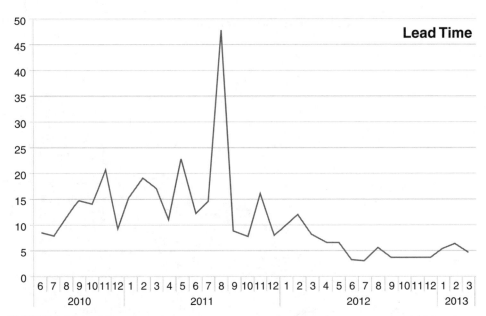

FIGURE A.28   Lead times trended downward as the team evolved ways of working with each new understanding.

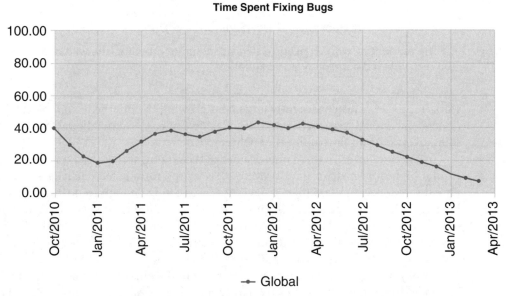

FIGURE A.29   An "incidental" result of the team's efforts was improved quality, as measured by the amount of time needed to address bug fixes.

Supplemental Information and Resources
Facilitating Difficult Conversations

A difficult conversation is anything we find hard to talk about because we fear the consequences. Even though they're a normal part of life, most of us opt to avoid engaging in these interactions. At best, strategies of avoidance allow problems to live on. At worst, they exacerbate them. If we want to create truly adaptive capabilities in our teams and organizations, we must nurture the following abilities in ourselves and in others:

- Not fearing difficult conversations
- Understanding how to make difficult conversations an opportunity to learn

Fortunately, leaders, coaches, and even Scrum masters have a good framework for guidance in this area, found in the book *Difficult Conversations: How to Discuss What Matters Most* (Penguin, Group 1999). Based on 15 years of research at the Harvard Negotiation Project, the authors help us recognize that when engaging in difficult conversations, we need to understand not only what is said, but also what is *not* said. In other words, we need to understand what people are thinking and feeling but not saying. The gap between what we are thinking and what we are saying is part of what makes a conversation difficult. Consequently, every difficult conversation should actually be viewed as an amalgamation of three different conversations:

- The "what happened" conversation—what the discussion is identifying as the area of disagreement or differing perspectives
- The "feelings" conversation—what the discussion may or may not be saying around what people are feeling
- The "identity" conversation—what the discussion is saying about me (the implications for our self-image)

Once we understand the challenges inherent in these three conversations (and the mistakes we make in each), we can begin to evolve the purpose of having particular conversations. We can better appreciate the complexity of perceptions and intentions, the reality that many things contribute to any problem, how feelings play a central role, and what the issues potentially mean to each person's self-esteem and identity. Along the way, our focus shifts from advocating for our own point of view to understanding what has happened, and to collaborating to find solutions that improve the situation or avoid similar problems in the future.

Some Additional Perspective on Effective Product Management

Like any other framework or methodology, Scrumban is simply a means to deliver great products and services to those we serve. All too often, this simple truth becomes lost in debates and machinations that really aren't relevant to what's at stake. Every role and function within an organization should be focused on continually improving how it approaches product management. To this end, I offer the following outline of what constitutes effective product management in a software development/technology delivery context.

1. *Continually evaluate your products and services.* Before any organization can develop a product/services roadmap that will lead to greatness, it's essential to invest time and effort in understanding what the market really wants and how it is using your current offerings.

    Rarely are the consumers of our products or services using all of the features and capabilities we offer. A simple way to visualize how many users take advantage of specific capabilities and the frequency with which they do so is to create a simple matrix like the one shown in Table A.10.

    Services and capabilities in the upper-right quadrant of this matrix are most responsive to marketplace needs, as almost all of your customers are using them almost all of the time. Generally speaking, services and capabilities resident in the lower portion along the y-axis represent opportunities to increase the frequency of use, and those on the left side of the x-axis represent opportunities to increase adoption. Of course, there's also the option of abandoning the poorly adopted/used features or capabilities altogether.

2. *Improve your products and services based on your conscious assessments.* Organizations can improve their services and capabilities by deliberately making them better, changing things so users will use them more often, or changing things so more users will use them. You can't deliberately make a service or product better, however, unless you understand what users value about it. Excellent product managers perfect how to discover this information and use this knowledge to drive better decisions.

TABLE A.10   Product / Services Review Matrix

Almost always used			Feature B	Feature A
Used most of the time	Feature C			Feature F
Used some of the time		Feature E		
Rarely or never used	Feature D			
	Used by few or none	Used by some users	Used by most users	Used by all users

This arena is also where the recognition and management of risk comes into play. Choosing to deliberately improve a widely adopted feature or capability represents a high-risk, high-reward endeavor. Get it right and you'll maximize value for the majority of your users; get it wrong and you'll negatively disrupt the majority of your users. Leveraging Scrumban's risk management mechanics like cost of delay profiles and classes of service represents a valuable capability with which to better navigate this landscape.

3. *Equip yourself to make better hard decisions.* If product owners/managers solely focus on identifying new features and capabilities, then you'll end up with a product or service that is wide and shallow. Focus too much on fixing what's wrong, and you'll fail to innovate and become irrelevant to the marketplace. In 2002, Anthony Ullwick proposed a simple algorithm that offers a pragmatic approach to better equipping ourselves to address this tension.[5] Ullwick's recommended approach identifies product or service shortcomings by getting customers/users to rank the things they need to do against how important those things are and how satisfied the customers/users are with the current capabilities. This relationship can be simply expressed as follows:

$$Opportunity = Importance + (Importance - Satisfaction)$$

More powerful than the simplicity of this formula is how it helps product managers highlight opportunities that would otherwise go unnoticed. In many instances, the greatest opportunities to increase the value we deliver to customers lie in areas that are deemed "complete" or "good enough." While it's true that 20% of features and capabilities will deliver 80% of what's valued, we can end up giving our customers a mediocre experience where it most matters—and that's rarely going to help us maintain leadership in the marketplace.

A related perspective depends on better understanding your return on development effort. Unfortunately, the perceived value of an output is not always directly proportional to the amount of effort that goes into producing it. Some high-development efforts (such as back-end architecture and code refactoring) are simply not appreciated by users, even though they may be necessary to deliver the experiences that are truly valuable. For this reason, good product managers will find ways to balance high-effort, low-value items with low-effort, high-value items so the customer perceives that continual delivery of added value is occurring.

---

5. "Turn Customer Input into Innovation," *Harvard Business Review*, January 2002. https://hbr.org/2002/01/turn-customer-input-into-innovation.

4. *Apply good process practices to nondevelopment workflows.* Unless customers use new features and capabilities, they may as well not exist. In fact, recognizing work that's valuable, prioritizing it appropriately, and improving the way it's delivered will all be for naught unless the completed work is recognized and used. Product managers exposed to Scrumban's deliberate practices have an opportunity to spread their use to other, integral parts of the customer delivery process.

Cynefin Framework

The Cynefin framework—a practical application of complexity theory to the science of management—is an example of other models that Scrumban teams can employ to improve understandings of their work and ultimately enhance their decision-making capabilities.

Scrumban's magic lies in the ease with which teams and organizations are enabled to visualize and measure the additional perspectives and information that frameworks like Cynefin and A3 Thinking bring to the table. As disciplined practices, these frameworks and models represent a way to make the thought process around continuous improvement both consistent and habitual within a team and across an organization.

It should be noted that complexity theory is different from systems thinking. Whereas systems thinking provides frameworks through which to elucidate the nature of a system (and suggests there is an ideal end state), complexity theory focuses on understanding the current state of a system and helping us best manage within that state. Pragmatically, the Cynefin framework allows managers to adapt their preferred management and decision-making styles based on context. This not only makes for better decisions, but also helps avoid problems that can arise when those preferred styles can lead to missteps and mistakes for a given context.

So how does it work? The Cynefin framework sorts issues into five contexts defined by the relationship between cause and effect. Four of the five contexts require diagnosis and reaction in appropriate ways. The fifth context—a state of disorder—applies when it's unclear which of the other contexts predominates in a given situation. These contexts are often visualized as shown in Figure A.30.

As the diagram reflects, the four primary states for a given context are simple, complicated, complex, and chaotic. Though the diagram resembles a quadrant-like form of categorization, it should really be viewed as a fluid series of states between which systems and situations can range. In other words, like systems themselves, the complexity of the states is constantly changing.

▪ *Simple contexts*: These contexts are stable, and there are clear cause-and-effect relationships that are easily seen by everyone. The right answer and approach to things is usually self-evident, so this is a domain where best practices are typically applied. Management is simple and straightforward—we want to sense what the situation is, categorize it, and respond appropriately.

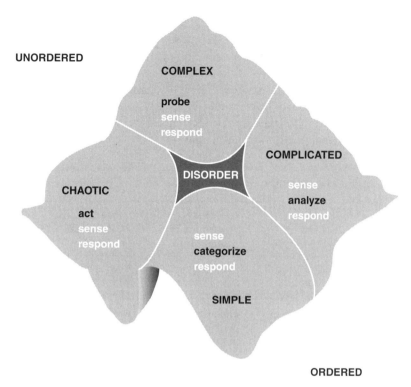

FIGURE A.30   The five domains of complexity.

- *Complicated contexts*: Unlike simple contexts, complicated contexts often have multiple right answers to a given situation. Cause-and-effect relationships are less clear except to those with a deeper knowledge and understanding of the context. This is the realm of the "known unknowns," where expertise is usually required to analyze the situation. Fittingly, the best management approach here is to sense, analyze, and respond.
- *Complex contexts*: In complicated contexts, at least one right answer exists to a given situation. In complex contexts, there is a high degree of unpredictability and flux, and no clear cause-and-effect relationships are evident (though patterns can emerge with proper observation). This is the realm of the "unknown unknowns," and the domain in which most businesses, and certainly software development teams, now operate. Instead of attempting to impose a course of action, managers must allow the proper path to reveal itself. The best management approach in this domain is to probe, sense, and then respond. Conducting experiments that are safe to fail is the preferred manner in which to probe.
- *Chaotic contexts*: In these contexts, there is no point in searching for a right answer because the relationship between cause and effect is shifting constantly. This is the realm of "unknowables." The immediate need here is not

to solve a problem, but rather to stop a catastrophe. Managers must act first, then sense where stability is present, and work to transform the situation toward one of complexity (where emerging patterns can be observed).

We can use the Cynefin framework to help us change our management style to better suit the changing state of our systems. We can also use the framework to better manage risks associated with individual work items. Table A.11 summarizes relevant characteristics and considerations for each context.

TABLE A.11   Summary of the Cynefin Domains

	Core Characteristics	Best Approach for Managing	Signals of Potential Danger	Best Response to Danger Signals
Simple	Repeating patterns and consistent events. Cause-and-effect relationship is evident to everyone. Known knowns. Right answer exists. Fact-based management.	Sense, categorize, and respond. Ensure best practices are in place and delegate to those practices. Minimal need to manage; keep communications clear and direct.	Complacency with entrenched thinking. Received wisdom unchallenged; overreliance on best practices if context shifts. Desire to make more complex problems simple.	Create channels for challenging convention. Recognize both value and limitations of best practices. Stay connected without micromanaging. Don't assume things are simple.
Complicated	Events and patterns are more complicated, requiring expert input to diagnose. Cause-and-effect relationship is discoverable, but not evident to all. Known unknowns. More than one right answer possible and discoverable. Fact-based management.	Sense, analyze, and respond. Create panels of experts with whom to consult. Evaluate any conflicting advice and direct appropriate response.	Experts are overconfident in their own solutions or the efficacy of past solutions. Paralysis by analysis and overreliance on expert involvement. Excluding viewpoints of non-experts.	Create an environment that encourages internal and external stakeholders to challenge expert opinions and entrenched thinking. Use experiments and games to force people to think differently.

TABLE A.11 Summary of the Cynefin Domains (*continued*)

	Core Characteristics	Best Approach for Managing	Signals of Potential Danger	Best Response to Danger Signals
Complex	Lots of flux and unpredictability in events. No clear cause-and-effect relationship, but instructive patterns can emerge. Unknown unknowns. No right answer. Creative and innovative approaches required. Pattern-based leadership.	Probe, sense, and respond. Create environments and experiments that allow patterns to emerge. Increase interaction. Encourage dissent. Experiment and monitor for emerging patterns.	The temptation to fall back into old habits (such as a command-and-control management). The temptation to look for facts and answers rather than allowing patterns to emerge. Being blinded by the desire for a quick solution.	Force yourself to be patient and allow time for reflection on what you sense from probing. Emphasize using approaches that encourage interaction so patterns can emerge.
Chaotic	Highly turbulent. No clear cause-and-effect relationship; no instructive patterns. Unknowables. No point in looking for right answers. Many decisions to make and no time to think. Pattern-based leadership.	Act, sense, and respond. Take immediate action to reestablish order. Look for what works. Clear, direct communication.	Applying a command-and-control approach longer than needed or chaos continues unabated. Failure to challenge leadership decisions after crisis. Missed opportunity for innovation.	Focus on actions that can help shift the context from chaotic to complex. Encourage others to challenge leadership's point of view once the crisis has abated. Set up mechanisms (such as parallel teams) to seize potential opportunities.

Cynefin can be applied in many different ways, but perhaps one of the most relevant applications within a software development context involves improving the assessment of risks inherent in the work—from market and regulatory risks (which inform us how work should be prioritized) to skill and technology risks (which inform us of the expected variability of time and effort needed to complete a particular feature or story). Scrumban lets us visualize and manage this intelligence in a variety of ways (from board and work card design to establishing classes of service), and Cynefin provides a framework through which we can gain a better sense of the best approach for dealing with the complexity associated with known risks.

For teams and organizations at the initial stages of adopting Scrumban, it's sufficient to simply be aware that many frameworks can be layered on one another to help us manage software development processes more effectively. Scrumban allows teams and organizations to easily incorporate other frameworks within its capabilities to visualize, measure, integrate, and direct work. It's this ease of integration that makes it such a powerful management framework.

Real Options

Real Options is a simple and powerful approach for making better-informed decisions by understanding and responding to the psychological effects that uncertainty has on behavior (both as individuals and within groups). There are two aspects to this framework—one mathematical, the other psychological. The math side has its origins in the financial markets (ironically enough, around options trading). It defines an optimal decision for what and when to trade. The psychological side is based on neuro-linguistic programming and cognitive behavior. These theories help us understand why humans are not wired to follow optimal decision-making processes and end up making irrational decisions as a result.

From the mathematical side, we learn three key principles:

- Options have value. An option is defined as the right, but not the obligation, to take an action in the future. To gain this right we have to incur some upfront cost. Options have a greater value when there are higher degrees of uncertainty associated with the decision tied to them.
- Options expire.
- We should never commit to a decision early unless we know why.

From the psychological side, we learn that humans tend to think of decisions in binary fashion—that there's either a right decision or a wrong decision to be made. The reality is that we have a third choice—no decision (or a deferred one). Because we fail to recognize the absence of decision as a valid choice, we commit to decisions early and, therefore, often commit to wrong decisions before we have to make any decision at all.

So how does options theory help us? It provides a framework that encourages us to create options around our most significant decision points, and to do so in a way that lets us understand both the cost and the value of those options.

In many ways, traditional Scrum limits the effectiveness of the Real Options framework when the methodology forces us to commit to completing items selected for a sprint backlog. While the duration of sprints is usually short enough to minimize the risk of early commitment, even a sprint backlog stands in sharp contrast to the "just-in-time" decision making associated with continuous flow.

That said, the benefits from the structure of a sprint often supersede any benefits from adjusting to extending our commitment point to the last possible moment (which requires continuous flow). As always, context dictates what makes the most sense for a given team or organization.

The GetScrumban Game

The GetScrumban game (http://GetScrumban.com) simulates how a software development team using Scrum can begin applying Scrumban's core principles and practices to amplify current capabilities, overcome common challenges, or forge new paths to improved agility. More importantly, the game allows players to experience how Scrumban evokes typical evolutions in how they work, and to experiment with how specific principles and practices can influence different outcomes in a variety of contexts (Figure A.31). Among the practices to which the game will orient new practitioners are the following:

- Expanded workflow visualizations
  - Value streams (e.g., moving from the typical Scrum task board reflected in Figure A.32 to more granular value streams such as those depicted in Figure A.33)
  - Types of work
  - Risk profiles

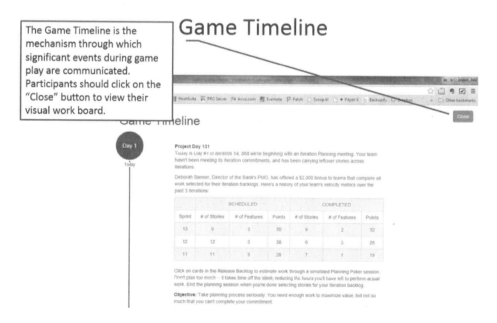

FIGURE A.31   In the GetScrumban game, players are exposed to a variety of conditions and events as they "perform" work during the course of several weeks of software development effort in simulated play.

Initial Task Board

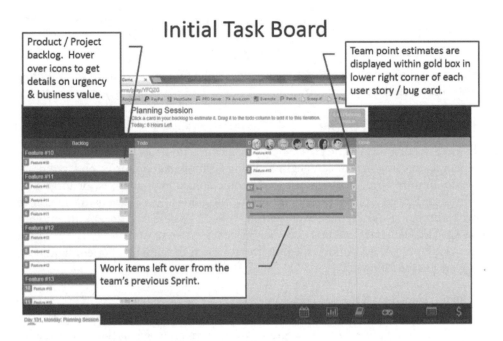

Product / Project backlog. Hover over icons to get details on urgency & business value.

Team point estimates are displayed within gold box in lower right corner of each user story / bug card.

Work items left over from the team's previous Sprint.

FIGURE A.32   The team's starting workflow visualization is represented by a typical Scrum task board.

Evolved Kanban Board

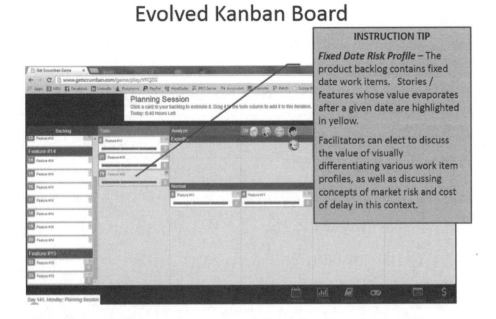

INSTRUCTION TIP

Fixed Date Risk Profile – The product backlog contains fixed date work items. Stories / features whose value evaporates after a given date are highlighted in yellow.

Facilitators can elect to discuss the value of visually differentiating various work item profiles, as well as discussing concepts of market risk and cost of delay in this context.

FIGURE A.33   Players quickly confront situations that demonstrate how evolving their workflow visualizations improves their shared understanding of both work status and factors influencing the flow of work through their "system."

- Pulling work versus assigning work
- Evolutionary adjustments versus radical change
- Cost of delay versus subjective prioritization
- Distinct classes of service versus single workflow
- Continuous flow versus time-boxed iterations
- Value of options
- And more . . .

Modeled on Russ Healey's getKanban Game (which is used by trainers around the world as an instructional aid for teaching Kanban principles), play in GetScrumban is most meaningful when participants play as a small team immediately following 1 to 2 hours of introductory instruction on Scrumban concepts. Having the game available for individual play thereafter is a great way for individuals to further explore key practices.

The game purposely introduces a significant number of events and changing conditions early on, then smooths out such events over time. The swift series of changing conditions helps simulate the impact of improved understandings and tools within fast-paced environments. It may result, however, in a lighter absorption of some concepts. The slower pace as the game progresses is intended to simulate the different experience of evaluating and responding to current ways of working in the context of a regular cadence.

Scrumban Tools: Examples of Key Features and Capabilities

Because Scrumban environments typically involve managing elements associated with both the Scrum and Kanban frameworks (and evolving how you use them over time), finding a tool that satisfies a majority of core needs can be challenging. Users have a variety of good options when it comes to selecting Scrum management tools. A slightly smaller number of robust Kanban tools is available in the marketplace, but variety still exists. Unfortunately, very few tools can satisfactorily meet the needs of Scrumban users. We're changing this reality by architecting critical changes to our own Scrum team tool, ScrumDo.

Because of its bias toward team member co-location, Scrum has historically frowned upon the use of virtual tools. In our experience, virtual tools can actually play a very important role in facilitating Agility, predictability, and business responsiveness (among other desirable outcomes). Let's review some of the key capabilities that ScrumDo is bringing to teams in 145 countries.

Planning: Iteration, Release, and Continuous Flow

As Scrum remains the central framework for teams that adopt Scrumban, it is important for a management tool to have the ability to meet the specific needs of the teams using those tools, and to be able to evolve with their changing practices over time. To this end, while most Scrum tools allow teams to manage release and iteration

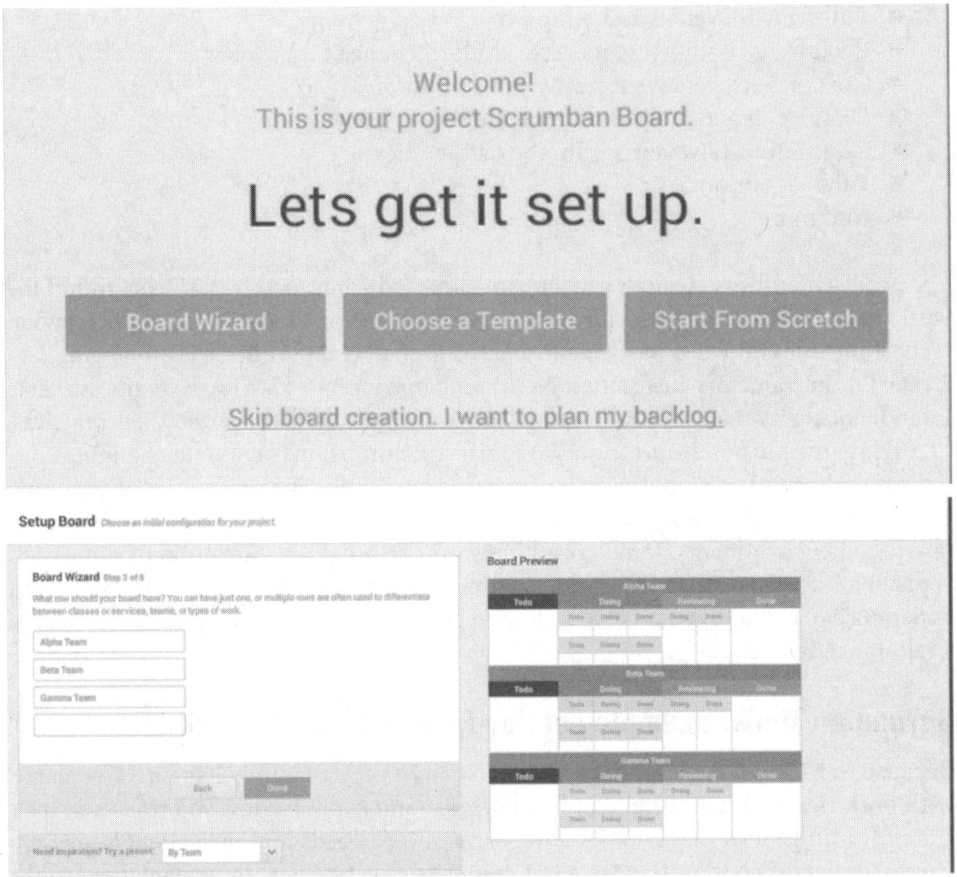

FIGURE A.34   You don't need to be a Kanban expert to set up effective board designs to get started.

planning in some fashion, few provide capabilities that support evolutions to continuous flow or nonsynchronized commitments around the acceptance and delivery of work. ScrumDo, however, makes this easy.

ScrumDo allows easy setup with a wizard and project planning at an iteration level or release level. It's easy to drag and drop stories to your iteration or a continuous flow board (Figure A.34 and Figure A.35).

Flexibility: Iterations Are Always Supported—And Always Optional

Because ScrumDo is built on Scrumban's core principles, it offers the flexibility to shift between iteration-based and continuous flow models as your business needs require (Figure A.36).

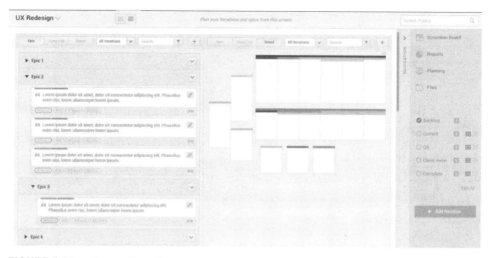

FIGURE A.35   ScrumDo allows you to easily assign epics and stories to appropriate cells in your visual board right from the planning tool.

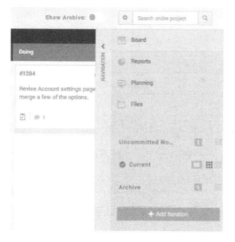

FIGURE A.36   Because Scrumban teams can opt to manage their work within time-boxed cadences or engage in a system of continuous flow, having a tool that provides capabilities for both is essential.

Integration with GetScrumban

ScrumDo helps users learn Scrumban easily thanks to its integration with the GetScrumban game (Figure A.37). This is particularly useful for teams at the Shu level, as members may not be fully aware of the framework's capabilities.

FIGURE A.37   ScrumDo users will recognize a lot of familiar capabilities when playing the GetScrumban game.

Setup Board *Choose an initial configuration for your project.*

Board Wizard Step 2 of 3

How should the columns look?

Todo	Standard	⌄
Doing	Sub Tasks	⌄
Reviewing	Split	⌄	Doing	Done
Done	Standard	⌄

Back   Next

Not sure which one? See some examples.

Board Preview

Todo	Doing			Reviewing		Done
	Todo	Doing	Done	Doing	Done	
	Todo	Doing	Done			

FIGURE A.38   Wizards help guide users in creating the right board visualizations for their context.

Flexible Board Designs

Boards are easy to create with simple mouse clicks and easy-to-use wizards (Figure A.38). In turn, new users can quickly set up simple boards to start tracking their workflow immediately, while still retaining the ability to grow with the team's understanding of the Scrumban framework. This is vitally important when new knowledge requires new perspectives, which your existing board setup may not support.

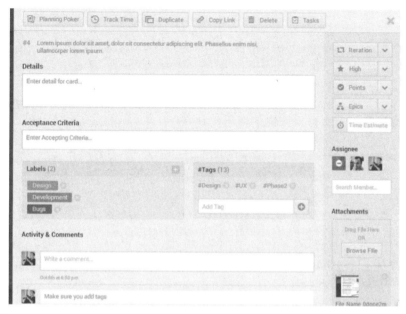

FIGURE A.39   ScrumDo's story editor interface allows users to visualize information uniquely employed in a Scrumban framework.

A Powerful Story Editor

ScrumDo includes a story editor that supports acceptance criteria (Figure A.39), prioritization based on cost of delay, and task breakdown. This helps teams identify bottlenecks and manage risk more effectively by giving them access to the data they need to make informed decisions. By changing the board along with your requirements, you can take advantage of new perspectives to enhance your visualizations.

Epic Breakdown

Work is easy to parse with the capability to break epics down to any level (Figure A.40). This facilitates working with sprints of any required duration, or even continuous flow. This functionality also contributes to Scrumban's ability to scale across multiple teams as necessary.

WIP Limits

Another important aspect of the Scrumban framework has to do with smoothing flow through managing the amount of work in the system. This is why the ability to set up WIP limits at the column and subcolumn levels is important (Figure A.41). Even when

FIGURE A.40   Epic management facilitates work prioritization and breakdown.

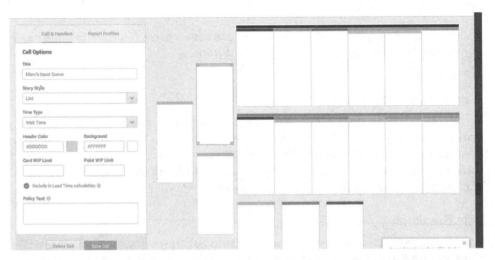

FIGURE A.41   WIP limits can be established throughout whatever workflow design users create.

appropriate WIP limits are set at the team level, it's important to ensure those limits apply at the developer level, as a single stalled developer can effectively stall the entire team.

Reports

To be effective, a Scrumban tool needs robust reporting capabilities that support, at a minimum, the following output: cumulative flow diagrams, lead time histograms, release burn-ups, flow efficiency, and burn-ups and burn-downs. Tools like ScrumDo

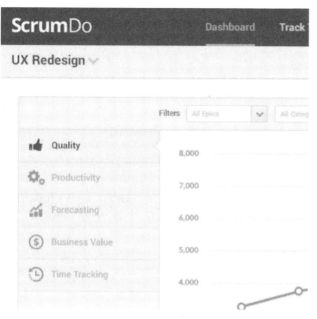

FIGURE A.42   Reporting is broken down by category, providing users and managers with easy paths to gain insight on the factors that are most important in the current context.

benefit Scrumban practitioners by integrating these reports with your existing boards, so you can immediately pull the data you need to make sound decisions based on business value (Figure A.42).

Decoupling board visuals from measurements is another important characteristic of a Scrumban tool. In other words, a board should support viewing the same stories from multiple perspectives. For example, a given container of stories might be in the "Waiting" column when viewed from one team's perspective but in the "Doing" column from another team's perspective. ScrumDo's report profiles different types of time, such as setup time, working time, wait time (Figure A.43), and done time, from different perspectives.

Integrated Functions

Features like integration of Planning Poker for stories can provide helpful consensus-building tools for teams that practice velocity estimation (Figure A.44). The more your Scrumban tool can automate the basic functions you need to effectively plan and visualize your work, the easier it is for your team to focus on doing the work.

Of course, there are also the usual features that any good Scrumban tool supports, including theming with tags and a context-sensitive notification system. For more information about Scrumban tools in general, and ScrumDo in particular, please contact support@scrumdo.com.

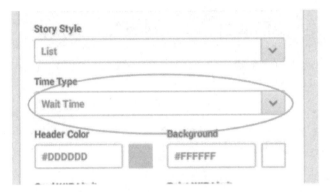

FIGURE A.43   One team's wait time may be another team's touch time. ScrumDo ensures the right metrics are created based on the viewpoint at hand.

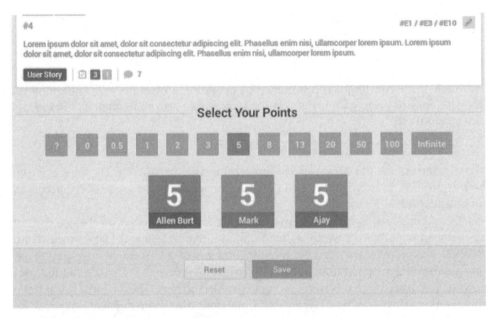

FIGURE A.44   Planning Poker is just one example of optional capabilities that a good Scrumban tool should provide.

Board Examples

Figures A.45 through A.46 represent other board designs that you can reference for ideas when developing your own designs.

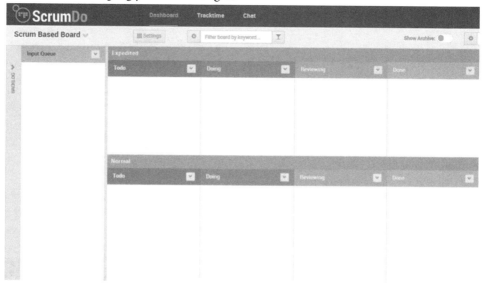

FIGURE A.45   A Scrum task board with a separate "expedite" lane for coordinated "swarming."

Source: ScrumDo.com.

FIGURE A.46   A board design for Scrum XP teams.

Source: ScrumDo.com.

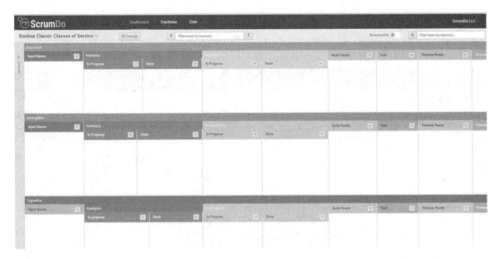

FIGURE A.47   A board design reflecting traditional Kanban classes of service.

Source: ScrumDo.com.

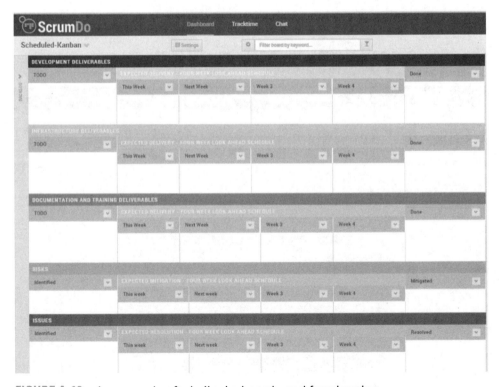

FIGURE A.48   An example of a heijunka board used for planning.

Source: ScrumDo.com.

INDEX

80/20 rule, 30

A

A3 Thinking. *See also* Design thinking.
    definition, 37
    description, 66–67
    at Toyota, 50
Acceptance, intrinsic motivator, 58, 196
Achouiantz, Christophe, 74, 209, 211–212
Ackoff, Russell, 298–299
Actions, aligning with marketplace needs, 23–24
Ad hoc requests, managing, 95
Adaptation. *See* Inspection and adaptation.
Adaptive budgeting *vs.* traditional method, 231
Adaptive buffer management, 140–141
Adaptive capabilities
    choosing the right metrics, 49–50
    core values, 45–49
    dealing with the most important problems, 50
    goals, 47–49
    importance of, 43–44
    mission, 47–49
    vision, 46–47
    "who you are" *vs.* "where you are going," 45
Adaptive risk assessment *vs.* traditional, 228–229
Adaptive risk management, 199
Advanced (Ri) learning stage, 4
Agile budgeting, 229–233. *See also* Costs.
Agile contracting, 233–235. *See also* Consultants.
Agile Impressions, 203
Agile Management for Software Engineering: Applying the Theory of Constraints for Business Results, 132

Agile Manifesto, core principles, 66
Agile practices
    holacratic approach, 32
    reasons for, 28–30
    spectrum of approaches, 32
Agile practices, adoption failure
    disillusionment, 34–35
    human factors, 35
    improving an unstable system, 36–37
    improving the wrong problems, 37
    intentional *vs.* emergent architecture, 39
    lack of commitment or effort, 33–34
    limiting responsibility for continuous improvement, 38
    negatively focused retrospectives, 38
    open Agile adoption framework, 32
    outside consultants, 35–36
    process *vs.* mindset approach, 31–32
    psychological elements, 38
    sacrificing quality for speed and results, 38
    tampering with things that work, 37
Agreement, core value of Kanban, 64
Aleatory (random) uncertainty, 104–106, 242
Anderson, David J.
    definition of the Kanban Method, 16
    on empowerment, 7
    Little's law, 132
    visualizing the depth of Kanban, 209
Ansoff matrix, 47–48
Aristotle, 220
Arrival rate distribution, quality metrics, 172
Authority, intrinsic motivator, 59
Average value calculation, lead time as substitute for, 138

335